From Pariahs to Partners

FROM PARIAHS TO PARTNERS

*How Parents and Their Allies Changed
New York City's Child Welfare System*

David Tobis

OXFORD
UNIVERSITY PRESS

Oxford University Press is a department of the University of Oxford.
It furthers the University's objective of excellence in research, scholarship,
and education by publishing worldwide.

Oxford   New York
Auckland   Cape Town   Dar es Salaam   Hong Kong   Karachi
Kuala Lumpur   Madrid   Melbourne   Mexico City   Nairobi
New Delhi   Shanghai   Taipei   Toronto

With offices in
Argentina   Austria   Brazil   Chile   Czech Republic   France   Greece
Guatemala   Hungary   Italy   Japan   Poland   Portugal   Singapore
South Korea   Switzerland   Thailand   Turkey   Ukraine   Vietnam

Oxford is a registered trademark of Oxford University Press in the UK and certain other
countries.

Published in the United States of America by
Oxford University Press
198 Madison Avenue, New York, NY 10016

Library of Congress Cataloging-in-Publication Data
Tobis, David, 1944–
From pariahs to partners : how parents and their allies changed New York City's
child welfare system / David Tobis.
    pages cm
ISBN 978-0-19-509988-1 (hardcover : alk. paper)
1. Child welfare—New York (State)—New York.   2. Foster home care—New York (State)—
New York.   3. Parent and child—New York (State)—New York.   4. Children—New York
(State)—New York—Social conditions.   I. Title.
HV743.N48T63 2013
362.709747'1—dc23
2013001124

This book is dedicated to my parents
Hazel and Jerry Tobis
who created a family in which love and
social justice were paramount.

CONTENTS

PREFACE

In the morning of March 16, 2011 it was raining in New York. Nevertheless by 9:30 Arnhold Hall at the New School University off Sixth Avenue in Manhattan was filled with close to 200 leaders of the city's child welfare system. The city and state commissioners, foster care agency executive directors, caseworkers, and parents had gathered to talk about parent advocates in the foster care system. Parent advocates are mothers and some fathers whose children had been placed in foster care. Whereupon, these parents changed the behavior that caused them to lose their kids, regained custody of them, underwent training, and were now working in foster care agencies helping other parents struggling with the types of problems they had overcome.

The forum was the culmination of 20 years of parents organizing on the outside, moving to the inside, fighting to have their needs addressed and their opinions heard, and finally having their work valued and funded by government and voluntary agencies. The forum was an acknowledgment that parents and the parents' movement had played an important role in reforming New York City's child welfare system.

The mood of the forum was festive. John B. Mattingly, commissioner of New York City's Administration for Children's Services, praised the work of parent advocates, but also joked that his middle initial stood for Bosco, which he said explained why he had so many problems as a child. Gladys Carrion, commissioner of New York State's Office of Children and Family Services, talked about the important contribution of parent advocates in casework, but joked self-critically that it took her a year and a half to change a line in New York State regulations—regulations that her office controlled—to encourage agencies to use parent advocates in their case-work. Jim Purcell, executive director of the Council of Family and Child Caring Agencies, which represents most foster care and preventive ser-vice agencies in New York State, said the system had reached the tipping point—he said we are no longer asking why parent advocates should be used in child welfare but when will agencies be able to hire parent advocates for every family that could benefit from one. The forum was a celebration not only of parent advocates but of how they have improved case practice. As Commissioner Mattingly said, "Everywhere you look in this city where we are doing our best work...where the best is happening, you will find parent advocates around."

The forum was organized by the Parent Advocate Initiative, an ad-hoc steering committee representing many of the key entities in New York's child welfare system—city and state governments, advocates, service providers, and parents. Parent advocates and their allies, who had once been at war with the city's child welfare administration, had collaborated with that administration for the previous 3 years to promote the hiring of parent advocates in foster care agencies. The advocates were parents who had overcome ordinary and extraordinary difficulties—fighting uncontrollably with their adolescent children, depression, drug and alcohol addiction, living on the street, and domestic violence. These parents had changed their lives, reunited with their children, and participated in training by the Child Welfare Organizing Project (CWOP) that prepared them to work in foster care agencies, where they coached parents who were going through what they went through. Other parent advocates had become community organizers and orators on behalf of parent advocacy, speaking truth to power—that families' needs must be met—before audiences ranging from city commissioners to the New York State Assembly. They were among the 100 or more parents who had become embroiled in the child welfare system now working in New York City foster care agencies, preventive service programs, law firms, and advocacy organizations.

In some ways the gathering was the culmination of a 20-year struggle for parents who had been pariahs and were now partners. Twenty years before, no parent who had had a child in "the system" had ever been employed by a foster care agency. Back then, and for as long as child welfare systems existed in the United States, poor parents had been pariahs, frequently demonized in the media and often disregarded or disrespected by the caseworkers and agencies that were supposed to help them and their families. They were usually voiceless on their own cases and invariably absent from the tables where heated battles for resources and power in child welfare took place. The March 16 forum was a sign of how much things had changed.

Several parent advocates spoke at the forum. One of them, Felicia Alleyne-Davis, had a successful 20-year career with Verizon as a customer service representative. But after she gave birth prematurely to a son, Tyrese, who was diagnosed with cerebral palsy, and her husband was arrested and put in prison, where he would remain for 8 years, she spiraled downward into alcohol abuse. When Tyrese was placed into foster care with New Alternatives for Children, Alleyne-Davis voluntarily entered an in-patient substance abuse program, which she completed, and began to repair her life. After several years she became a parent advocate at the same agency and described her experience working there:

> From being a client to a colleague as a parent advocate in the beginning was a tough pill for some workers to swallow. Upper management of the agency received me with open arms. When it came down to the supervisors and the case planners, it was a brick wall. Are you here to side with the parents against us? No, I'm here to level out the playing field. I'm here to give parents a voice. They have rights too.

The five executive directors of voluntary foster care agencies who spoke were in unanimous agreement that parent advocates improve case practice. Bill Baccaglini, executive director of New York Foundling Hospital, one of the oldest, largest, and most powerful child welfare agencies in the city, described the importance of hiring enough parent advocates to work with the thousands of families who could benefit from their coaching. Richard Altman, executive director of the Jewish Child Care Association (JCCA), one of the oldest and largest Jewish child welfare agencies, said he was inspired by the parent advocates and has used them in his agency for many years. Jeremy Kohomban, executive director of Children's Village, one of the oldest and largest Protestant child welfare agencies, closed the event by saying:

> I am convinced that I will never know the true excitement of this work until our organizations are overflowing with parents and youth who are imbedded in our day-to-day struggles.

But the forum was also a time of concern about the future. As the chairman of the steering committee that organized the forum, I spoke about my worry that although everyone—parents, caseworkers, supervisors, and executive directors—agreed that parent advocates improve case practice, parent advocacy might remain a boutique program on the margins of the child welfare system. Baccaglini expressed a similar concern. He praised the two parent advocates working in his agency, but then added that New York Foundling has 1,000 children in its care; most of their parents, he said, could benefit from a parent advocate. He wondered whether government would allocate the money needed to hire them.

The forum grew out of a movement of parents and their allies working over a span of 20 years to reform New York's child welfare system. This book is about that movement and the people in it—parents whose children were placed into foster care who then turned their lives around, and commissioners, lawyers, foundation officers, social workers, and agency executives who implemented changes in the system. It is about the unprecedented changes parents and their allies brought about.

ACKNOWLEDGMENTS

I've had a contract with Oxford University Press to write a book on child welfare for almost 20 years. Originally I intended to write a history of the cycles of crisis, reform, and crisis in child welfare over the past 200 years. Although I realized that I was not the right person to write that book, I also realized the pattern was there, and I had a theory as to why that pattern existed: There wasn't a countervailing force in child welfare to overcome the forces of the public bureaucracies and private agencies pushing for the status quo, or as they might couch it, stability or predictability, or even the best interests of the child.

The book I've written presents the story of the creation of a countervailing force—organized parents and their allies—that developed over the past 20 years. During that time as both a participant and as an observer, I've worked with and learned from many people.

Many authors in their acknowledgments thank their wives last. I'd like to thank mine first. Not only is Risa Jaroslow a fine and rigorous editor in all things, she has been and is the love of my life during the 45 years we've been married. Almost 20 of those years have been tied up with writing this book, which drew me away from her more times than either of us wanted.

Peter Carry edited the entire manuscript, some parts multiple times. His questions were as helpful as his gracious and elegant editing. My editor at Oxford, Dana Bliss, was a pleasure to work with, very supportive and very helpful. I would also like to thank Maura Roessner, editor at Oxford who was always encouraging and supportive but left before the manuscript was completed.

John Courtney and I have worked together for more than 30 years, and in the same office for more than 20 of them. His sage advice and vast knowledge of the child welfare system helped me and countless others who work in, or are affected by, the child welfare system.

Richard Lieberman, Jim Cohen, and Steve Rosenheck have read count-less chapters, providing helpful guidance and, more importantly, life-long friendship.

Berny Horowitz, a scholar of child welfare, sharpened my thinking and my work for more than 30 years; most recently he nailed the focus of the book.

Many parents shared their stories with me. Some are included in the book. I thank you all for your honesty, openness, and fighting spirit for justice.

Many administrators, researchers, journalists, lawyers, and advocates responded to my many requests for information. The child welfare community and I are lucky to have so much data and to have journalists and others who write about it so well.

I would like to thank the many foundations, large and small, who supported the reforms in New York City's child welfare system in the past 20 years. I am happy to say that their insightful and courageous funding supported services and social change, and while I worked closely with several of these groups over that period, this book was written independently and was not funded by any organization.

I would like to thank three giants in child welfare who I had the good fortune to work with: Trude Lash, Jim Dumpson and Peter Forsythe. Special thanks to another giant from that generation, Julius C. C. Edelstein who believed in government's responsibility to serve its people. He also believed in the reforms we were bringing about and in the Child Welfare Watch which he helped launch.

Finally, I would like to thank the anonymous donor of the Child Welfare Fund. She gave me an opportunity that few people have. I had the chance to have resources—limited in comparison with the $2 billion annual budget of New York City's child welfare system—to help children and families. She and her husband who first suggested that she and I work together have been devoted to the well-being of children for decades. I thank them for their generosity and trust.

Parents play a big part in this book; my parents played a big part in my life. My mother died in 2002 and my father died in 2012. He read the manuscript of this book and enjoyed it just as my parents enjoyed the work of each of their three children. I would like to dedicate this book to my parents, Hazel and Jerry Tobis, who created a family that nurtured each of the children to become who we wanted to be.

Until lions have their historians,
tales of the hunt shall only glorify the hunter.

African Proverb

INTRODUCTION

Tracey Carter[i] is an attractive, middle-aged, hard-working African-American mom. She wears neat jeans and a bright blue slicker with "Bridge Builders" written in large white letters on the back. She is a parent organizer who works in the storefront office of Bridge Builders on the corner of Ogden Avenue and 164th Street in the Highbridge section of the southwest Bronx. She helps parents who are struggling to come back "from the other side," as she describes her former life. No one would imagine that six of Tracey's 11 children had been in foster care and that she spent 13 years on the streets smoking crack.

Tracey is part of a growing number of mothers and some fathers in New York City and elsewhere who have been through hell. They were victims of domestic violence, homelessness, and poverty. Some became dependent on drugs. Many neglected their children, and some were subjects of a malicious, false report of abuse or neglect. They all had the crushing, enraging, and at times transforming experience of having their children taken from them and put into foster care by the city government's child protective service department.

These parents changed their lives over several years. Many recognized their role in the harm they caused their children; others, whose children were removed in violation of the parent's rights, fought to right the wrong. They all battled to regain custody of their kids. Many entered drug treatment programs, got intensive counseling, moved out of their abusive relationships, got jobs, filed lawsuits, and were reunited with their children.

Some like Tracey took the next step and were trained as parent organizers. They learned how the child welfare system operates, how to help themselves and others, and how to fight against child welfare policies

---

i. All parents profiled in this book agreed to have their real name used. The names of parents in stories they wrote in other publications are also their real names.

and practices that too often leave families victimized by a system that is supposed to help them.

Hundreds of these parents in New York City—mostly women, mostly African-Americans and Latinas, almost all poor—have found what is best within themselves, have transformed their lives, and are working one-on-one to help other mothers and fathers transform their lives. A few work as community organizers who strive to end the systemic abuses of the enormous, impersonal, often mismanaged child welfare bureaucracy. They worked alongside their allies to change child welfare—child welfare commissioners who recognized that their bureaucracies have mistreated many families, social workers who collaborated with parents, foundation officers who used their resources to help parents and advocates, and lawyers who protected the rights of these indefatigable parents.

The book presents their perspective as the product of participant observation. During most of the period covered in the book I was the executive director of the Child Welfare Fund, which provided grants to parent organizations, advocacy groups, child welfare agencies, and the Administration for Children's Services (ACS) to reform the city's child welfare system. In addition, I had a direct role in administering two programs, Bridge Builders in the south Bronx, which helps families stay together, and the Parent Advocate Initiative, which promoted the hiring of parent advocates in foster care agencies. As a participant in the changes brought about in the past 20 years, my beliefs, or biases if you disagree with them, are woven into the pages of this book. First I believe that except in extreme situations when a child is in imminent danger, it is better for children to live with their families than to live in someone else's family or in a group home or in an institution. Decades of research support this conclusion.[1] Nevertheless, many families need help—child care, a job, better housing, health care, counseling, guidance to parent better—so that children can remain safely at home. Second, child welfare, and the movement to reform it, should be based primarily on rights not on service needs. That principle is enshrined in the United Nations Convention on the Rights of the Child (UNCRC), and in countless other documents that are often disregarded when it comes to families of children in the child welfare system. The United States is the only country in the United Nations that has not ratified the CRC, now that Somalia has agreed to sign.[2] And finally, I look at social change as a sociologist not as a social worker. My focus has been to analyze power, to influence how power is used, and to create a countervailing force to change a system as large and intransigent as New York's child welfare system. I believe that organized parents and their allies are the main constituency to create that countervailing force.

The book describes the significant changes in child welfare that occurred in the past 20 years. The number of children in foster care decreased from almost 50,000 in 1992 to under 14,000 today. More families receive preventive services so that their families can remain safely together. And many parents now have quality legal representation when they appear in family court. But the book argues not just that parents and their allies contributed to these changes, but that parents were decisive in bringing them about. Without their personal, active, and organized involvement in a movement, the changes would not have been as deep or lasted as long, though there have been setbacks and limits to the reforms. Child welfare improved during this period in other cities and states in which there was not a significant parents' movement, but those changes were not as profound and did not last as long, except when there were court-ordered consent decrees.

Other social welfare systems have parent advocates. In mental health, parents of children with mental illness have become fierce and powerful defenders of their children's rights. In the field of disabilities, parents have become major service providers. In education and Head Start, parents play important roles in shaping policy and programs. Child welfare is one of the last fields in which parents have found their voice. This book presents their story.

NEW YORK CITY'S CHILD WELFARE ROLLERCOASTER

New York City historically has had a troubled child welfare system. Over the years, the system, which is meant to care for abandoned, abused, or neglected children, repeatedly has been the subject of investigations by government, the media, and research centers that have revealed abuses of children by the system that is supposed to protect them. After the public became aware of these shortcomings, government often implemented reforms to curtail the abuses. More often than not, it was not long before the reforms were defunded, undermined, or shown to be unsuitable to solving the problems they were supposed to address. Then a new crisis would emerge. New York's child welfare system has been a rollercoaster ride from crisis to reform and back to crisis.

In 1979 I jumped onto that rollercoaster almost by chance.[ii] Carol Bellamy, president of the New York City Council at the time, hired me to

---

ii. I actually began working in child welfare, totally by chance, 3 years before in New Jersey's state child welfare agency, the Division of Youth and Family Services (DYFS). Having studied medical sociology in graduate school, I was hired as a health planner by Bill Resnick, the quirky lawyer who directed DYFS's Research Bureau. My involvement with New York City child welfare began in 1979.

lead her human services department. As a social liberal and a fiscal conservative, she wanted to improve government while spending less. She asked me to find a sector of the city's troubled social welfare system that could be fixed in such a way that the reforms would save the city money and help her constituents.

After surveying a number of options I zeroed in on the child welfare system, the last resort for poor abused or neglected children. Typically child welfare has relied too heavily on foster care—the state's legal removal of a child from his or her family and placement in another person's home, usually that of a stranger, but sometimes that of a relative—as its first and main response to family problems.

New York City's child welfare system in 1979 was again in crisis. A *New York Magazine* article in December 1978 by Nicolas Pileggi described mistreatment of children by religiously affiliated private foster care agencies that operated on contracts with the city government.[3] A lawsuit filed 5 years earlier by the American Civil Liberties Union had documented discrimination against black children by some of the same agencies.[4] According to city government data, children languished in foster care for an average of more than 4 years, though their placements were supposed to be short-term. Children who entered foster care as infants routinely were not adopted until they were 7 years old or older. The city comptroller's financial audits of the religiously affiliated foster care agencies were 10 years out of date, and no oversight agency conducted programmatic audits. No one knew how the hundreds of millions of public dollars devoted to foster care were spent or how the children in out-of-home care were doing.

I organized a campaign from the council president's office to reform the system. The documents used in the campaign included an inventory describing a dozen recent reports pinpointing numerous shortcomings in New York City's foster care system and a new financial analysis by Gerald Finch titled *Good Money After Bad*, showing that foster care performance tends to decline as total expenditures per care day increases, showing that poor performance could not be blamed on inadequate funds.[5] The council president's staff joined forces with the office of City Comptroller Harrison Golden and drafted resolutions to be put before the city's Board of Estimate, the body that then effectively controlled city contracts.[iii] The

iii. The now-defunct Board of Estimate then was the New York City government body that approved all city contracts above $10,000. It was composed of the mayor, the council president, and the comptroller, who each had two votes, and the five borough presidents, who each had one vote. In 1989, the Supreme Court of the United States declared the New York City Board of Estimate unconstitutional on the grounds that the city's most populous borough, Brooklyn, had no greater effective representation

board unanimously passed the resolutions authorizing dramatic reforms.[iv] Perhaps the most important was the requirement that private foster care agencies, which annually received $300 million in public money, would be evaluated yearly to make sure that foster children received at least adequate care. As a result of the reforms, New York City's child welfare system improved for several years. Fewer children were in foster care, more children visited their birth families, on average children returned to their homes more quickly, and fewer children were abused while in care. Three of the worst foster care agencies were closed.[6]

In fewer than 10 years the system was in crisis once more. In the mid-to-late 1980s, the city found that it could not cope with the number of children coming into care. Infants were living for months in hospital wards. Children slept in the city's stark child welfare reception center. Adolescents spent nights in city offices. The shortage of beds abated by the end of the decade, but the underlying ills were not cured.

Then, in the early 1990s, the city, responding to pressure from the voluntary agencies and budget constraints, eliminated the evaluation system that had contributed to the improvements of the early 1980s.[7] This dramatically reduced New York's ability to determine how well agencies were caring for children. The number of children in out-of-home placements in 1992 reached the staggering level of almost 50,000, more than twice the previous record.[8] In 1995, 6-year-old Elisa Izquierdo was killed by her mother after the city's child welfare agency returned her to her mother from foster care. Another round of reforms began.

I wrote my doctoral dissertation on the child welfare rollercoaster in New York City and received a Ph.D. in sociology from Yale University in 1989, 22 years after I had entered graduate school. Working in the real world of child welfare slowed down my academic work, but by then I was hooked on trying to fix the system on which I had stumbled.

on the Board than the city's least populous borough, Staten Island. This arrangement was a violation of the Fourteenth Amendment's Equal Protection Clause. Under the 1990 New York City Charter most of the responsibilities of the Board of Estimate were delegated to the New York City Council.

iv. When the mayor's office learned that we had introduced resolutions to hold foster care agencies accountable, which would embarrass a mayoral agency (Special Services for Children, the name at the time of the city's child welfare agency), his representative to the Board of Estimate, Victor Botnick, called me to his office, offering to implement an accountability system if we would withdraw the resolutions. By that time we had the votes on the Board of Estimate to pass the resolution without the mayor's support. Eventually Botnick, Mayor Koch, and even the agencies publicly supported the reforms, although they had strongly opposed them in the meetings before the May 4, 1979 Board of Estimate session. Financial concessions by the comptroller in a closed door meeting changed their minds.

I was intrigued by the pattern I saw. Not only did the child welfare system in New York City in the last quarter of the twentieth century have a pattern of crisis, reform, and crisis, but when I looked back over American history, the same pattern emerged throughout the country. The system designed to protect abused, destitute, orphaned, and/or abandoned children repeatedly failed those children. In response, government and private agencies implemented reforms that sometimes led to modest improvements and at other times dramatically changed the system of child protection. However, after each period of reform, the aspects of the system harmful to children reappeared.

Poorhouses, which sheltered destitute, abandoned, and/or orphaned children with insane adults, adult paupers, and criminals in the eighteenth and nineteenth centuries, had annual mortality rates above 25%.[9] By the mid-nineteenth century, orphanages had widely replaced poorhouses as places to shelter and protect children. In time orphanages were found to be isolating institutions that were harmful to children and costly to operate. The Children's Aid Society developed Orphan Trains in the mid-nineteenth century as a progressive alternative to orphanages. The trains transported poor urban children from the East Coast to the Midwest for placement with farm families. When it became known that this program hurt children because of lack of supervision, by encouraging child labor and by placing Catholic children in Protestant homes, moderate reforms were periodically put into place. But the ills persisted. The Orphan Trains stopped running in 1929 at the start of the Great Depression, when child labor was no longer in high demand. The Orphan Trains were replaced by foster boarding homes, which now constitute the principal way abused or neglected children are sheltered.

This is true, though foster care in New York City and throughout the United States is frequently criticized for harming children and neglecting their families. Foster care reforms have repeatedly been implemented, but the same shortcomings resurface: Too many children are removed from their families, too many children remain in foster homes too long, and too many children end up severely damaged or homeless when they leave foster care.

In the 1990s, Family Preservation was the reform that was hailed as an antidote to the ills of foster care. Family Preservation programs provided assistance to families in their homes, enabling some children who might have been placed into foster care to remain safely with their families. The concept was consistent with research that showed the importance of maintaining family bonds, and it was less expensive per child than foster care. Most evaluations of the programs, however, found scant evidence of substantial success. According to Duncan Lindsey, a sociologist at UCLA, "the most rigorous tests of family preservation to date fail to find evidence of its effectiveness in either protecting children or keeping families together."[10] The way the programs were implemented—they attempted to solve a family's immediate problems but did not possess the resources to confront the larger obstacles poor families confront, such as the lack of good housing or jobs—doomed them to largely insignificant results.

Each of these reforms was a response to the shortcomings of the previous system. But in each case the solution was defined narrowly as improving poor supervision, augmenting insufficient funds, and/or upgrading inadequate facilities or programs for the small group of abused or neglected children. The bigger issues of society's or the child welfare system's responsibility to poor children and their families were not addressed.

In each case, a more advanced service system replaced a more primitive one. But each time a new system was implemented or a new reform was introduced, it was done in a way that left the underlying problems unaddressed, or if the reform did confront a fundamental issue, over time the reform was revised, diminished, or defunded. As *New York Times* reporter Nina Bernstein writes in *The Lost Children of Wilder*, arguably the best book written on child welfare:

> The two hundred year history of American child welfare is littered with programs once hailed as reforms and later decried as harmful or ineffective, only to emerge again in the guise of new solutions to past failures.[11]

The result has been the rollercoaster pattern of child welfare. And that posed the questions that intrigued me: Why does the child welfare system never permanently improve? Why does it continue to harm children and families, even after substantial reform? And most important, what can be done to break the pattern?

WHY THE ROLLERCOASTER

The causes of the child welfare rollercoaster are complicated and require an historical analysis that is beyond the scope of this book. Nevertheless, I will briefly mention some of the most salient factors that keep the rollercoaster rolling. Then I will focus on the last of the above questions, which is the heart of this book: What has been done and can be done to change the pattern?

Taking good care of poor children, especially children of color, has never been—and is not now—a high priority in the United States. The kids in the child welfare system are almost all poor and a disproportionate number of them are children of color. In New York City, 96% of the children in care in 2007 were children of color.[12] Because meeting the needs of these youngsters and their families is not a priority, the system devised to help and protect them is pulled in many directions at once as it works to attain its nominal goal of protecting children and helping their families. Alfred Kadushin, a seminal thinker in the field and the author of an encyclopedic child welfare textbook, writes that "Although the needs and rights of children are a matter of great concern within the individual family, this concern has not been reflected in public policy."[13]

As other concerns shape the system and the way parents and children are treated, the system adopts measures that are often harmful to children and their families. It is partly because of these divergent pressures that the child welfare system performs its purportedly principal functions so poorly.

One of those competing priorities is regulating the behavior of the poor. David G. Gil, a professor of social work at the Heller School for Social Policy and Management at Brandeis University, argues that child welfare services are designed to compensate for various shortcomings in our society's primary systems of socialization and social control. He writes:

> [Child welfare's] function is simply to complete and correct the unfinished tasks of the primary systems, namely the adaptation of children to prevailing class determined patterns of life. Child welfare policies and services are therefore supplementary tools of the state employed in reproducing and preserving the social status quo and its ideology.[14]

This function of preserving the societal status quo and regulating the behavior of the potentially disruptive poor is easy to see historically and, as described later in this introduction, is easily seen in other cultures. It is more difficult to recognize this function in our own culture. The Orphan Trains of the nineteenth century, for example, were nominally designed to improve the well-being of children, but they also had the explicit function of protecting New York City from delinquent, immigrant Catholic youth. Charles Loring Brace, the Protestant minister who founded the Children's Aid Society and the Orphan Trains, described this function of the program:

> These boys and girls, it should be remembered, will soon form the great lower class of our city. They will influence elections; they may shape the policy of the city; they will assuredly, if unreclaimed, poison society all around them.[15]

Today, the social control function of the child welfare system is more directed at the mothers of poor children than at the children themselves. A recent groundbreaking study looked at all children born in California in 1999 to determine the percentage of youngsters whose families were investigated by child protective services at some time before the child turned 7 years. The rates were higher than the researchers expected: The families of 19.8% of all children and 38.5% of black children in the state were reported to child protective services.[16] As the researchers in the California study conclude, "If a family has not been touched by the child welfare system directly, it knows many others—friends, neighbors and relatives—who have been."

The pervasiveness of these investigations and the resultant child removals have created a widespread and profound fear in inner-city neighborhoods. As African-American, Latino, immigrant, and other impoverished parents repeatedly jump through hoops to keep their children or to have their children returned to them, they become fearful, preoccupied, and compliant. That is exactly what a child welfare system focused on social control seeks to accomplish.

This orientation toward social control has also limited the decision-making role parents are afforded in their own cases and has excluded them until very recently from having any input in shaping the programs that are supposed to help them and their families.

Under the social control model of child welfare, victims of poverty and racism are blamed for their condition, thus obscuring the true sources of their problems, such as overcrowded apartments, double-digit unemployment, lack of health care, and bankrupt schools. This model promotes the idea that the mother is the primary cause of her family's plight. When a child falls from an unguarded window, the mother's other children are placed into foster care because of her neglect.[17] The landlord who failed to provide the required window guards does not go to jail. The impoverished single mother who leaves her sick child alone while she goes to buy medicine sees her child placed in foster care because of her neglect. The welfare system that won't provide respite care or cut thousands of publicly funded daycare slots is not responsible.[18] The father who must collect empty cans to supplement his meager income has his child placed in foster care if he unleashes his rage at home. The business that just laid him off has no responsibility. Parents are responsible for their actions, but so are the individuals and institutions who create the intolerable conditions under which some parents and children must live. The child welfare system, however, singles out parents, primarily poor minority mothers, for blame.

Another competing concern for the child welfare system in the United States is that it must serve as a cover for the country's refusal to give support to vulnerable families at a level comparable to that provided by most other industrialized countries. America's child welfare policies, programs, and funding focus on reporting and investigating child abuse and neglect and on removing children from their homes. Most of the rest of the industrialized world concentrates on assistance as the first response to family problems.[19] In Germany, for example, if child abuse or neglect is reported in a home, a social worker from a private agency visits the family to assess its needs and ensure that services such as child care, therapy, or housing are forthcoming. If the inappropriate treatment of the children continues, the social worker then contacts the state to have the children removed from the home. In the United States, children at risk are often removed from their families without consideration being given to what the families need to address their problems.

Americans declare their concern for poor children by supporting a massive system to report abuses and remove children from their families, rather than a program that would help struggling families by improving the difficult environments in which they live and reducing the stresses in the home that contribute to abuse and neglect. As Martin Guggenheim, Fiorello LaGuardia Professor of Clinical Law at New York University Law School, writes:

> Child welfare has become an extremely important component of modern government in the United States because it furthers the interests of those who generally oppose spending tax money on children but who need to deflect criticism that they are anti-child.[20]

A third complicating factor for the child welfare system is that it serves as a resource for organizations that receive money from the government to provide services.[21] In New York City, the children in out-of-home placements are cared for by large, powerful, politically connected organizations, many of which are affiliated with Catholic, Jewish, or Protestant religious institutions. The organizational requirements of these institutions often take precedence over the needs of the children and families they serve. These foster care agencies have successfully pressed government to reimburse them on a per diem basis. They receive a specific amount for each day a child is in their care. Once a youngster is discharged, the money stops coming in. This creates a disincentive to discharge children. The negative impact of this scheme is dramatic. The Adoption and Safe Families Act (ASFA) was passed by the federal government in 1997 to reduce the length of time children remain in foster care, so that they go home or are adopted more quickly. However, ASFA did not change the way foster care agencies are reimbursed. Ten years after the federal legislation was passed, according to the research team at the University of Chicago that evaluated the impact of ASFA, the average length of stay of foster children in New York City had *increased*. And, according to the Chicago research, "Children in the post-ASFA years had an even lower rate of family reunification [nationwide] when compared with children served in the mid-1990s."[22]

PATHS TO REFORM

A countervailing force is needed to create a child welfare system that meets the needs of children and families and breaks the cycle of crisis, reform, and crisis. Parents and children who have been subjected to the child welfare system have begun to speak about the needs of children and families and stand up for their rights. Alone they cannot break the recurring cycles of crises, but they are working with foundations, lawyers, and like-minded supporters in government and child welfare agencies. Together they have created a paradigm shift, at least for the moment. The shift is toward assisting families when they are having difficulty rather than removing their children as the first response. It includes ensuring that parents' rights are protected through adequate legal representation. And it promotes listening to the concerns of parents and young people whose lives have been changed forever by their contact with the child welfare system.

This book not only tells their stories, but it also recounts my journey as a participant-observer. I traveled three different paths to gain appreciation of the vital role of parents and youth in changing child welfare.

The first path was one I followed long before I had thought much about child welfare. In the 1960s I worked as a civil rights organizer in Mississippi and then as an antiwar activist while in graduate school in New Haven, Connecticut. I saw that community organizing—registering sharecroppers to vote, demonstrating in the streets, walking on a picket line, and researching and publicizing a shared problem—could change things. It was amid that ferment that I learned that people should have the right to participate in the decisions that affect their lives. I also found that if people act together, they can make a tremendous difference, not only in their individual lives but also in the institutional structures that shape and constrain so many of their choices.

Over the next 30 years, two other paths connected to child welfare informed my views about what will make a difference. One shaped my thinking about the functions of child welfare and the importance of social reformers working with government. The other shaped my thinking about solutions to the crises in child welfare.

The second path led me to UNICEF and the World Bank. After the fall of the Berlin Wall in 1989, the world saw the horrors of Romanian orphanages. UNICEF asked me to help it reduce the number of children entering Romania's large residential institutions. The team I worked with in Romania identified key decision points that led to children being placed into residential care and created community-based services as alternatives to out-of-home care so that poverty and its related problems would drive fewer children into orphanages.

I shuttled back and forth to Romania for about 10 years, and, according to recent reports, the number of children in institutions there has fallen dramatically,[23] though the conditions in the remaining orphanages range from unsatisfactory to cruel. A stipulation for Romania's accession to the European Union—reducing the number of children in residential institutions—provided the pressure that allowed the work with children of UNICEF and others to take hold.

The World Bank learned about my activities in Romania and asked if I would perform the same function for it in Lithuania, not just for children but also for the disabled and the elderly. I began working as a consultant to the bank. In the 1960s the World Bank was, in my view, the center of an evil empire. I still feel that many of its structural adjustment loans do more harm than good, but I was able to develop an effective, humane, and, of particular interest to the bank, cost-saving approach to helping children and adults in need. In concert with Stockholm University's Department of Social Work,[v] my colleagues and I created community-based social services in Lithuania, which we then helped to replicate in other countries of Eastern Europe and the former Soviet Union. These programs provided family services and foster care for children, shelters for battered women and their children, day programs for the disabled, and home visiting for the elderly. One of the great ironies of my life was proudly working for the World Bank.

---

v. The international work of Stockholm University's Department of Social Work was overseen by Ronald Penton, a passionate, peripatetic, kind, and incomparable teacher and implementer of social welfare programs. He died in 2007 having influenced or transformed the child welfare systems of dozens of countries from Lithuania to Vietnam, leaving a great void in international social work.

Learning about child welfare systems in other parts of the world shaped my understanding of the shortcomings of child welfare in the United States. I wrote a report at the World Bank's request on residential child care in Eastern Europe and the former Soviet Union, which it published as a monograph in its Prague Series. I said in the report:

> Residential institutions...in most of Central and Eastern Europe and the former Soviet Union...served a dual role of social protection and social regulation. They also socialized individuals into the collectivist culture; deculturated ethnic minorities such as Roma (gypsies); educated and trained children and channeled them into the work force...[24]

The competition between the multiple functions of residential institutions in the former Soviet Union—protecting children and, more important to the powers-that-be, regulating their behavior and the behavior of their families—was visible to anyone who looked. Seeing the conflicting multiple functions of the child welfare system in a different culture made it easier for me to see the analogous circumstance in the United States. Working with the World Bank and UNICEF also made it clear that programs to help poor children and families were not sustainable without government's political and financial support.

The third path that shaped my thinking about solutions leads from the Child Welfare Fund. In the early 1990s a friend who had acquired an inheritance asked me to help her give it away with two main requirements. First, that we use the funds to help children and, second, that she would remain anonymous. We created the Child Welfare Fund, which for the next 18 years focused on changing New York's child welfare system. The Fund's approach was to provide both direct service grants to help children and families, and other grants to bring about reform of the child welfare system. Because I had worked as a community organizer in my youth, I believe that people have a right to participate in decisions that affect their lives. That right was almost universally denied in child welfare. One of our main activities was creating and supporting programs that give voice and power to parents and young people who are touched by the child welfare system.

My plan was to create a countervailing force to push child welfare to change. Over the next two decades, the Child Welfare Fund became a powerful force, supporting dozens of projects that enabled people embroiled in the child welfare system to speak for themselves. These include *Rise* and *Represent*, which are publications written by and for parents and young people, respectively, touched by the child welfare system; the Child

Welfare Organizing Project, which trains parents undergoing scrutiny by the child welfare system to be advocates for themselves and to press government to meet their needs and respect their rights; Bridge Builders, a collaboration of foundations, government, service providers, and community residents with child welfare experience who are now working to help their neighbors; Voices of Women, which organizes battered women to push for changes in public policy; and the *Nicholson v. Scoppetta* lawsuit, which protected battered women from having their children taken from them because the children had witnessed their mother being abused.

These projects helped those of us at the Child Welfare Fund to see that trained and organized parents who have hit bottom can find the best in themselves, change their lives, and fight back. Tracey Carter became sober and an activist after 13 years of crack addiction and losing six children to foster care and four to adoption by her sister. Julia McGuire voluntarily placed her children in foster care and then spent 10 years trying to get them back. She then helped other mothers do the same. Carlos Boyet, a self-described "former deadbeat father," spent 4 years getting his disabled son out of foster care. He then led support groups for parents who confronted the same challenges. These activists work or have worked with the Child Welfare Organizing Project in New York City, but there are also parent activists struggling to change the culture of child welfare in cities across the country.

At the Child Welfare Fund we learned from our work that if parents and children articulately, forcefully, and collectively express their needs and fight for their rights, those needs and rights will more likely be met and respected. Over the past two decades the voices of parents and youth have been loudly heard in New York City's child welfare system, which improved dramatically, albeit with ups and downs.

We now realize that part of the solution to the crises in child welfare lies in parents, young people, and their allies playing a significant role in shaping child welfare programs and policies. Their exclusion from decision making is a big reason that other concerns have dominated child welfare decision making.

MOVEMENT

In New York City and elsewhere the situation has begun to change. A movement has slowly developed in which parents who have had children taken from them and young people who have lived in foster care are taught their rights and are trained to serve as advocates for themselves and others, to testify at legislative hearings, to work in child welfare agencies as mentors and coaches for parents with children in foster care, and to advise senior government officials. And they have learned how to organize and demonstrate in the streets when those other avenues fail to bring the results they want. They have begun to shift child welfare's focus toward rights and assisting families rather than primarily focusing on needs and deficits.

The goal of these parents, young people, and their allies is to help families deal with problems in the home rather than have government remove children as the first response; to provide assistance so children who are placed in foster care can return home to a safe family environment, or to live satisfying lives if they cannot return home; and to ensure that the legal rights of parents and young people are protected when they must deal with the child welfare system.

This book tells the stories of these parents, their allies, and the organizations in which they work, describing the impact they are having on the system. The stories are not without their dark moments. Some parents' groups have remained small and others have folded. Efforts to organize youth in foster care have foundered against the often-grim reality of their lives. And some reforms that parents successfully implemented have been sidetracked. The rollercoaster pattern of crisis, reform, and crisis is changing very slowly, and only in a few cities and states, most prominently in New York City. Perhaps the pattern won't change completely and permanently without a stronger, permanent countervailing force, but parents, youngsters, and their allies are beginning to make unprecedented change.

THE CHAPTERS

Chapter 1 describes the child welfare playing field in New York City, and although some of the story takes place in the shadow of both the new and the old Yankee Stadium, even the Bronx Bombers couldn't play on a field as uneven as this one. The chapter describes the child welfare system, or at least the main elements of this vast $2 billion industry, in the 1990s at a time when parents had no voice and New York City had one of the worst child welfare systems in the United States. The chapter looks at who had the power—the religious agencies that had defined child welfare in New York City for at least the past century and the city child welfare bureaucracies.

Chapter 2 presents four mothers who have had their children placed into foster care: Sandra Killett, the articulate, feisty mother of an even more feisty adolescent who crossed every limit she set; Wanda Chambers, who spent 15 years off and on crack before 3 years in prison broke the cycle; Jeanette Vega, frightened, enraged, and a struggling young mother who hit her toddler when she saw him wander from her apartment building's courtyard onto the street; and Youshell Williams, who spiraled downward when her much older partner left her. She lost her job and became increasingly depressed and anxious, which led to her keeping her son and daughter home from elementary school.

The chapter discusses what at times might seem inexplicable: How can parents who have been through hell make such dramatic changes—to not only overcome their addiction, or control their rage or depression, or escape a violent partner—and then help other parents do the same? The chapter describes the circumstances that have allowed parents to find the best parts of themselves and become activists.

Chapter 3 discusses the three most important organizations pressing for change. Together they created an environment in which parents cornered by New York City's child welfare system could play a meaningful role in their own cases and could have a voice, along with their allies, in shaping child welfare programs and policies. These organizations are the Child Welfare Fund, the mouse that roared through the voice of parents, youth, and the hundred organizations it funded; Children's Rights, Inc., which used the *Marisol v. Giuliani* lawsuit and the Special Child Welfare Advisory Panel to restructure and strengthen the bureaucracy and, in spite of not intending to do so, to give parents greater influence in the new system; and the city government's Administration for Children's Services, which embraced and then championed reforms that put parents in the front seat instead of at the back of the bus or, as parents often felt, under the bus. Together these organizations unleashed a countervailing force that successfully pushed the system to reduce the number of children in foster care and to change in other ways, and allowed parents and their allies to be at the policy-making table, though parents report that they feel the real decisions are made at a different table.

Chapter 4 describes how parents and their allies took advantage of the opportunity to change child welfare policies and practices. The chapter profiles a new organization,[vi] the Child Welfare Organizing Project (CWOP), that quickly became the country's preeminent organization for training and organizing parents who had become embroiled in the child welfare

vi. New of course is a relative term. CWOP was founded in 1994 giving it more than an 18-year track record and $600,000 annually. The bureaucracies in New York City that oversee the child welfare system, on the other hand, go back at least to the middle of the twentieth century and it could be argued that their organizational

system. It also profiles three key people in CWOP: its long-time leader, Mike Arsham, who worked inside the system as a social worker and then came outside the system to change it; Sharwline Nicholson, the chairperson of CWOPs board of directors from 2006 to 2011 and the named plaintiff in the Nicholson lawsuit that ended the city's right to remove children from their home merely because they had witnessed their mother being beaten; and Tracey Carter, a CWOP-trained parent advocate who had been on the streets for 13 years and lost six children to the system.

CWOP is not the only parent-led or parent-focused organization working to reform the New York City child welfare system. There are other such organizations, but the impact of some of them has begun to wane and the sustainability of all of them is uncertain. Chapter 5 briefly describes several of these parent-led and parent-focused organizations and profiles four of them.

Rise magazine is the first. It publishes on-line and hard-copy editions in which appear the compelling, painful, and instructive stories of parents whose children have been placed in foster care. It operates on a shoestring but is read and used nationwide.

The second is Bridge Builders, a collaboration of parents from the Highbridge area of the South Bronx, some of whom have been involved in the child welfare system; social service agencies in the neighborhood; private foundations; and the city's child welfare agency. Together these groups have lowered the rate of reports of abuse and neglect and reduced the rate at which children from Highbridge are placed into foster care. Although its impact grew over several years, its funding has decreased as a result of government and foundation cutbacks; its impact is declining and its sustainability is uncertain.

The third is Voices of Women, an organization of survivors of domestic violence who provide support to each other and organize campaigns to reform particularly egregious aspects of child welfare. As often happens, when the founding director left the organization after 8 years, its focus shifted and its impact decreased.

The fourth organization, People United for Children, was created in the early1990s by Sharonne Salaam after her 15-year-old son, Yusef,

roots go back to public bureaucracies in the nineteenth century. Combined, their budgets are several billion dollars. The religiously based voluntary child welfare agencies that have dominated the system have been around for longer than even the public bureaucracies. The Children's Aid Society (Protestant), the New York Foundling Hospital (Catholic), and the Jewish Board of Family and Children's Services (Jewish) were incorporated in the latter half of the nineteenth century. The combined budgets of just these three agencies is close to half a billion dollars.

was arrested along with four friends for assaulting and raping a 28-year old female jogger in Central Park. All the boys were convicted and spent a combined total of 44 years in prison. They were freed after Matias Reyes, who was convicted for another rape, confessed to the attack on the Central Park Jogger. Sharonne created People United for Children (PUC) to work on behalf of youth in New York's juvenile justice system, but she soon realized that problems for children in the juvenile justice system begin farther upstream, in the child welfare system, and that became her focus in the mid-1990s. For a while, PUC had a significant impact, but it closed its doors in 2009 though Sharonne continues to fight the good fight.

Chapter 6 surveys the activities of parents and their allies across the United States. It describes a new bill of rights for parents embroiled in the child welfare system, and focuses on three areas: parent organizing to reform child welfare policy, legal representation for parents in family court, and the work of the Annie E. Casey Foundation and Casey Family Programs in promoting parents as mentors for mothers and fathers struggling to be reunited with their children in U.S. cities.

Chapter 7 gauges the effectiveness of child welfare reform efforts in New York City during the past 15 years. What has changed, what has not, and what has begun to slip? The short answer is that the system has improved dramatically, with reforms of unprecedented depth and duration. The most dramatic change is that the number of children in foster care has decreased from almost 50,000 to fewer than 14,000. The full story, however, is far more complicated. Much hasn't changed, and some reforms have begun to slip

The conclusion analyzes why these changes came about and have in many instances been sustained. It reviews the impact of parents who have been ensnared in the child welfare system working alongside their allies—two commissioners with a vision and a commitment to families, social workers and administrators in and outside foster care agencies, foundation officers, lawyers, and other advocates. Together they created a new force for change. Will that pressure for reform continue? Will another crisis cause the child welfare rollercoaster to accelerate downward? The chapter speculates about the future.

The epilogue briefly describes what has happened since Ronald Richter became commissioner after John Mattingly resigned in July 2011.

The annex presents a vision for the future of child welfare and a strategy to get there, describing what needs to be done by those involved in child welfare and by readers who care about children and having government serve its people.

This book tells the story of the energy and experience of parents who have been pariahs and are now partners. It recounts how their courage and resilience were tapped and harnessed. It describes what they and their allies have done to bring about reforms that meet the needs of poor mothers and their families, rather than punish them. It was written both to help readers to understand the child welfare system and to change it.

From Pariahs to Partners

CHAPTER 1

New York's Child Welfare System before the Reforms

Until about 1995, New York City's child welfare system was on a perpetual roller coaster ride from crisis to reform to crisis. The system operated outside the public consciousness, except when it burst into view after a foster child or a child at home was killed or a lawsuit charging the system with widespread abuses was filed. Although it helped some children and families, this large, costly, fragmented, and in many ways archaic system had failed to help many of the children it served, harmed countless others, regularly neglected families with desperate needs, and frustrated the people who worked in it. Of course, New York's system did not operate in a vacuum, and cities across the country were on their own wild rides. To understand and appreciate the extent of the reforms in New York within the larger national context, some background on the role of the federal government is useful.

FEDERAL ROLE IN CHILD WELFARE

The contemporary child welfare system in the United States began in 1935 when the federal government began to fund and regulate child welfare through the Social Security Act.[1] In 1961 Congress allowed welfare payments (Aid to Families with Dependent Children, AFDC) to follow children into foster care, contributing to an increase in the number of children in care.[2]

In exchange for government funding, states are required to comply with federal standards for the care of children and for the administration of child welfare programs. The federal government's Administration for Children and Families, a branch of the Department of Health and Human Services, administers the federal government's funding, regulatory, and oversight roles in child welfare.

In 1974 the federal Child Abuse Prevention and Treatment Act (P.L. 93-247) created the child protective services system with mandated reporting and investigation of abuse and neglect, again increasing the number of children in care.

As one of the last initiatives of the Carter Administration, Congress passed the Adoption Assistance and Child Welfare Act of 1980 (P.L. 96-272). It was the first federal law to set time limits on how long children could stay in foster care (18 months) and required "reasonable efforts" to assist families before removing children. Nevertheless, the number of children in foster care throughout the nation continued to rise, in part because foster care reimbursement remained an open-ended federal entitlement for states and localities. Far less is available to prevent foster care.

In 1993 Congress passed and President Clinton signed what is now called the Promoting Safe and Stable Families Act, which provides additional, though limited, funding for family preservation. In spite of the legislation, the national foster care population continued to grow, reaching an all-time maximum of 567,000 in care in 1999.

As the numbers in care increased nationally, Congress passed the Adoption and Safe Families Act of 1997, again trying to reduce the number of children in care. The legislation required, with few exceptions, that states seek the termination of parental rights if a child is in foster care for 15 of the previous 22 months. After 1999 the number of children in care began to decrease. With passage of the Fostering Connections to Success and Increasing Adoptions Act of 2008, which provides funding to support relatives to care for children and improves incentives for adoption, the number of children in care continued to decrease, dropping to 400,000 in 2012.[3]

In cities across the country, especially in large urban areas, child welfare had been repeatedly criticized or sued for wasting public dollars, harming children, or contributing to their deaths. In the mid-1990s 25 state child welfare systems were either being sued or were operating under court order.[4] New York City was being sued. Since 1995 improvements have occurred in child welfare systems in New York and across the country. In New York City, the number of children in foster care decreased by 72% between 1995 and 2012; nationally in the same time period the decrease was only 17%.[i,5] This book looks at the movement of parents and their allies in contributing to that difference.

THE NEW YORK SYSTEM

Federal involvement in child welfare did not create an integrated national system. In other cities and states across the country, as in New York, the child welfare system is a conglomeration of numerous—in New York's case the number reaches into the hundreds—of poorly coordinated government organizations and voluntary agencies: powerful and weak, religious and secular, progressive and archaic, exemplary and incompetent.

What was—and still is—unique about New York City is the extent to which child welfare services were privatized.[ii] New York City has the only large child welfare system in the country in which foster care has been entirely privatized.[6] Since the nineteenth century most foster care in New York has been provided by voluntary, primarily faith-based, service providers with names like Catholic Guardian Society, Jewish Child Care Association, and Episcopal Social Services. These agencies, some of which have provided child welfare services for more than 150 years, have had enormous influence in shaping the system, though that influence has waned in the past decade.

i. Even if we look at the high point of children in care nationally, 567,000 in 1999, and compare it to 400,000 children in care in 2012, the decrease is only 29%, less than half the decrease in New York City.

ii. The first significant growth in contracting out of child welfare services across the country began in the early 1960s with amendments to the Social Security Act. State and county efforts at privatization in child welfare have increased in waves since then. By 2001, according to a report by the U.S. Department of Health and Human Services, nationwide child welfare agencies contract out 58% of all family preservation services, 42% of all residential treatment services, and 52% of case management services for adoption. [Child Welfare League of America (2003), *An Assessment of the Privatization of Child Welfare Services* (Washington, DC: CWLA, 2003): 13, citing USDHHS (2001), *National Survey of Child and Adolescent Well-Being.*] The CWLA, trying to cast as positive a light as possible on contracting out since it represents private child welfare service providers, concludes in its book reviewing privatization: "in some ways these efforts [at privatization] have been successful, and in other ways, they have presented substantial challenges that have not been readily overcome." [(CWLA (2003): 293).]

In 1980 there were 79 voluntary foster care agencies in New York City; in 2011 there were about 30, a decrease reflecting two facts: that fewer children are in foster care and that the average size of foster care agencies has increased. Half of the children in New York City foster care are in Catholic agencies connected to the Archdiocese of New York or the Diocese of Brooklyn and Queens.[iii] Several of the voluntary child welfare agencies are large, with budgets above a hundred million dollars each. The money they receive to operate their child welfare programs comes almost exclusively from public coffers, about a third each from the federal, state, and city governments.

These agencies are funded in part and regulated by the Administration for Children's Services (ACS), New York City's public child welfare agency. ACS also administers child protective services, which investigates reports of abuse and neglect of children. New York State's Office of Children and Family Services licenses child welfare agencies, regulates them, establishes rates at which agencies are reimbursed, administers the State Central Registry of Child Abuse and Neglect, and monitors the performance of local districts, such as New York City.

The New York City Family Court is the other center of power in child welfare. Its judges decide if a child should be removed from a parent's custody, if a parent's rights to rear a child should be terminated, or if a child should be returned home.

More than 100,000 children New York City families are caught up in this mix each year—either investigated by child protective services, having a child in foster care, or receiving services to prevent child removal.[7] Most of these families are from poor, black, and Latino neighborhoods. These families had little role in the decisions made about their own cases and no role in shaping how service programs designed to assist the parents and children or child welfare in general worked. Although the center of power in child welfare over the decades has shifted between the voluntary agencies and the public

iii. In 1987 53.4% of the children in foster care were in Catholic agencies, 6% were in agencies affiliated with the Federation of Jewish Philanthropies, 26.8% were with the Federation of Protestant Welfare Agencies or were unaffiliated, and 7.3% were in the city's direct care program. [David Tobis, "The New York City Foster Care System, 1979–1988: The Rise and Fall of Reform" (PhD dissertation, Yale University,1989): 22.] In 2011, after the elimination of the city's direct care program, the percentage of children in Catholic foster care beds (including family foster homes, residential care, specialized family foster care, and other settings) was 50.1%. [New York City Administration for Children's Services, *Foster Care Awarded Slots by Borough, Contract Term Begins: July 1, 2011* (New York: Administration for Children's Services). Calculation by the author.]

bureaucracy, neither the children nor their parents were ever part of the power equation—until recently.

This vast, complex, and changing system is difficult to summarize in spite of or, more accurately, because of my having spent the past 30 years studying and trying to reform it. Rather than drown the reader in the details of child welfare, this chapter focuses sharply on the players with the power—the religious and secular agencies that provide the services; the New York City public bureaucracy that investigates families and underwrites and regulates the system; and Family Court, which authorizes both removal of children from their homes and their discharge from foster care.

CHILD WELFARE AGENCIES

Religious agencies have been involved in the delivery of child welfare services from the time the city was the Dutch colony of New Amsterdam. Orphanages run by religious organizations proliferated in New York and other large port cities in the middle of the nineteenth century to care for destitute and street children who were often the by-products of industrialization and immigration.[iv] Religious organizations created orphanages to meet the needs of their own poor, to protect them from the encroachment and proselytizing by other denominations, and to shield the rest of society from these troublesome children.[8]

The Children's Aid Society, founded by a Congregational minister, Charles Loring Brace, developed the Orphan Trains in the 1850s to transport vagrant, delinquent, or neglected children to farms in the Midwest. That many of these children were Catholic immigrants who were sent to Protestant homes contributed to the creation by Catholics of New York Foundling's orphanage in the late 1860s.[9] Jewish orphanages expanded in the middle to the end of the nineteenth century to care for the children of impoverished Eastern European Jews fleeing pogroms and ghettoization.

Over the years the influence of these faith-based agencies has ebbed and flowed, depending on the political and financial climate and the number of children in foster care. By the middle of the twentieth century, faith-based agencies were the dominant force in New York's child welfare system. Although almost all of the agencies' money came, as it still does,

iv. City and state government promoted these agencies and led to their expansion. Public funding not only supported the religious institutions from the early nineteenth century but state law permitted the establishment of public institutions only if no private ones existed. [S. Imbrogno, "Subsidy in New York State to Voluntary Child-Care Agencies" (PhD dissertation, New York University, 1965).]

from the government, as late as 1979 neither the city, the state, nor the federal government conducted programmatic evaluations assessing the care the agencies provided to children with the hundreds of millions of taxpayers' dollars they received. Financial audits were routinely filed 10 or more years late, which not only rendered them useless as a regulatory tool but also meant that government was allowing the agencies to operate in violation of the law without any repercussions.[10]

The agencies decided which children in the state's custody they would accept into their care. As a result, children who were not the cream of the impoverished, abused, and neglected crop were rejected and left with no one to care for them. Similarly, the influx of blacks who moved north after World War II as part of the Great Migration, led to a flood of their children into the foster care system. Catholic and Jewish agencies often refused to accept Protestant children of color, falling back on the argument that they existed to serve children of their faith and ethnicities. In response, the city created a direct care program in 1949, which was soon serving 10% of all the foster care children in the city.[v] Responding to the discrimination against black children by the foster care system, the American Civil Liberties Union in 1973 filed *Wilder v. Bernstein* on their children's behalf against Catholic and Jewish foster care agencies and the city.[vi] The lawsuit dragged on for 25 years because it was such a political hot potato. It touched on hot-button issues such as separation of church and state, racial discrimination, provision of family planning, and whether the government, as the funder of the child welfare system, should decide which children should be cared for by which agencies. The story of the lawsuit is told in riveting detail by Nina Bernstein in her book *The Lost Children of Wilder*.[11]

One source of the foster care agencies' power is their affiliation with politically influential religious denominations. They are also part of faith-based federations that coordinate their activities.[vii] In the area of

v. For the next half century the city directly provided out of home care to foster children whom the voluntary agencies did not want to serve. The settlement of the *Wilder v. Bernstein* lawsuit gave the city more control over placements. As the number of white children in care decreased, as did the total number of children in care, agencies were more willing to serve children whom they might not have served in the past. In 2008 the city ended its direct provision of foster care.

vi. In legal terms the plaintiffs alleged that religiously affiliated child care agencies provided foster care services with public funds in violation of the Establishment and Free Exercise Clauses of the First Amendment, and that policies of racial and religious matching of foster children denied equal access to services in violation of the Equal Protection Clause [78Civ. 957 (S.D.N.Y.) June 14, 1973].

vii. Catholic Charities of the Archdiocese of New York, Catholic Charities of Brooklyn and Queens, UJA Federation (Jewish), and the secular Federation of Protestant Welfare Agencies.

child welfare this coordination is done through the Council of Family and Child Caring Agencies (COFCCA), which is a lobbying organization and a trade association of businesses in child welfare. It represents virtually the entire New York foster care industry in negotiations regarding government policies, procedures, and funding. The agreements on these issues that COFCCA reaches with the city are then incorporated in the purchase of service contracts between each foster care agency and New York City. COFCCA plays a similar role with the state government regarding state regulations, reimbursement rates, and funding levels. It is both ironic and a sign of the foster care agencies' power that the city permits them to use public funds to pay their annual dues to COFCCA to influence government policy.[12]

The city's reliance on these agencies over the past two centuries and the influence they exert have shaped the city's child welfare system. Although the individual agencies and the religious federations and denominations that stand behind them are often unnamed players in child welfare crises, their actions shape how children and families experience the system.

THE FOSTER CARE BED CRISIS

The behind-the-scenes story of the foster care bed crisis in the mid-1980s illustrates the influence these agencies have had. After 10 years of steady decline in the foster care caseload, which reached 16,200 children, the lowest total since at least 1960, the caseload began to rise in the spring of 1985 because of a flood of crack-affected[viii] babies entering the system, the housing shortage, and the increase in teenage pregnancies. At first the cumbersome child welfare system had difficulty changing direction from shrinking to expanding its bed capacity. That created a bed shortage. But a campaign by voluntary agencies, in which John Cardinal O'Conner, the Catholic archbishop of New York, took the lead, turned a bed shortage into a bed crisis.

Nine months after O'Conner was installed as archbishop, Mayor Ed Koch invited him to participate in a news conference on housing. At the December 1984 press conference the archbishop surprised the mayor by announcing he was examining ways to withdraw the archdiocese from the city-funded foster care system. "We will not sell souls for city contracts," he said.[13] From O'Conner's perspective, many city policies menaced Catholic

---

viii. Children were placed into foster care if their crack-addicted mothers were incapable of caring for them or if they had any signs of crack-cocaine in their blood.

doctrine, restricted the independence of foster care agencies, and upset their financial bottom lines. Henceforth, the city's contracts with all voluntary foster care agencies, he correctly feared, would contain new policies that would restrict the agencies' independence that they believed was in the best interests of children. Three issues were particularly salient from O'Conner's perspective. First, Koch's recent Executive Order 50 required any agency that contracted with the city not to discriminate against gays and lesbians in its hiring practices. Second, the *Wilder v. Bernstein* settlement, which was being negotiated at the time, seemed certain to demand that all agencies, including Catholic ones, make family planning available to teens in their care. The *Wilder* settlement also seemed likely to strip the agencies of control over which children were placed in their care. Cardinal O'Conner, fearful that increased government regulation would not stop with child care, said in a speech at the time in Washington, "Will the A.C.L.U. [which filed the Wilder lawsuit] stop with child-care institutions? We expect nursing homes to be next and then our hospitals. How long can we fight the legal battle that already has cost us a fortune?"[14]

Third, the reforms mandated by the New York City Board of Estimate in 1979 were having an impact on foster care agencies. The reforms required city government, for the first time, to conduct on-site monitoring of agencies' care of children through a Program Assessment System. It raised performance standards and required sanctions against agencies that performed below the new standards. At its height, in the mid-1980s, the city's Program Assessment System had approximately 100 staff members reviewing the performance of foster care agencies. Four agencies had their foster care contracts terminated because they were unable to improve their performance; others were in jeopardy of being closed.[15]

O'Conner followed through on his threat. At a time when the crack epidemic was increasing the need for beds, Catholic agencies, which had more than half the foster care beds, continued to withdraw beds from the system. Archdiocesan agencies with upstate residential facilities reduced the number of children accepted from New York City and replaced them with children referred from upstate counties. Some of these residential foster care facilities were converted to serve children from the mental health and developmental disabilities systems. In addition, the archdiocesan agencies did not initially cooperate when the city asked them to provide more beds, turning a shortage into a crisis.[16]

For many agencies, withdrawing beds from the system was a result of business decisions, not a political response to unwanted government regulation. As the foster care caseload was decreasing and fewer foster care beds were needed, agencies logically decided to shift beds to other systems that were not shrinking, such as mental health, mental retardation, or juvenile justice. Similarly, during the years that the foster care caseload was decreasing, agencies cut back on recruitment of foster homes, shifting their foster home recruiters to other responsibilities or not replacing them when they left the agencies. These business decisions made it difficult to shift gears to recruit more homes when that became necessary.

Soon the city's child welfare agency's main executive conference room on the 16th floor of its headquarters at 80 Lafayette Street was converted into a daycare center and then into an overnight nursery to care for children for whom permanent foster care placements could not be found. At least 100 infants, so-called "boarder babies," were living in hospitals beyond medical necessity. The New York State Department of Social Services authorized some foster care facilities to operate over capacity. In April 1986, 60 workers stormed into the office of child welfare Commissioner Eric Brettschneider, demanding more foster care beds in which to place children. The following month the Legal Aid Society filed *Doe v. New York City Department of Social Services* in federal court, alleging that the city did not provide a bed for every child in foster care as required by law.[17]

O'Conner eventually achieved his child welfare goals—more independence and less government interference—though he used other means in addition to the bed crisis to achieve them. He and the Salvation Army, a large Protestant foster care agency, Agudath Israel, an orthodox Jewish social service agency, together with the Chamber of Commerce and Industry brought suit in New York Supreme Court against the City of New York to overturn Executive Order 50. In September 1984, the New York Supreme court struck down that part of the executive order that prohibited discrimination based upon "sexual orientation or affectional preference" on the grounds that the mayor had exceeded his authority.[18] *Wilder v. Bernstein* was not completely settled for another decade. When a partial settlement was reached in 1988, faith-based agencies were not required to provide family planning to children in their care, but the city child welfare agency, not the individual agencies, was directed to ensure that all children had "meaningful access to the full range of family planning information, services and counseling."[19] The Program Assessment System that the city's child welfare agency used to evaluate the performance of foster care agencies was slowly weakened. Over the years standards were lowered, exceptions to standards were allowed, and agencies were no longer sanctioned or closed as a result of unsatisfactory assessments. The assessment system was finally eliminated in 1992 because it no longer was useful to evaluate agencies and improve their performance; its elimination would save the city money.[20]

The influence of religious agencies on child welfare has ebbed and flowed since the mid-1980s. The Catholic agencies, the most powerful faith-based organizations in child welfare, reached perhaps the apogee of their influence under O'Conner. With the conflict between the religious child welfare agencies and the city behind them, Koch and O'Conner formed a political alliance, immortalized in the book they co-wrote, *His Eminence and Hizzoner* in 1989 when Koch was running for a fourth term as mayor.[ix]

Since the time of the Koch–O'Conner alliance the influence of the religious child welfare agencies has diminished. Edward Cardinal Egan, who replaced O'Conner as archbishop in 2000, and Archbishop Timothy Dolan, who replaced Egan in 2009, both played a lesser role in child welfare. The dramatic decrease in the number of children in foster care in the past 20 years also diminished the influence of the voluntary agencies. When the foster care system is expanding, as it did in the second half of the 1980s, the agencies find themselves in a seller's market. In the period after 1985, the city was desperate to have more beds and was at the mercy of the agencies that provide the beds, which greatly increased their influence. When the system is shrinking, as it has been since the 1990s, the city can pick and choose which agencies it uses to provide the decreasing number of beds it needs, greatly strengthening the city's hand.

As a result, the city has more recently been able to pursue an agenda that at times has conflicted with the interests of the faith-based and other voluntary agencies. The commissioner of New York City's Administration for Children's Services, John B. Mattingly (2004–2011), summarized the agencies' influence as follows:

> I think Giuliani [Rudolph Giuliani, mayor of New York City, 1994–2001] and his rough and tumble ways, and the fact that over the years there were fewer kids in care, the administration didn't need the voluntaries as much as they did in the past. I think that began the process. Since Giuliani and this mayor [Michael Bloomberg, mayor of New York City, 2001–2013], they haven't had

---

ix. As the conflicts between the faith-based agencies and the city's child welfare agency were resolved on terms favorable to the voluntary agencies, the Brooklyn Diocese led the way in providing additional foster care beds. Little Flower Children and Family Services of New York, for example, reports it "eventually provided family placement for over 2,670 children by the time the acute [bed] crisis ended in 1991." [Complaint, June 14, 2010, Supreme Court of the State of New York, *Little Flower Children and Family Services, v. City of New York*, New York City Administration for Children's Services, p. 9.]

the access.... Of course they can always get heard. Sister Paulette [executive director of Good Shepherd Services] can always call Linda [Gibbs, deputy mayor for Health and Human Services].[21]

CHILD WELFARE SERVICES

Child welfare agencies provide three main types of services: in-home services (called preventive services), out-of-home services (foster care and group care), and adoption. These services are briefly described below.

IN-HOME SERVICES (PREVENTIVE SERVICES)

Preventive service is an odd name for services that are generally provided only after a family is found to have neglected or abused a child. It can be said that the U.S. child welfare system provides an ambulance to a family after it has fallen off the cliff.[x] In most other industrialized nations, preventive services (often called family support services) are provided to prevent problems before families are overwhelmed. In the United States, a family has to have been reported, been investigated, and found to have abused or neglected a child to receive services such as anger management, counseling, therapy, parenting classes, homemaking assistance, drug or alcohol treatment, or emergency financial aid.[xi]

Although other social welfare systems provide assistance to poor families, the child welfare system assists only families that have been found to have abused or neglected their children. In the 1990s, even after a family had been found to have abused or neglected a child, if the child was not placed in foster care, the family rarely received assistance. As late as

---

x. In formal terms the child welfare system in New York and throughout the United States is a reactive, residual, remedial system, rather than a proactive, preventive, universal system. [See Duncan Lindsey, *The Welfare of Children* (New York: Oxford University Press): 25, quoting A. Kadushin and J. A. Martin, *Child Welfare Services* (New York: Macmillan, 1988): 7-8.]

xi. The New York State Child Welfare Reform Act of 1979 does allow a small percentage of families served by preventive service agencies to be walk-ins, people who voluntarily come to the agency for help before a child is neglected or abused. The contracts the Administration for Children (ACS) has with preventive service agencies allow for a few families to be helped before they have abused or neglected a child but these cases are discouraged by ACS as it tries to have more higher risk families served.

2006, 38.4% of families in indicated reports of abuse or neglect, received no services.[22]

Commissioner Mattingly describes current cases he reviewed that were also reported to child protective services for abuse and neglect in the past:

> If you sit in the child stat conferences,[xii] you see cases with seven or eight or nine prior reports [of abuse or neglect] during the past 15 years, and we didn't do anything to help them. This has to change.[23]

The family support services provided by some child welfare agencies are exemplary. Harlem Children's Zone in Manhattan and the Center for Family Life in Brooklyn are nationally renowned for helping troubled families. Many other preventive service programs also are helpful to those they serve. Some, however, provide little more than an arm around the shoulder or a class teaching how to raise a toddler when the parent is dealing with an out-of-control teenager. Parenting classes and anger management classes are almost universally required hoops parents have to jump through to get their children back, though the effectiveness of those programs has rarely been evaluated.[24] What families often need, however, are social services or material assistance to deal with problems associated with poverty, the factor most often associated with abuse and neglect.[25]

Part of the reason that the effectiveness of these programs varies so much is that very few of the roughly 118 programs that provide preventive services in New York City (or the thousands of others that provide them elsewhere in the country, for that matter) have been evaluated to determine if they improve a family's functioning or keep children safe. In 2010, New York City did not evaluate the performance of the $235 million it spent on preventive services for almost 30,000 children, which is hardly surprising because it has never done such a performance assessment.[26] The city gathers numbers on how many families are served and how many times a worker contacted a family by phone or in person, but the city does not determine if the children were abused or neglected again, if the life of the family changed after the receipt of services, or if the parents felt they received the help they needed.

Nevertheless, even relying on unevaluated programs, it is much wiser policy to keep a family intact, if the children's safety can be assured, than

---

xii. Child Stat conferences are weekly reviews held by Commissioner Mattingly of child protective service cases. Each week a different unit of CPS workers presents randomly selected cases for review by the commissioner and his senior staff.

to take the extreme and often harmful step of removing children from the home. Services such as providing child care, a larger or safer dwelling, family counseling, a homemaker to help manage the household when a parent is incapacitated, or an outpatient drug treatment program, with a social worker periodically visiting the home, are what families need and often want.

FOSTER CARE

Foster care—placement with a relative or with a stranger—is a necessary but unfortunate way to care for children.[xiii] It should be used only when it is not possible to ensure a child's safety in his or her home. When a child is placed into a foster home, a family bond is broken that is very hard to repair. Children often are traumatized by being removed from their family and often blame themselves for the removal. Although some children in care feel nurtured by their foster family, children more often report feeling like an outsider, like a guest in the foster home, or like nothing more than a source of income for the family in which they are placed.[27]

Compounding the problems of separation, parents until recently had been excluded from participating in most decisions about their children while the kids are in foster care. They were often not allowed to decide simple matters, such as whether their adolescent daughter should continue to see her pediatrician or should switch to a doctor nearer her foster home or what school their first grade son should attend. And, as has recently been revealed, many parents whose children were in foster care were not asked permission for their youngsters to participate in experimental research for an HIV drug.[28]

When a child protective service worker from the city's child welfare agency determines that a child cannot live safely with his or her family, New York State law requires that the child welfare agency petition Family Court for authorization to remove the child from the home and to put the child in the care of a voluntary foster care agency. However, more often than not in the 1990s, the child was first removed from the home and then child protective services went to court to have the removal approved.

---

xiii. Foster care formally refers to the placement of children into an individual family home. The term, however, in contemporary child welfare parlance has come to mean any out-of-home placement for a child who is in the custody of the state, which is how the term is used in this book. When other types of settings are discussed— group homes, campus settings, or large residential institutions—that modality is specifically mentioned.

Today, child removals before court approval, except in emergencies, are less common. In most instances today, the child protective service worker meets as a group in what is called a child safety conference. In attendance is the family, family friends and relatives, and perhaps a minister or someone from the neighborhood, at times a parent advocate to discuss the family's ability to care for the child before child protective services goes to Family Court for authorization to remove the child.

Children in state custody can be placed into kinship foster care with a relative, usually a grandparent, an aunt, or an older sibling, or with a stranger.[xiv] Kinship placements are generally preferable to placements with strangers. In kinship care the child is in a familiar environment and can more easily maintain connection with his or her biological family. In the early 1990s slightly less than 60% of the children in foster care were placed with strangers; slightly more than 40% were in kinship foster care with a relative. The percentage of children in kinship had decreased somewhat to about 35% in FY 2010.[29]

Foster care is supposed to be a short-term placement until a permanent solution for the child is found. In New York City as well as throughout the country, foster care in the 1990s had become a long-term solution, often with harmful consequences to children. Children in New York City in 1995 remained in foster care an average of 4.4 years, considerably higher than the national average stay of 2.4 years.[30,xv]

Children with more serious behavioral, emotional, or developmental problems and some teenagers are placed in congregate facilities that house as many as 40 or so children, rather than in foster homes. Depending on the number of children housed, these facilities are called group homes, group residences, or residential treatment centers for emotionally disturbed

xiv. Children who are not in state custody can be informally placed in the family of a relative. These children are not part of the child welfare system and are not discussed in this book.

xv. There are two main ways of measuring how long children stay in foster care. The first is to look at how long all children in care on a specific day have been in care. Using this approach, in 1995 children were in care an average of about 4.4 years. This approach looks at all children who enter foster care. Children who remain in care for long periods of time, sometimes from birth until they are 21, bring up the average.

The second approach is to measure how long children who enter care for the first time during a given year remain in care before leaving care for a specific destination—to parents, to adoption, or to independent living. Using this approach, in 2000 children who were discharged to their parents remained in care an average of 6.4 months. This approach looks only at children who have left care, not at children who remain in care. It looks at subgroups of children, excluding, for example, children who are discharged to independent living, who often are in care for many years. The city changed its reporting system to use this approach in about 2000 preventing comparisons of the two approaches in comparable years.

children. New York City no longer uses large residential institutions housing hundreds of children, which until the mid-twentieth century were the main way that foster children in New York and throughout the nation were housed. Though Newt Gingrich, a Congressman from Georgia then serving as Speaker of the U.S. House of Representative, and others in the 1990s championed the revival of large residential institutions, such facilities have been almost universally discredited as a healthy way to care for children. Smaller group facilities have a useful place in a continuum of care.[31]

New York City now contracts with 28 agencies to provide foster care and 20 agencies to provide residential care (all but four of the residential providers also provide foster care) for a total cost in 2010 of $789 million.[32]

As a result of the difficult lives they had before entering care, the trauma of separation, and their often painful experiences in foster homes, many children are severely damaged emotionally when they leave care. In New York City, 19% of teens in foster care in 1991 were in homeless shelters within 3 years of discharge.[33] Nationally, the outcomes have been similar. A 2007 study by Chapin Hall at the University of Chicago looked at adolescents formerly in foster care in the Midwest when they turned 21. It found that 18% had been homeless at least once, 25% did not have a high school degree, 29% had been incarcerated, and 50% were unemployed.[34]

ADOPTION

As much as adoption[xvi] might seem redolent of motherhood and apple pie, it is a controversial and problem-fraught element of the child welfare system. Many aspects of adoption had been contentious. Should single parents or gay parents be permitted to adopt? Should adoption be as much a priority as reunification with a child's family of origin? Should black children be adopted by white families, or is cross-racial adoption genocide, as the National Association of Black Social Workers has declared in 1972?[35] Should Caucasian children be adopted by black families, as the character played by Steve Martin was in the hilarious 1979 movie *The Jerk*? Each of these issues has been resolved in favor of widening the range of people who can adopt, though Martin is the only white boy I know of who was adopted by a black family.

xvi. In this book adoption—the permanent transfer of legal rights of parenting—refers to children placed for adoption through a child welfare agency that is part of the city's public child welfare system. Independent or private adoptions or international adoptions occur outside of the public U.S. child welfare system. Those adoptions are not discussed in this book.

Adoption is a complicated and delicate process, made more difficult by fractured decision-making and conflicting goals. In 1992 only 1,784 children, about 12%, were adopted from among the 14,463 children who had a goal adoption in New York City.[36] At that time it took almost five years for a child in the care of New York City voluntary foster care agencies to be adopted, among the longest adoption delays anywhere in the U.S.[37]

In response to the delays and the very low number of children who were being adopted across the country, Congress passed the Adoption and Safe Families Act (ASFA) of 1997, which provided a stick and a carrot to improve adoption. The stick was that agencies had essentially 15 months to reunify a child with his or her family, often too short a time to solve the many family ills that had brought the child into care. If the agency could not return a child home in time, it was required to terminate the parents' right to the child and to move to have the youngster adopted. Getting many of these children adopted was not easy, resulting in an increasing number of children in limbo: Their parents' rights had been terminated, but the children remained unadopted.[38] In addition, as more attention was focused on children being adopted, reunification rates for children with their biological families fell in the post-ASFA 1990s.[39]

The carrot was that jurisdictions received an additional $4000 to be distributed to agencies for each child that was adopted, as an incentive to complete more adoptions. Earlier legislation, the Adoption Assistance and Child Welfare Act of 1980, provided funds to parents who adopted special needs children from the child welfare system. These are older children, children with disabilities, and children from ethnic minorities, terms that describe essentially all children who are adopted from the New York City foster care system. As a result, at present almost all families that adopt a child from the public welfare system in New York receive a monthly payment that is the same as the foster care payment.

The result of these changes was that annual adoption rates doubled nationally and more than doubled in New York City, where in 1999 3,806 foster care children were adopted, equaling 34% of youngsters with a goal of adoption.[40] As the number of children in foster care has decreased over the years, the number of children adopted has returned to earlier levels. In FY 2010, only 1,165 children were adopted, but the percentage of children with a goal of adoption who are adopted remained high, at 30.3%. Nevertheless, today children who do get adopted still remain in care an average of more than 3 years before their adoption is completed.[41]

Until the beginning of the twenty-first century, New York City had a troubled child welfare bureaucracy with commissioners leaving or being fired after very short tenures and with mayors reorganizing the agency and changing its name almost as frequently. The Bureau of Child Welfare (BCW) became Special Services for Children in 1969, which became the Child Welfare Administration (CWA) in the late 1980s, and finally became the Administration for Children's Services (ACS) in 1996. Until ACS was created, the city's public child welfare agency was an ineffective, mismanaged, underfunded part of a mega-bureaucracy, the Human Resources Administration.

The murder of 6-year-old Elisa Izquierdo in November 1995 by her mother once again exposed the child welfare system's profound failings. The city had been notified multiple times by social workers, school officials, relatives, and neighbors that Elisa was being mistreated, then brutalized, and then tortured, but the city failed to act appropriately. A memo from Katherine Kroft, then the Giuliani administration's child welfare commissioner, a month before Elisa's death complained that city staff cuts made it impossible to train child abuse case workers or to measure their competence. City, state, and federal cuts had reduced the city's child welfare budget by one-sixth in the preceding years. Child protective workers who received the complaints about Elisa had caseloads that were three, four, and even five times larger than regulations required.[42]

Hoping to improve child welfare services and to limit the political fallout from Elisa Izquierdo's death, Giuliani in 1996 created ACS as an independent agency, reporting directly to the mayor, with Nicholas Scoppetta, a former prosecutor, an experienced city administrator and a former foster child, as its first commissioner. The creation of ACS laid the foundation for a long, slow process of reform in the city's child welfare system.

New York City's public child welfare agency, whatever its name at a given time, signs contracts with and allocates the money to the voluntary agencies that provide preventive services, foster care, and adoption services. It also monitors their performance and, along with the state and federal governments, sets the standards for their performance. The city's public child welfare agency also directly administers child protective services, which investigates all reports of abuse and neglect and recommends to Family Court whether children should be removed from their home.

CHILD PROTECTIVE SERVICES

Child protective services are the gateway to the child welfare system. Doctors, social workers, teachers, and other professionals are required by the federal Child Abuse, Prevention and Treatment Act of 1974 (P.L. 93-247) to report to the state whenever they suspect that a child might be in danger of being neglected or abused. They are called "mandated reporters." Anyone else can report a suspected case of abuse or neglect but is not required to do so.

A person who suspects that a child is being abused or neglected calls the New York State Central Registry to report the allegation. The registry is administered by another large bureaucracy, the New York State Office of Children and Family Services, which refers the report to the local district, in this case New York City, to investigate the allegation. In fiscal year 1996 the city's child welfare agency investigated 52,994 reports of abuse and neglect, an average per case worker of 24.1 cases, far higher than would allow workers to adequately investigate reports; in fiscal year 2010 ACS investigated 65,114 reports of abuse and neglect, with the average caseload per worker of 9.1, the lowest it has been in over a decade.[43]

Investigating reports of abuse and neglect is one of the most difficult jobs in the city. CPS workers, who generally have little more than a college degree, 10 weeks of classroom training, and 3 months of field training, go into apartments in the worst neighborhoods in the city, often alone and after dark. They have to make quick decisions that might contribute to the death of a child on the one hand or to the destruction of a family on the other.

In the 1990s, child protection workers had few ways to help, other than removing the child, when a family was overwhelmed or a child was at risk of neglect or abuse. Today workers have access to more services to help families than they had in the past. Nevertheless, in May 2007 14% of families who have been found to have abused or neglected their children received no services.[44]

The culture of the protective services has added to the difficulty of responding in a measured way to reports of abuse and neglect. The protective service workers not only see abuse and neglect under every bed but also see almost any situation as one that could lead to a child being put in danger or killed. This culture is a logical outgrowth of conditions in the field. With few resources available to help families in trouble, a worker is faced with the choice of removing the child or leaving him or her in a home with little or no assistance and being held responsible for harm that might befall the child, no matter how unlikely. Not surprisingly, workers gravitate toward taking the child from the home. In 1995, 7,949 children were removed from their families and placed in foster care.[45] After the death of Elisa Izquierdo at the end of 1995, Scoppetta promulgated a policy that stipulated: "Any ambiguity regarding the safety of a child will be resolved in favor of removing the child from harm's way."[46] In fiscal year 1997, 11,453 youngsters went into foster care[47]—an average of one child removed from his or her family every 45 minutes.

That policy and the general culture of child protective services contributed to unnecessary removals of children. Although it is hard to find agreement on what is an unnecessary removal, the following is illustrative. In fiscal year 1997 when 11,453 children were removed from their families, 30 children died in cases known to ACS. In fiscal year 2003, the first full year after Scoppetta left office, 6,901 children were removed but only 24 children died in cases known to ACS. According to this indicator, removing more children does not increase their safety. In fact, fewer children died when fewer children were removed from their families.[48]

There is an additional factor that compounds CPS's woes: the high rate of turnover among its investigators, who for reasons cited above find their job daunting. In 2006, 49% of child protective service workers had less than 1 year of experience on the job.[49] The combination of inexperienced workers, few resources to help families, understaffing, limited funding, and the vulnerability of children has made child protective services the area that comes under fire when a child welfare crisis arises, causing a commissioner to be fired or the abandonment of well-intentioned reforms that have not done enough. Even though there have been significant improvements in ACS's child protective services since its nadir in 1995, it is still a troubled area.

FAMILY COURT

The New York State Family Court Act of 1962 created Family Court to be an objective judicial authority that would make independent, equitable, and timely decisions when the state decides to remove a child from his or her family.[xvii] The reality of Family Court in New York City, created as a result of the Act, is very different. At the end of the twentieth century, Family Court in New York City had evolved into an institution that was

---

xvii. In addition to child protection proceedings, Family Court also handles cases involving child support, custody and visitation, domestic violence, and juvenile delinquency.

almost universally criticized for failing to provide equitable or timely justice for families embroiled in the child welfare system. The Special Child Welfare Advisory Panel, as part of the *Marisol v. Giuliani* settlement, in 2000 prepared a "Special Report on Family Court" containing withering criticisms.

The report described pervasive delays in the resolution of cases, with "multiple, routine adjournments of virtually every case." When cases came before the court, "With rare exceptions, hearings lack sufficient docket time for a true examination of the issues...Some caseworkers appear in court late; some are unprepared to testify; some are dressed inappropriately, and some do not appear at all, without prior notice." The panel found that parents lacked adequate legal representation. "Parents must appear at court in order to have an attorney assigned," the report said. They were represented by independent lawyers who worked without institutional support, were inadequately compensated ($45 an hour for courtroom time; $35 an hour for time out of court), and, in some boroughs, "hearings have to be postponed because there is no attorney available for assignment." The report concluded that "It is common for court orders (for example, for specific services or evaluations to be provided) not to be carried out.... Judges see themselves as powerless victims of the system rather than as powerful change agents."[50]

In many ways these shortcomings persist.[51] According to Children's Rights, Inc.'s 2007 study *At the Crossroads*, which reviewed changes in Family Court, "Indeed, by most accounts, the court continues to be chaotic, with families and attorneys sometimes waiting the better part of a day for their hearings to be called; fact finding hearings are long delayed, sometimes resulting in permanency hearings being held prior to the court even having made the finding that abuse and neglect had occurred; and permanency hearings are not occurring in a timely fashion."[52] Another problem is a lack of services to help families resolve the situations that caused their children to be placed in care, as well as services needed for children to return home. According to Clark Richardson, supervising judge of New York City Bronx Family Court from year 2000 to 2009:

> The difference between a well-handled case and one that is not well-handled is access to services and supports for families. There is a lack of services in general, and the services that do exist are poor services.[53]

In addition, many of the decisions made in Family Court by judges are social work decisions, not legal decisions. For example, should a child be moved from one foster home to another? Should family visits be supervised?

Which services should a family receive? Family Court proceedings have turned making social work judgments into adversarial legal proceedings rather than a mediated, supportive, collaborative process to help families solve their problems.

There is one exception to the persistent problems in Family Court. Beginning in 2007 in the Bronx, Brooklyn, and Manhattan and in 2011 in Queens, half of the families who appear in New York City Family Court proceedings involving the removal of their children are represented by publicly funded lawyers who work for legal organizations— Bronx Defenders, Brooklyn Family Defense Project, and Center for Family Representation[xviii]—rather than for themselves. These lawyers are members of a team—that also comprises a social worker and often a parent advocate[xix]—that represents the parent in court. Adequate legal representation has begun to move New York City's Family Court toward a system in which justice can occur.

SUMMARY

The protection and care provided to children and families by New York City's child welfare system by most accounts were dysfunctional in 1995. The power of the faith-based voluntary foster care agencies was at an all-time high, despite the fact that government provided almost all of the money the agencies used to provide foster care to children and preventive services to families. Families whose children were in care or who needed help from the city or the child welfare agencies had little influence on their own cases and no influence in shaping child welfare programs or policies. After a 10-year decline in the number of children in foster care, which reached an all-time low of 16,200 in 1984, the crack and HIV/AIDS epidemics, the housing shortage, and the rise in teenage pregnancies caused the number of children in foster care to rise rapidly, reaching an all-time high of almost 50,000 in 1992. The voluntary agencies successfully used their political power and the city's need for additional beds to undo,

xviii. In 2007 the New York City's Office of the Criminal Justice Coordinator began contracting with these organizations for legal representation for half of the parents who appear in child protection proceedings in Family Court in the Bronx, Brooklyn, and Manhattan, respectively. The Center for Family Representation received the contract for Queens in 2011. Staten Island is not yet covered.

xix. A parent advocate is a person whose child was in foster care. Generally the parent advocate has been reunited with his or her child and has been trained to assist other parents and help them negotiate the child welfare system so they can be reunited with their children.

prevent, or delay reforms that would have improved the system but would also have restricted their independence.

In 1995, the death of Elisa Izquierdo, a 6-year-old child under the supervision of the city's child welfare system, exposed the system's pervasive problem: overwhelmed and unsupported staff was failing to help overwhelmed and unsupported families. In the aftermath of *Marisol v. Giuliani*, Giuliani created in early 1996 a new child welfare agency, the Administration for Children's Services, that began reforming the child welfare system.

CHAPTER 2
Parents Change

Every year thousands of children from poor families, most of them black or Latino, are put in New York City's foster care system. They are placed there for many reasons.[i] Poverty is an underlying cause in almost all cases. And it is not just the poor whose children go into foster care, but the poorest of the poor.[1] Child abuse is present in all social classes, but child removals occur disproportionately among children of the poor. The stresses of poverty amplify other problems, such as a parent's medical issues, or a child's hyperactivity, or living in close quarters, or residing in a shelter.[2] These in turn create tensions that can lead to neglect or abuse.

Neglect is the most common reason a child is put in foster care. The neglect is often a by-product of an overwhelmed single mother, living in poverty, trying in vain to cope with myriad problems, possessing few

i. The Administration for Children's Services (ACS) regularly reports the specific reasons that children are reported to the State Central Registry. It does not, however, report the specific reasons that children are placed into foster care. In 2009, 59,249 reports involving 93,988 children and 100,194 allegations were filed. Of the 100,194 allegations, 68% were for neglect, 18.6% were for physical, sexual, or psychological abuse, and 13.4% were for other unspecified reasons. [New York City Administration for Children's Services, "Child Abuse/Neglect Statistics for Selected Highbridge Census Tracts, Bronx CD4. Bronx, and NYC 2009."]

material resources, and having only a frayed safety net and a small social network to assist her. Abuse is much less common, though media coverage of the occasional, sensational abuse cases gives the public the false impression that most parents lose children to foster care because they have battered them. Domestic violence in which mothers are battered is often part of the family dynamic in which a child is removed for having been abused. Substance abuse is often present as well.

Sometimes placement in foster care is necessary to protect a child; in other cases, financial assistance, help in rearing a difficult child, and/or child care or a homemaker to help an overwhelmed single parent cope would go a long way to solving a family's problems without the drastic measure of removing a child from the family home.

RACIAL DIFFERENCE THROUGH NEW YORK CITY'S CHILD WELFARE SYSTEM

Nationally, 60% of the children in foster care are black, Latino, or other races.[3] In New York City in 1998 and continuing through the present, 96% of the children in foster care were children of color—primarily black and Latino.[4] The disproportionality increases at each step in the placement process. Figure 2.1 prepared by ACS shows the percentage of African-American children at each step in the placement process in 2007. Whereas African-Americans were 27% of the city's child population, they

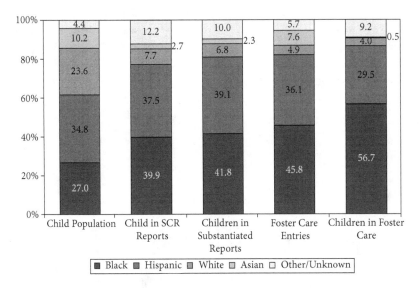

Figure 2.1: Race/Ethinicity and the Path through the Child Welfare System, CY 2007

constituted 39.9% of children in abuse/neglect reports, 41.8% of children in substantiated reports, 45.8% of children who entered foster care, and 56.7% of children in foster care.[5]

PARENTS CHANGE

The four stories recounted later in this chapter represent common situations that can often lead to mothers losing their children to foster care. Each of the mothers in these stories changed her life as a result of her experience with the child welfare system. Some were helped to change by a person or a program; some changed in reaction to the injustice they felt they had experienced. All the mothers have become activists or advocates who work to improve the child welfare system or to help other families.[ii]

Most of us change during our lives. Often the changes we make are far greater than we imagined they would be when we were young. When a parent dies, we shift from being a child to becoming a senior member of our family. When a job or career ends, we find new ways to make a living, to feel fulfilled, or at least to be occupied. An illness or disability strikes us or someone close to us, and we learn to cope with or embrace the life we now have. We become involved in a dead-end relationship, it ends, and we move on. We struggle with and sometimes overcome the countless large and small addictions that trap us in a lifetime—food, money, praise, clothes, alcohol, cigarettes, drugs, sex, cell phones, email, or Crackberries. Often we change, but not always. Parents who have been involved in the child welfare system are similar. Some change and some don't. This chapter describes parents who have changed and have overcome adversities that to many of us seem overwhelming.

How is it possible that parents who have abused or neglected their children, or have been charged with doing so, can change so dramatically that they are not only able to care for their children well but also are able to help other parents? An analysis of the emotional, psychological, cultural, and social factors that go into a person's change, let alone identifying the shared reasons that a group of people change, is beyond the scope of this book and perhaps beyond human understanding. Instead, the stories of the four mothers whose children were placed into foster care recount the changes in their lives.

Like all people, these parents have complex personal histories that define their choices and contribute to their behavior. Parents charged with abuse

ii. A few fathers are parent advocates. One, Carlos Boyet, is profiled in Chapter 4 on CWOP.

or neglect, however, are often presented in the media as two-dimensional, cardboard figures. This portrayal leaves out their humanity, their limited choices, and, not infrequently, their innocence. The complexity of their pasts contains the seeds of their unexpected futures. With changed circumstances, different aspects of a person can flourish.

Sometimes we make enormous changes on our own; sometimes we change with help from another individual, a program, or a better environment. Parents who become parent advocates generally have not changed on their own but have been encouraged and supported in their efforts by other parents and organizations that believe in them and work on their behalf. To solve their immediate problems, they received help—better housing, drug treatment, a job, or a new school for their children. Sometimes counseling helped, though often the parenting and anger management classes required by welfare agencies were of scant discernible benefit.

Becoming a parent advocate demands additional support. Among other things, it requires learning how the child welfare system works, how to identify key people to contact, how to influence decision makers, and how to do grassroots organizing. It involves participating in a peer support group, learning how to be a leader, and overcoming the fear of speaking in public.

Working alongside others who have had a child put in foster care and being part of a movement of likeminded people are aspects of their lives that sustain them. Having a paid job as an advocate, having a positive impact on other people's lives, and having an effect on the system that caused them so much pain are affirming, energizing, and life-changing experiences.

Finally, not everyone who is charged with abuse or neglect or whose child is placed in foster care is guilty or needs to change dramatically. Sharwline Nicholson was a struggling mother doing a fine job raising her two children alone when her ex-boyfriend returned to New York and began beating her as soon as she opened the door of her Brooklyn apartment. He was enraged because he thought she was involved with another man. While she was in the hospital recovering, child protective services removed her children because one child had witnessed the assault. The *Nicholson v. Scoppetta* lawsuit later overturned the city's right to remove children merely because they witnessed abuse.[6]

Nicole Bush feared for her son's safety after a male school aide took him to unknown locations during school hours for a "suspension" hearing. She complained to the school and was subsequently reported by the school to child protective services, according to an article in the *Daily News*. The article stated, "Friction with principals and fights with teachers have led to visits from child welfare investigators, numerous parents have told the *Daily News*."[7]

Examples of mothers' whose children were wrongly removed from their custody by the state occur with painful regularity in every jurisdiction in the country as summarized in the study by the U.S. Health and Human Services, Children's Bureau cited below.

What proportion of parents whose children have been put in foster care can change sufficiently to be successfully reunited with their kids? And what proportion of parents who are reunited with their children can or should become parent advocates? Some data give a rough answer to the first question. First, many children have been removed inappropriately from their parents' custody, and those parents do not need to change. For example, according to a study reported by Paul Chill, clinical professor of law, University of Connecticut School of Law, "According to statistics published by the U.S. Department of Health and Human Services (HHS), more than 100,000 children who were removed in 2001—more than one in three—*were later found not to have been maltreated at all*" [emphasis in original].[8]

Among children in New York City discharged from foster care in 2010, 69% were reunified with their families, 16% were adopted, and 15% were discharged to a nonpermanency discharge (independent living).[9] Presumably this means that ACS believes that almost 7 out of 10 parents who have had children placed in foster care have changed enough that their children can rejoin them.

Some of the children who are discharged to their families, however, return to foster care within 2 years. In 2009, 11% of children discharged in New York City returned to foster care within 2 years of discharge. This would reduce the successful family reunifications to closer to 60%.[10]

The second question—what proportion of parents who are reunited with their children can or should become parent advocates—is harder to answer. Working as a parent advocate or a parent organizer is not for everyone. Few people in the general population work as community organizers or have social service jobs in which they help others. The proportion of parents who become parent advocates or organizers is similarly small.

THE MOTHERS WHOSE CHILDREN WERE REMOVED AND THEN BECAME PARENT ADVOCATES

What follows are the stories of four mothers who had their children removed from the home and how and why they changed, were reunited with their children, and became parent advocates. All of the mothers agreed to have their names used. Unless otherwise noted, the quotes are the voice of the mother.

I originally interviewed the mothers between February and June 2009.[iii] I remained in touch with the parents profiled in this book and reinterviewed them in April and May 2011 to find out how their lives had evolved in the 2 years since we first spoke. I spoke with them again in August 2012.

The mothers' accounts have not been corroborated with ACS records or court records. These stories are not presented in an effort to establish the "truth" of what occurred in the situations involved, if such a thing could be determined. Rather they are here to show the perceptions of people who have had their children put in foster care. These perceptions reflect the attitudes of the clients toward a system intended to help them and their children. In doing that, the stories offer valuable guidance to the people who run that system. These stories are also presented because, in my 30 years of experience, they are typical—in their import, if not in their details—of the accounts given by people who have had to deal with the child welfare system. Beyond that, the stories show not only the complex, difficult lives that bring the system into these mothers' living rooms but also the need for empathy and in-depth explorations of each family's history to develop an effective, appropriate, and humane course of action for the child and his or her family.

Perhaps these stories understate the parents' role in the child's placement in foster care, just as an autobiography of politicians or corporate executives might understate their errors and overstate their achievements. And if the stories underplay the mothers' responsibility, their transformation into advocates for other parents becomes all the more impressive.

Each of these mothers made mistakes that brought ACS into their lives. Some tried to get help from ACS, schools, medical centers, or social service agencies; most often they did not receive the help they needed for themselves or for their children. Wanda, who was deeply involved with hard drugs, should have had her children removed. The other parents' situations are more complicated. Would quality parent training or medication for a hyperactive 2-year-old child have enabled Jeanette to safely care for her child? Would therapy, a support group, or medication have helped diminish Youshell's depression, or would a more responsive school system have enabled her children to attend school regularly? Would a top-notch boarding school have cooled things out between Sandra and her angry adolescent? As costly as that might be, it would likely be no more

iii. Three of the stories are amplified with information from articles the mothers wrote about their lives in *Rise* magazine.

expensive than the average cost of keeping a child in New York City foster care, $49,000 in 2010.[11]

Could the supports that these parents received after they fell off a cliff—a job, a parent support group, leadership training, good therapy, a community of similarly struggling parents—have made a difference had that help been available earlier in their lives? I think so.

SANDRA KILLETT: PHYSICAL ABUSE OF AN ADOLESCENT

According to New York City's Administration for Child Services (ACS), Sandra Killett beat her 13-year-old son, Sam, with a baseball bat. According to Sandra, before the incident with the bat, she contacted ACS several times, seeking help to deal with her angry, defiant adolescent son. The assistance she received failed to resolve their conflicts. When one of their fights escalated out of control, she hit him on his leg with a bat to defend herself. Sam was in foster care for 2 years in four different foster homes.

Sandra is a bright, articulate, loving mother. Today she readily acknowledges she should not have hit her son with a bat. Sandra contacted ACS early on to get help but they did not provide what she needed, allowing things to escalate to an explosion. A humane social welfare system would not have allowed the family situation to get to that point. Sandra went to a medical facility to have her son evaluated but they missed seeing the depth of Sam's defiance and extent of the family's conflicts. Help should have been provided to Sam to deal with his anger and defiance. As Sandra says, the system treated her as if "He did nothing. It was all about me. You are the out of control person, the parent. You don't know what you're doing. You're clueless."

Sandra, now in her 40s, grew up in the Bedford-Stuyvesant section of Brooklyn. "I lived on a block where everyone cared about everyone" she says. "It was that village. I remember our garbage not being picked up, and a neighbor chastising the garbage men because they were late."

When she was 14 she went to the welfare office with her mother after her parents had separated and her mother had lost her job. "I remember my mom going to the welfare office and not being respected. At the time I thought, 'So this is how it works.' I wanted to do something about that."

Sandra said to the guidance counselor at William H. Maxwell High School in East New York, "I want to be a social worker." According to Sandra, the guidance counselor said, "There's no money in that," and steered her to an internship with Chemical Bank, where she worked for the next 15 years, first as a clerk and finally as "an officer of the bank, where I got to sign off on a lot of money."

She then married and moved with her husband to Atlanta, where he had a job in a rental furniture company. In 1992 she gave birth to Sam and a few years later to a second son, Simeon. Sandra and her husband moved back to New York City before separating in 1997. With two young kids, no husband, and no job, she applied for public assistance, which she received after a long struggle. She eventually got a job in an after-school program near her home in Harlem. She was working there when she called ACS for help.

In June 2005 Sam was about to turn 13, an often difficult age in parent–son relationships. They got into an argument over a lost birth certificate he had taken to photocopy. Sam yelled and screamed and an argument and tussle ensued. "Though his teachers had said he had been aggressive in school and we were in counseling, he had never been that way with me." During the struggle Sandra scratched Sam on the neck. She said to him, "You can't jump in my face like that. We're not going to live like this. We're going to ACS."

ACS, to its credit, connected Sandra's family to Harlem Children's Zone, a well-respected preventive services program. The social worker who visited the family helped set limits for Sam and found another family's home in the Bronx where Sam might stay to allow things to cool off between him and his mother. That home was unable to accommodate Sam so he stayed with Sandra's niece on Staten Island for a week. When Sam returned to live with Sandra, he continued to be explosive, and the conflict between mother and son escalated. In October, according to Sandra, "Sam pulled out a hanger and put it in my face. I was scared to even say anything. I called the ACS worker and said, 'There's something wrong with him. He needs to be evaluated now.'"

The ACS worker suggested that Sandra take Sam to Columbia Presbyterian Medical Center's pediatric psychiatric emergency room, which she did. According to Sandra, the clinician who evaluated Sam said, "He's not a threat to himself or to anyone else." "Oh, I begged to differ," Sandra says. "They wouldn't keep him, and I didn't want to be in the house with him. I called ACS, but they wouldn't take him either. I called a friend, who let Sam stay there for a couple of nights. I went back to ACS and said, 'He can't live here. What am I going to do?'"

Sam came back home, and for a short time he was calm. Then a dispute developed over schoolwork. Sandra, exasperated said, "You cannot live here and not do what you're supposed to do." Sam left and went to his father's house without telling Sandra, causing her to contact the police who brought Sam home that night.

"The next morning Sam was still angry," Sandra says. "When he was upset, his anger never left him. There wasn't a cool down period when you could talk." Against her better judgment, she said to Sam, referring to a call she had received from his school, "Why would you lie and tell your teachers that I was not around?"

"The anger that came out of him I cannot describe. He was in my face, yelling and screaming. I responded, and it escalated. Before I knew it we were fighting. He grabbed my arms, and I couldn't move. He was holding me. It went out of control. My son had me down on the floor. He was kicking me. I was kicking and hitting him. I wasn't thinking at the time. I grabbed the closest thing to me. It was a bat. I hit my son on the thigh one time, and he let me go. I was so upset, I called my mom. I called the police and told them what was going on in the household. When the police came, I had the bat still in my hand because Sam was that agitated. 'We need to speak to your son,' the police said."

"When they came out, they said they are going to arrest me. And they did. I was in jail two days. The DA called me in and said, 'You can go home if you admit to abusing your son with a bat.' I didn't abuse my son with a bat. Should I have been fighting with him? No. Did I fight with him? I did. I did not just get a bat and beat my son. I say 'hit,' you say 'beat,' and there's a difference." Sandra was represented by a friend who was a lawyer; the criminal case was dismissed.

In early December the Family Court put Sam in foster care; Simeon, Sandra's younger son, was released to Sandra's care. About a week passed before Sandra was allowed to see Sam. They met at a case conference with representatives of the Edwin Gould foster care agency. According to Sandra, "They brought Sam in. When I saw my son, he immediately reached out for me. I reached out for him, too. There was no separation. But the worker said, 'No, you can't touch.' This was the first onset for me of how the system tears you apart. They didn't allow the natural bond to occur, they made it hostile. At the conference he could not sit with me, he could not talk to me. They're telling him, your mother did something bad. And that's exactly how it played out. He was in placement for 2 years."

SANDRA'S ACTIVISM

After her husband left her, with two kids and no job, Sandra moved back to New York City from Atlanta. While on public assistance in 1999 she went to a meeting at the Federation of Protestant Welfare Agencies. "I was looking for something to do. I found a flyer and went to a meeting about welfare. There were other moms on welfare, including students. Sandra Youdelman from Community Voices Heard (CVH), who was there, said

'You might want to come to one of our meetings.' I went. Immediately I thought, 'Oh, my god. Women out there are fighting the struggle, trying to change the system.' I felt I had found what I was looking for, so I just stayed."

She began volunteering with CVH, handing out flyers when she went to the public assistance office, talking to people in the neighborhood, and getting more involved in community activism. Her energy, commitment, and articulate and passionate speaking were soon recognized. She was asked to join the board of directors of CVH and served for 7 years, until 2007.

While working with CVH during the time her son was in foster care, she heard about the Child Welfare Organizing Project (CWOP) and joined its 6-month training program. She became a full-time parent advocate with benefits in 2007, working at Children's Village, a large, progressive, foster care agency.

According to Sandra, "My role is to assist families in navigating the child welfare system as well as navigating the agency. I help families engage in services such as parenting and anger management. I help them understand why they would want to engage in services as soon as possible. I help them understand their rights, and they still do have rights, though most families believe they don't have any rights at all."

The first family she worked with, and still worked with 2 years later, stands out in her mind. "Children's Village had just about given up on the family. The mother is a young mom who had four children removed because of medical neglect and deplorable living conditions. The children were in care for 2 years, and the case was stuck. The mother was not accepting any services."

"I've been able to help her understand why she needs to be in services. I don't think she understood what medical neglect was and what was considered to be deplorable living conditions. "When I met her my question was simply, 'Do you want your children back? If you want your children back, I'm not going to say they are going to come home tomorrow or in 3 days. They may not even come home in six months. But you're going to get your children back. I will work with you to do that.'"

"There was an immediate something with the mother. She had a feeling that someone really cared and really wanted to see her come through this. More often than not, the mother feels the worker doesn't understand what she's going through." The mother now has unsupervised, extended visits with her children, a major milestone toward being reunited with them.

Sandra handles about 25 to 30 cases at a time. "When we knock on that door, we need to always be saying to ourselves, 'Perhaps it's not what it looks like.' If we come in with the attitude that the situation is absolutely what it looks like, I don't believe we're open to receive what the family has to say about where they are in their life. It's how you come in to the family's life that matters. If you come in judgmental, it's not going to work. You need to ask, 'Why is it like this?'"

Sandra feels her work at Children's Village is not enough. "I don't want to just help parents navigate. I don't want them to have to navigate. I want to change policy." She serves on the advisory board of the *Child Welfare Watch*, a publishing project of the New School University's Center for New York City Affairs that provides in-depth investigative reporting, news, and analysis on children and family services in New York. In that role she presents her views and the perspective of parents during policy discussions with child welfare advocates that influence the content of the *Watch*. She's a member of ACS's Parent Advisory Work Group, which met quarterly while Mattingly was commissioner. CWOP asked Sandra to join its board of directors, which she accepted. She became the new chair of the board replacing Sharwline Nicholson, who resigned as chair in early 2011.

Sandra was more ebullient than usual when we spoke in April 2011. Her son Sam, 18, had graduated from LaGuardia High School, and with his girlfriend and most of his friends away at college, he moved back home. "We fight, but it's normal stuff," Sandra says. Before Sam moved in, he and his mother talked about what his living at home would look like. "No drinking, no drugging, and no sexing in the house. We worked out an agreement of what I couldn't accept and what I'd be flexible about, and how he could express himself to me."

Although he had been diagnosed as bipolar, he didn't want to take medication. Three weeks after living at his mom's home, according to Sandra, he changed his mind. He began taking medication, had a job working in a restaurant, and was going for an interview and an assessment in hope of studying architecture at City College near their home. An earlier diagnosis, perhaps when Sandra took Sam to Columbia Presbyterian Medical Center, might have prevented a lot of subsequent trauma.

Sandra enrolled at Metropolitan College of New York a few years ago. "That was stressful. I was growling at everyone. I couldn't be in school and on the phone with parents [for my job]." She left Metropolitan about a year and a half ago. Subsequently she got a scholarship from Road 2 Success (a college scholarship program set up at CWOP, and funded by the Child Welfare Fund, for parents who had experienced the child welfare system), transferred to Empire State College, and completed two semesters. She didn't return to school the next semester because Sam was living with her. "It was a struggle, not the coursework but balancing it all. I have a second chance with Sam, and I can't be fully involved with him, work, and be in school."

When Sandra and I spoke in August 2012, things had changed again. Sandra was diagnosed with multiple myeloma, cancer of the blood and bone marrow. She's had chemotherapy, a bone marrow transplant, and has been on sick leave for 6 months from Children's Village. Her continued low immunity to infection has caused her doctor to recommend that she not return to work in September as had been planned.

Sam moved out of Sandra's apartment in May 2012. According to Sandra, the conflicts between them resurfaced. He could not deal with her illness and he stopped taking his medication for his bipolar condition. In August he tried to kill himself with a drug overdose. He went to the emergency room at St Luke's Hospital and was transferred to Roosevelt Hospital's psychiatric unit. "I saw him there and broke down. He's really a good kid." He was discharged to a shelter after 3 days and was given medication.

Sandra doesn't know where he is living or if he is taking his medication or in therapy as the doctors recommended. She does know that he's enrolled in City Technical College in Brooklyn and has been approved for a scholarship since she received confirmation from the financial aid office.

Sandra's life has had wild swings from pain and sadness to joy and celebration, and then back to pain. Nevertheless, her indomitable spirit shines. "I feel fine," she said in our most recent conversation. "I haven't gotten a raise in 3 years, but I'd probably do this work for free." That is, once she is able to work again.

WANDA CHAMBERS: PARENTAL SUBSTANCE ABUSE

Wanda Chambers is the third generation in her family to abuse drugs or alcohol, using crack cocaine and other drugs off and on for 20 years. Her arrest and incarceration for selling a controlled substance and the loss of her children to foster care broke her cycle of drug involvement. In prison she became sober, briefly used when she got out, and has been clean for more than 10 years. She eventually regained custody of one of her four children, her youngest daughter, and became a parent advocate who works at Brooklyn Family Defense Project helping other parents change their behavior and take back their children.

Wanda was born in Harlem when her mother was 13. "My mother had some issues and was always on drugs," she says. "I never knew her as a sober person. We kind of grew up together. She was always using something—shooting, crack, methadone. She caught the virus [HIV] in the streets. My mom passed when she wasn't even 50, while I was locked up on Rikers Island."

"My mom never was parented. She didn't know how to parent. I was totally out of control. I had to be the mom for her and for my younger sister. I had to do a lot of things a child shouldn't have to do to eat and to have a place to stay—steal, sleep around." When Wanda was 12 she became involved with a man who was 20. "I stayed with him because I didn't have anybody else. I got on drugs real bad. There was a lot of domestic violence. We lived in my mother's house. I think they were sleeping together. They always were locked up in the bathroom. I think she was in there washing his car."

He kept Wanda high and got her pregnant at 18. "It was an abusive, sick relationship. I can remember my mom selling our apartment, which she didn't own, to these Dominican guys who moved in and turned it into a crack spot. I was 8 months pregnant with Levar when the police kicked the door in and raided the apartment. My girlfriend and her husband let me move in with them. I was clean for about 3 weeks before Levar's birth. He came home from the hospital with me."

Wanda and her infant son lived briefly with the girlfriend in the Bronx. The girlfriend was going to Arizona and didn't want Wanda staying with her husband, so she put Wanda and Levar out. Levar went to live with his father, and Wanda began using drugs again. She says, "I remember being on 174th Street in the Bronx. I was like done. I had run for so long, I was so weak. This has to stop." Wanda walked into a program called V.I.P. and said she didn't want to use anymore. A worker drove her to Mount Eden Rescue Mission, a small home-like shelter run by Christians. Wanda stayed there for a couple of years, marrying Calvin, the son of a woman who worked there. "That was another horror story. VD and drugs. I couldn't catch a break." After she and Calvin had a son, Devere, and married, the relationship soured.

Eventually Wanda left Calvin and moved with her two children to her sister's apartment in Harlem. She periodically stopped, but mostly she was abusing drugs. "I was using with the guy next door. I had a job working with mentally challenged adults. My sister would watch the kids till I got back home. I was still using on the low and trying to hide it."

Calvin called child protective services, alleging that Wanda had burned Devere with a cigarette when she was high. According to Wanda it was a malicious report. When the protective service worker came to investigate, he saw no burn marks and according to Wanda, he said, "You should kick his ass," meaning the allegation was false. "It was the summer. Devere had mosquito bites, and he scratched them," Wanda said. Although there is no way to confirm the truth of the allegation, I know how frequently malicious reports occur. Having known Wanda over several years, I doubt she would ever intentionally hurt her children. ACS confirmed a lesser allegation of child neglect. Wanda, who did not have a lawyer and did not know her rights, and who wanted to be honest, told ACS she had been using drugs. "I ran my mouth. I told them that I had been on a binge and things like that. They took me to court and did a removal. When they scratch the surface, they find other things."

ACS put Levar and Devere in kinship care with Wanda's grandmother, who lived near Wanda. "He was in care, but I didn't consider it care," Wanda says. "If the children are with family, a parent is not going to work that hard to change. The children were basically with me. The worker absolutely knew that."

Wanda went to a drug treatment program called NARCO Freedom and took a parenting class. "I stayed off drugs long enough for ACS to leave me alone," she says. But she wasn't clean for long. "It was a sick suffering cycle. It surely wore me out. Because of what I had to do to get by, my body still hurts today. I remember going to buy crack and saying, 'God, I am so stupid. I cannot help myself.'" She was arrested and spent about 2 1/2 years in prison. Levar was in kinship care with his maternal grandmother; Devere lived with his father.

After she got out, Wanda gave birth to her third child, Shaquelle, in 1993. Because Shaquelle was born with drugs in his bloodstream, child protective services took him from the hospital and placed him in foster care with a friend of his mother. Shaquelle was adopted, is now 16, and has never lived with Wanda.

Ebony, Wanda's fourth and final child, was born in 1998. "I stayed clean the whole pregnancy. I wanted to keep her. I'm coming home from the hospital with my baby, thinking, 'They didn't get this one.' Walking home from the hospital, going up into my building, I ask someone to go get me something. How sick is that? I was using again for a couple of weeks when I was busted for possession of a controlled substance." Ebony was placed into foster care with a stranger and Wanda served a little more than 3 years in Bedford Hills and Albion." In prison, Wanda stopped using drugs. While she was there, she decided to communicate with the child welfare agency that had custody of Ebony. "My daughter [Ebony] had been in care a year and a half at that point. I asked for reports and pictures of her, but I never got visits. She was 3 years old when I saw her again."

Wanda got out of prison in July 2001 but was soon locked up for 30 days on a parole violation because of a positive urine test for marijuana. For reasons she still cannot explain, in the fall of 2001 she stopped using.

"I was done," she says. She went to the Daytop Drug Prevention Program as an outpatient for 6 months, was clean throughout that period, and has been clean ever since. She took parenting classes, found an apartment, and connected with a preventive services agency. "My grandmother was my backbone through it all. She supported me when I didn't believe in myself."

After Wanda came out of prison, Lutheran Social Services, the foster care agency that was caring for Ebony, required Wanda to receive family support services to prepare her for Ebony's return. Wanda also wanted to get as much help as she could to learn how to care for her daughter and to learn more about how the child welfare system works. She found a preventive service program on 125th Street, a few blocks from her home in Harlem.

"When I began visiting, my daughter couldn't stand my living guts. She wouldn't talk to me, she'd scream when I got near her. She'd sit under the desk for the whole visit or keep running out in the hall to see the foster mother. I would keep reading, 'And the bear said…' and if she looked at me, I'd say, 'Hello Ebony.' Of course I went home and cried. We got closer when we had weekend visits. I could do little things like wipe her face and do her hair and put on her shoes."

A year after Wanda was released from prison, when Ebony was 4 years old, Wanda regained custody of her. "Ebony's former foster mother is still part of our lives. Her foster mom and I don't always agree—she thinks I'm too strict, and I think she lets my daughter stay up too late eating anything. I'm big on boundaries because I didn't get any when I was a child. My daughter spends the summer with her foster mother because I'm getting my college degree in psychology and working as a parent advocate at the Brooklyn Family Defense Project."

WANDA AS PARENT ADVOCATE

Wanda also wanted to be trained to learn more about the child welfare system. She said, "Me being bold and brazen like I am, I went to ACS, which was near where I lived, to find out what trainings they had. I sat in on their trainings. I got 26 certificates on gang violence, mental health, all sorts of things."

The day Lutheran Social Services agreed to allow Wanda's daughter, Ebony, to go home on a trial discharge, the social worker said, according to Wanda, "Your daughter is lucky to have a mom who will fight for her as you did. You could be a parent advocate because you're an amazing advocate for yourself." Tony Taylor, a social worker at Lutheran, told Wanda that ACS was hiring parent advocates for the first time and that she should fax her resume quickly, which she did. "Like a bat out of hell I faxed my resume." Twenty-six people were interviewed by ACS. Wanda was one of three who got a job.

She worked as a family specialist in the ACS Office of Advocacy for 3 years. "I loved working there, but I wanted more hands-on work." She made presentations about her experiences and ran a parenting group called Bridging the Gap, but she and the other family specialists who worked at ACS couldn't go with parents into court as their advocates because of possible conflicts with ACS. "I felt a little stifled," she said.

A supervisor with whom she worked at ACS told her about a position to advocate for families at the Brooklyn Family Defense Project, a newly created legal services office that represents parents when their children are about to be or have been placed in foster care. Wanda got the job. She and three other parent advocates at the Family Defense Project help parents get benefits to which they are entitled and refer parents and accompany them to various health and social service organizations. She also makes home visits to comfort the parents and see how things are going in the household. Often a mother will call and ask Wanda to come to the home when a child protective services worker is coming for an inspection, so the mother has an ally and doesn't feel alone while she is being investigated.

On May 27, 2010 Wanda graduated from the College of New Rochelle and was accepted at Columbia University's School of Social Work, to start in the fall of 2011. "I'm really excited," she says. Things with her children are more complicated. According to Wanda, her relationship with her oldest child, Levar, is good. Her relationship is distant with her other children who experienced her life when she was involved with drugs. Ebony, who is 13, lives with her godmother, with whom she has a much tighter bond than she has with Wanda. "One thing I've learned: However much you try to right a wrong, you can't change what happened."

Her work as part of the legal team at the Brooklyn Family Defense Program continues to be a lot of "hand holding" as she says. "I go to court with the parents to make sure the process is fair and families are respected. I refer the parents to drug treatment or anger management or other services." Where she feels most effective is with teen parents. "They are impressionable if they believe you're not going to abandon them."

JEANETTE VEGA: A HYPERACTIVE CHILD HIT WITH A BELT

Jeanette Vega was a teenage mother living with her hyperactive toddler who years later would be diagnosed with attention deficit hyperactivity disorder

(ADHD). Upon finding that her child had climbed out of his crib, had opened the front door, and was in the courtyard adjacent to the street, she panicked and hit him with a belt. He was placed in foster care for 3 years. Before that, Jeanette had tried unsuccessfully to get medication for him and guidance for herself about how to raise a hyperactive child. The only help provided for the boy was speech therapy. Perhaps additional assistance would have created a safe family situation, making foster care unnecessary. Jeanette subsequently worked part-time as a parent advocate for the Child Welfare Organizing Project and now works full-time at Episcopal Social Services, helping biological and foster moms work together to raise a child in foster care.

When Jeanette, the youngest and only daughter in a family of eight children, was 1 year old and living with her family in Philadelphia, her father was shot and killed in a taxi. Her mother moved in with another man, creating a household with 12 children. That man used drugs and abused members of the family. When Jeanette was 4, he had a religious conversion. He began going to church and gave up drugs and beating Jeanette's mom.

The family moved to New York City in about 1994. Jeanette describes her mom as "easy going," though she did not allow Jeanette to date until she was 17. Her brothers made sure she adhered to her mother's prohibition, never letting boys get too close. Still, she became pregnant shortly after she met her first boyfriend, Lucas. They moved in with his mom.

"Lucas was kind of happy with his hands, kind of violent," says Jeanette. "He didn't like it when I got too dressed up. He wouldn't let me go out. I was to be home before he got home from work. I wasn't allowed to visit family or friends because they would see the bruises."

When their son, Remi, was 3 or 4 months old, and Jeanette was 18, she said she couldn't take it anymore. She called her brothers to get her. "They took me and Remi to my mother's house, and they took care of Lucas."

But after a few months, she found staying at her mother's house wasn't easy. She still wanted her boyfriend, despite his mistreatment of her. When she began staying out late and her mother learned she wanted to move back in with Lucas, her mother reported her to child protective services for neglecting Remi. The ACS investigator agreed to let the child remain with Jeanette if she would continue to live with her mom. Jeanette said she would do that, and the neglect allegation was dropped.

For a while things were fine. "Everyone helped out, so I had easy babysitting. Remi was so cute, so cuddly, no one could stay away. When Remi was one and a half, Jeanette and her new boyfriend, Reggi, moved into a basement apartment. "I got my life on a schedule: Remi in daycare by 8:00 a.m., me in school from 9:00 a.m. to 1:00 p.m., then straight to work. After work

I'd get Remi, go home, cook something quick, put him to bed, and do my homework."

Being a mother became harder as Remi grew older. "Many days Remi would come home from daycare full of energy, throwing toys, papers, clothes. I had to find games to take his mind off of destroying things. If I wasn't close by, he'd run wild. I was always watching him and wondering, 'What's next?' Starting when he was one, he stayed up until 1:00 a.m., running around the house instead of sleeping. People who were so eager to help when Remi was a newborn suddenly had the attitude, 'Do it yourself. I never told you to have a baby.' I needed their help, but they said, 'You wanted him, you raise him.'"

When Jeanette went to her mother's house, Remi would break her figurines then say he wanted to go home. "My mother said I was too soft on him. I see now that she was right. If I had limited him when he was young, he could have learned that bad behavior wouldn't get him anything. But I rewarded bad behavior, laughing with him at the silly things he did. I loved him and wanted him to be happy, and I thought that meant giving him everything he wanted."

As Remi got more out of control, Jeanette decided something was wrong with him. She contacted three or four different social service centers to have him evaluated. Each place said that Remi's behavior was normal for a 2 year old. An early intervention program that provides help if a baby's development is delayed provided speech therapy twice a week. "The idea was that if he could express his needs better, he would be less frustrated and behave better. But his behavior did not improve," says Jeanette.

Two nights before Remi's second birthday, in June 1999, Reggi was at work. Remi was in his crib, which he knew how to climb out of. As Jeanette came out of the shower, "I saw the front door was open. I freaked out, ran to the door, and there he was, just playing outside in the courtyard all alone, saying he wasn't tired. God forgive me, but I flipped out. I was scared for me and for him. Someone could have taken him or hurt him. I panicked and made the biggest mistake of my life. I hit Remi twice with the belt I was wearing. He had a bruise on his arm, his face, and a red mark on his back. "I hugged him to stop his crying. He cried for 10 minutes; I cried for an hour, walking around the house with him in my arms to calm him and myself. I apologized over and over again, rubbing him until he fell asleep. I felt terrible. I never meant to hurt my little man."

The following day Jeanette's mom and her aunt came to take Remi for the weekend. Jeanette told them what had happened, hoping they would offer to help the next time she was feeling overwhelmed. "All I got was a mouth full of it," Jeanette says. With the aunt's urging, Jeanette's mother called child protective services to file a report of child abuse.

Monday morning a child protective services worker called Jeanette and said that her child was in custody of the child welfare system and that she must appear in Family Court that day. Jeanette went to court and was immediately taken to a police precinct.

A police officer said Jeanette could see her son once she wrote out and signed a statement of exactly what happened. She thought, "I've never been in trouble. I'm in school, I'm working. I thought the system would help me." Still a teenager and without a lawyer, she thought that honesty would be the best approach. She told the police and then wrote out and signed a statement of what had happened. She was immediately arrested, fingerprinted, and held in jail for 3 days.

The authorities put Remi in the care of Jeanette's mother for a week. She couldn't handle him. He was then placed with Jeanette's aunt for 2 weeks, but she couldn't handle him. He was then sent to a foster home. During visits Jeanette saw bruises on him. After 5 months in that home, he had four stitches in his forehead from "crashing into a computer table," according to the foster mother and Remi's social worker. When Jeanette saw the stitches, she demanded that Remi be moved to another foster home. ACS agreed.

According to Jeanette, "The second foster mother was the best foster mother in the world. She was an older, church-going woman, who had a private house. She wasn't rich, but she was comfortable and shared that with Remi." It was a long and frustrating process for Remi to be returned home from foster care where he remained for 3 years. Despite the kindness of the foster mother, Jeanette wanted Remi to be with her and felt she was now old enough and patient enough to deal with his difficult behavior. It took her 3 long and frustrating years to regain custody of her child.

For Remi to come home from foster care, Jeanette did the standard things that ACS and foster care agencies require of mothers: parent training, anger management, and counseling. "I couldn't do all of those things at once and stay in school and work. Since getting Remi back was my priority, I quit school, quit my job, and got public assistance, so I could do what ACS required."

"The parenting class wasn't very useful. They were teaching me how to feed my baby and how to change Pampers. But my baby was not a baby anymore. I said, 'Teach me how to deal with him bugging out, throwing toys at me, taking off his Pamper, and putting it on the wall.' They didn't teach that."

After a year Jeanette was excited that Remi would come home. "I finished all the services requested of me and was getting ready to get my man back. I had an apartment, I was working again, I had unsupervised visits, and things were looking brighter. Then I found out that since my fiancé lived with me, he had to do all the classes. Why wasn't I told that at the beginning?"

After the fiancé spent a year completing all of the classes he was required to take, Remi still did not come home. "The caseworkers were coming and going like flies. I had a new caseworker every 5, 6 months. I had to wait until they got acquainted with my case. And then I would be called in to talk. That was never pleasant."

After 3 years, Remi came home, but, according to Jeanette, "Remi was no different at 5 years than he had been as a baby. He was still hyperactive with strong emotions." It wasn't until many years later, after Jeanette took Remi to many different social service agencies, therapy programs, and medical facilities that Remi, by then 11 years old, was diagnosed with ADHD and was given medication. "Now, with medication, he's great, but every child has his moments. Since he's been on medication, his grades have improved greatly. He's been taken out of special ed. and put into regular education. He focuses on his homework. He does his chores without a problem. He plays with his brother without getting upset. It is a severe change."

Her fiancé, who has become her husband, has always been an involved father and stays home with the children while Jeanette works. Jeanette began volunteering at CWOP the year after Remi came home from foster care. Jeanette's best friend, Teresa, with whom she had grown up in the Highbridge section of the South Bronx, told her about the CWOP training. Jeanette's immediate response was: "I don't need no one to tell me how to work the system. I got my son back. 'Where were they when I needed them' was my first reaction."

Nonetheless, Jeanette took the 6-month CWOP course in 2005. A year after she graduated, CWOP offered her a one-day-a-week job to attend child safety conferences. These conferences had recently been set up by ACS in a few locations in the city. Right before or immediately after a child is put in foster care, a meeting is held with the parent, the child protective case worker, family members or friends of the parent, and at times a parent advocate. They review the situation in the family's home and determine if the child can live safely in the family or must be put in foster care. Jeanette attends the safety conference as a parent advocate.

Jeanette graduated from TCI College of Technology with an associate degree in December 2009. She is the first person in her family to have a high school diploma and the first in her family to have a college diploma. In September 2010 she enrolled in Adelphi University to complete a bachelor's degree in social work. "It's harder than I thought it would be," she says. "Living it, working, and going to school make it complicated." She was expecting to graduate in a year and was considering extending the program by 2 years to get a master's degree in social work.

In early 2011 while Jeanette was working part-time at CWOP, she was hired as a full-time parent advocate at Episcopal Social Services, a New York City foster care agency. Among other responsibilities, she facilitates parent-to-parent meetings in which the biological mother meets the foster parent for the first time. "So far no parents have flipped out," she says.

At home things are improving. She moved from a basement apartment into a fourth floor apartment in the same building in the south Bronx where she has lived for 9 years. It is a one-bedroom apartment in which Jeanette, her husband, and their three sons live. Since her children are all boys, the city housing agency from which she receives a subsidy requires the boys to share one room. They sleep in the living room, which is larger than the bedroom she and her husband share.

Reginald, her 5-year-old son, is doing well, though he has what Jeanette calls a "social disability." "He doesn't like change. Starting kindergarten next year will be hard for him." Problems with her youngest son, 3-year-old Zachary, are reminiscent of the problems with her oldest son, Remi, when he was a toddler. "He's a little hyper, but now I know how to deal with it. He gets 'time-outs.' That calms him down."

Remi, who had been in foster care is now 14. "He's off meds and is doing great in high school. He's in occupational therapy, and it's working. Everything is about girls and phones. He lives on the phone. He's done a 360 turn around."

YOUSHELL WILLIAMS

Youshell had a very difficult childhood. She tried to kill herself twice—once in her teens and once in her 20s. After leaving her emotionally abusive husband, it was difficult raising two young kids, and though she had a well-paying job, she began to spiral downward and gave up her job. She became so depressed and concerned about her children's safety in a public school in Bedford-Stuyvesant that she kept them home. The school reported her to ACS for educational neglect.

The children were placed into foster care with Youshell's sister, where they remained for 3 years while Youshell got help from a variety of therapies and from participating in the CRADLE, an ACS-sponsored community-service program in Bedford-Stuyvesant. Youshell slowly recovered from her depression and was reunited with her children. She worked for a time as a parent advocate and wrote regularly for Rise magazine. She now spends her time raising her youngest child, blogging, and working hard to feel good about herself.[iv]

Youshell grew up in Detroit. "My father was not a nice man. He was mean to my mother, abusive of her. He once threw her down the staircase because he wasn't done beating her. She threw him in jail. We had to run to New York to live with my mom's sister. I was eight."

Living in New York with her aunt in Starrett City in Brooklyn was not much better. "She worked hard for everything she had. She had a very structured life and believed in etiquette. We had to follow her rules. She thought we were unkempt." In time Youshell and her family moved out, but her mom couldn't make it on her own and the family had to move back in with Youshell's aunt. Soon after, her mother, who had been diagnosed with cancer before they left Detroit, died. Youshell was 14; her mother was 43.

Youshell was miserable living with her aunt and without any other member of her family. One sister was in college, her brother was in the navy, and her other sister was back in Detroit with her boyfriend. "My aunt's daughter resented me. My mom had just died. It was not good. I tried to kill myself. I mixed roach poison with other things. I drank it, and it came back up. My aunt didn't know anything was wrong. I went shopping with her, though my lips were white. I didn't go to the hospital or anything."

"I didn't have a good opinion of myself. I actually hated myself. I started acting out and doing bad things with boys. My aunt sent me to live with my dad. I hated it. I didn't trust him or like him, but we were both readers and at least we had that in common. I went to Martin Luther King High School but hated every minute of it. My sister, who has always been there for me, was living in East New York and sent for me to live with her when I was 19. I got a job in a factory packing fruits and candies and met Janelle and Ramel's father who was twice my age. It was a very bad choice." They married in July 1989 when she was 19 years old and he was 36. "My father

iv. Her story is based on interviews with Youshell and stories she wrote about her life that appeared in *Rise* 16 (Summer 2010): 8–9, "What's Going on Here? What Parents Need to Know about Mental Health Evaluations"; *Rise* 14 (Fall 2009): 8–9, "It's Truancy, Not Neglect"; *Rise* 13 (Summer 2009): 1–2, *Rise* 11 (Fall 2008): 8, "Do Over: Changing as a Parent Takes Courage and Practice"; *Rise* 10 (Summer 2008): 6, "Stopping the Clock: Many Parents in Prison Are at Risk of Losing Their Rights Permanently"; and from the *Rise* website: http://risemagazine.org/PDF/Rise_issue_16.pdf
http://risemagazine.org/PDF/Rise_issue_14.pdf
http://risemagazine.org/PDF/Rise_issue_13.pdf
http://risemagazine.org/PDF/Rise_issue_11.pdf
http://risemagazine.org/PDF/Rise_issue_10.pdf
http://risemagazine.org/featured_stories/It_wont_happen_again.html

was abusive, my mother had died, and I felt lost. I already hated myself, but he made me feel like I was beyond dumb. When he wasn't calling me names, he was out in the streets getting drunk and having affairs."

It wasn't easy taking care of two small children alone. She moved, found childcare, and started looking for a job with the help of America Works, a program that prepares young people for work. In 1994 she was hired on a trial basis at a cancer research firm. "They liked my hard work and kept me." Soon she was making good money and had worked her way up to lab technician. She was successful, yet she was not happy. "I just did not feel right. I was short-tempered and angry and cried a lot. I didn't know what was wrong with me. I had wonderful support at my job. One nice man suggested that I see a therapist. I didn't listen. I felt I was too strong for that nonsense. Yet I felt myself getting weaker and weaker and crying more and more." Then things got worse at home. The Catholic school her children attended told her that her son could not continue on to first grade because he didn't listen and disappeared from class.

She switched both kids to public school, but their new school was deplorable. "The teachers didn't care, and my son was often beat up by a bully. I rushed to the school from work one day only to be told by the teacher that my son was "around here somewhere." Well, I found him walking down the street, away from the school. At 6 years old! I lost it. I felt my children were being treated very badly."

She was soon having lots of problems at work. She was late almost every day and had to leave early to pick up her children. Finally, she asked her firm to lay her off. "Once I stopped working, I became so depressed that some days I wouldn't bother taking my kids to school. I just wanted to keep them home with me where I knew they were safe and taken care of. I was overwhelmed and needed help." She talked to a social worker at the school and told her, "'I can't take it anymore.' She didn't ask me what I was talking about but did take it upon herself to call the abuse and neglect hotline and report educational neglect. An ACS caseworker began coming to my home. She had a very nasty attitude, and I refused to bow down to her. Instead I responded in the same nasty way."

A worker from a preventive services program began visiting, too. "She approached me tentatively, in a nice way, but I felt she did not know how to help me. I really did not trust preventive services or know what they were about. Looking back, I wish I had asked more questions of the preventive worker. I wish I'd asked her to provide me with the services I needed, but I didn't even have a clue what those would be or even how I could help myself."

Eventually, when her son was 6 years old and her daughter was 7, she broke down. "One day, after another horrible visit from the demon worker,

I called her and asked her to take my children to my sister's house. The children were placed with a stranger."

"My son suffered for my mistakes. My daughter suffered for my mistakes. And I suffered, too. I feel I will never forgive myself for giving up. After my kids went into care, I just barely kept living. The first month was terrible, because the worker put them with a stranger instead of with my sister, until a judge ordered them moved. I was so scared and angry when I didn't know where my children were." For a short time, she was hospitalized to deal with her depression. She went to support programs and worked to have money to give her sister for her kids. "I only had two good reasons—my kids—to keep trying."

AFTER FOSTER CARE

Her children were in foster care with her sister for 3 years. The Children's Aid Society was the supervising agency. "I had a nice worker who really cared, and my sister was wonderful. She did above and beyond what a sister or aunt should do. But the separation took its toll. As time passed I became afraid to get my children back, afraid to fail again. Life felt like one big messy hell for me. My sister woke me up. She said, 'It doesn't seem like you want them back.'" Youshell's new social worker helped, too. She explained what steps to take to get her children home. "Without her, I believe my case could've dragged on forever."

When the children came home there were tensions and conflicts. "After such a long absence it took a long time for my children and me to get back in the groove. My kids acted like I was no longer the parent, Aunt Gina was. I felt like they were thinking, 'Mommy showed how weak she could be.' Now the respect was gone. My son was especially angry. He did not want to face the new man in my life, my future tormenter and second hell."

When her children came home, she was required to go to a preventive services agency, Family Dynamics, which she liked. When her worker left the agency, she found another agency in her neighborhood, Brooklyn Bureau of Community Services. A sympathetic counselor at Brooklyn Bureau helped Youshell deal with her depression and ease the rocky transition when her kids came home from foster care. "I loved my second worker, Julia Kim. She started us on family therapy, and I was hooked. I found out a lot. My children were fearful and disappointed in me. I had seemed so strong to them that it had been shocking to them to watch me fall so hard. They were bitter and scared that I might fall once again."

After several years of belittling treatment, physical abuse, and a new baby by the "tormenter" in Youshell's life, the therapist Youshell was seeing called protective services after she saw bite marks on Youshell's hand. "She felt she needed to do it. I thought she was decent, but that was not good to call it in. My trust [in the therapist] fell right there." The therapist is required by law to report abuse or neglect. However, Youshell reports that the therapist knew she was in a program, Sanctuary for Families, that was helping her move out of the abusive relationship, that had a lawyer for her and was helping her find an apartment. ACS came to investigate. "ACS tried to take my kids away. The therapist and her supervisor didn't speak up for me."

ACS did not take her kids away but her boyfriend left and the family moved into a much nicer apartment, where each child got his and her own room. The move eased the tension some, but Youshell still didn't get the respect she wanted from her children.

Ramel's truancy put her family at risk. "I've had child protective caseworkers come to my house three times. They've investigated not only my son's attendance problem—which I believe should be considered truancy, since he's 15—but they also looked into every corner of my life. They even made me get my youngest daughter tested for psychological problems. A psychologist found nothing wrong. I've been able to fight these allegations so far. The cases were closed because I was already taking Ramel to counseling and had sought family counseling. But these investigations have terrified my children and me, and I have not seen much improvement in my son's attitude toward school or attendance, even though Ramel understands that he's putting his family at risk of separation."

"Counseling is helping Ramel and me communicate better, but it feels like a Band-Aid on the sore, not healing. We made a deal recently. Ramel would attend school all week, and I would get his PSP [video game] fixed. I was desperate. But it didn't work. I am worried about Ramel and his future. I am afraid that, to protect my family, I will have to give up on my son. I wish my kids' lives could have been better. My daughter is another story waiting to happen. She is a difficult child."

Julia Kim, the aforementioned social worker at Brooklyn Bureau of Community Services, also linked Youshell with a program administered by ACS called CRADLE,[v] a program for parents from Bedford-Stuyvesant

v. CRADLE, Community Responsibility for Assisting Developing Life and Empowerment, was a 5-year federally funded demonstration project administered by ACS. The CRADLE was a collaborative of families, concerned community residents, community-based organizations, civic leaders, and governmental entities engaged in

to engage with child welfare agencies. "People were nice. There was not judgment, no put down. It amazed me that such a program could come out of ACS." Youshell worked at CRADLE as a paid intern for 2 years. During that time, Nigel Nathaniel, director of the office of community partnerships at ACS, told her about CWOP. "I came to a CWOP meeting. I met Mike [Arsham, the head of CWOP], and that was it. CWOP is parents who experienced the same thing. They are not judgmental. We're able to talk and to connect with each other. After something tragic happens, you're really learning and helping others come through the same thing. When you're going through things like that, you don't think anyone else goes through that. And you come into a room, and they've gone through worse. And they've survived. There's a lot of strength and perseverance. Once you get through it you know you have strength. It's beautiful and the people are beautiful. CRADLE was different. They didn't want to hear the pain and suffering you went through."

Youshell took CWOP's 6-month parent advocate course. A writing workshop led by Nora McCarthy from *Rise* was part of the training. "I did not want it at all. Nora said, 'Write down what you feel.' She's pushy. She didn't allow people to just come in and put in their time sheet. I would write and not disclose a lot. She would say, 'I would like you to write more about this.' She's able to bring out the best and the worst. You can't hide from her. She has those x-ray eyes. You want to talk to her. This is the best therapy I ever could have had."

Youshell recovered from her depression though she still struggles to feel good about herself. She left her abusive partners, but her son feels 'she lets people walk all over her.' She reunited with her two older children after 3 years; she has always lived with her younger daughter Lina. She has been able to care for them and have a genuine, though complicated relationship with them.

She has written often for *Rise* magazine, not only telling her story but trying to help other parents by writing on topics such as what parents need to know about mental health evaluations or how to become a terrific parent even if you didn't have one. As she says, "Once I started writing I couldn't stop."

Youshell lives in Bedford-Stuyvesant, Brooklyn with her younger daughter Lina and her older daughter Jinelle. "My children are doing great," she says. "My daughter Lina is in sixth grade. She is a healthy, happy,

a partnership to enhance services that promote safety and well-being of infants and their families in the Bedford-Stuyvesant community. The program began in 2003 and ended in 2008 when government funding ended.

bright child, though she has asthma." Her older children are also doing well according to Youshell. Her 20-year-old son Ramel is working and her 21-year-old daughter who was in college has taken a year off and moved back in with Youshell.

Youshell had been depressed and isolated in the past but that has changed in recent years. She has chosen to focus on herself and her young daughter. She is active in the PTA, a healthy eating program, and was a parent coach on her daughter's track team. "I am happy. I know where I'm going and feel blessed to be here."

To focus on her daughter and her own well-being Youshell has distanced herself from the child welfare system. She hasn't had contact for months with CWOP or *Rise*. She writes instead on Facebook. Her postings are positive short notes about loving yourself and feeling positive about what you have.

***

Two observations stand out from learning about the six mothers profiled in this book, four in this chapter. Although some of the women are currently on a straight line trajectory toward more fulfilling lives, they all have had significant ups and downs since their children left foster care, probably more extreme than most people experience. They have had severe personal illnesses, loss of work, continued conflicts with their children, and children struggling to find their own path after the traumas of their earlier lives and foster care. Nevertheless, each mother is hopeful about her future, engaged in what she is doing, and happy with the road she is on.

Second, three of the mothers continue to be advocates and activists in child welfare. They delight in their work and feel proud of helping others. One of the mothers, Youshell, has had to distance herself from the child welfare system, including her earlier efforts to reform it, to find peace and fulfillment. She is focusing instead on her children and herself. Why she and other mothers, such as Sharwline Nicholson profiled in Chapter 4, have left child welfare activism is not surprising given the trauma associated with their child welfare experience, the low pay as activists, and the difficulty of the work. That three of the four mothers in this chapter have stayed active for 5 years and other mothers have been activists for longer than that is more interesting. I think their continued activism is the result of being part of a group with a common purpose and a shared identity and of being able to find "collective efficacy" in what they do as part of the parents' movement. As Mike Arsham said, parents get more than their kids back. "They get a sense of their own value and worth . . . to fight back and not just be a victim."

CHAPTER 3

Tilling the Soil: The Groundwork for Parent Activism

In the past two decades New York City parents and their allies fought for and won more influence, affected more change, and garnered more respect in child welfare than parents had at any other time in the history of the United States. To achieve this, they organized and worked collectively rather than as isolated individuals as parents had in the past. Nothing like this collective action by parents and their allies had ever occurred in child welfare.

As Linda Gordon describes in her book *"Heroes of Their Own Lives,"* a history of parents in child welfare from the 1870s to the middle of the twentieth century, women who were battered by their husbands or had their children taken from them by child protection agencies fought back individually against the men who beat them or against the public and private agencies that took their children.[1] This type of individual activism continued into the twenty-first century with mothers and fathers fighting on their own to be reunited with their children, or parents finding lawyers who were willing to take their case, or activist lawyers finding parents whose case represented a violation of law or principle they wanted to rectify. But until the recent parent activism in New York, which later blossomed in other cities, the women (and the few men) who were accused of neglecting or abusing their children never organized as a group to fight for their rights, to help shape programs and services that would meet their needs, or to press for a less punitive child welfare system.

This chapter describes the individuals and organizations that helped shape the environment in which parents could unite, create their own organizations, and gain influence in New York's child welfare system. The next two chapters describe the activities of parents and their allies once an environment had been created in which parents could organize and be heard.

ORGANIZATIONS AND INDIVIDUALS THAT
HELPED PARENTS GAIN INFLUENCE

The child welfare system in New York City is a $2 billion dollar enterprise,[2] employing about 14,000 people in city bureaucracies and voluntary agencies that are involved in the lives of roughly 100,000 children and their families a year.[3] In a system that large, fragmented, and entrenched, many forces work to keep things as they are. Even when all forces align to bring about a reform that everyone wants, change is painfully slow.[i] Usually, though, the forces that shape the direction of the child welfare system do not coalesce behind change.

More often than not, change begins in one corner—a commissioner wants to improve the way agencies interact with families, or the mayor wants to cut the child welfare budget, or agencies want more autonomy or more funding to cover their expenses. When a change is proposed in one sector, powerful actors in other child welfare sectors push and pull to

---

i. One small example was referenced in the preface of this book. Very early in 2009 leaders of New York's child welfare system agreed that a provision in New York State social services regulations should be changed to allow agencies to receive credit for parent advocate contacts with families when the state evaluates the agencies. John Mattingly, commissioner of New York City's Administration for Children's Services, Gladys Carrion, the commissioner of New York State's Office of Children and Family Services (OCFS), Jim Purcell, the executive director of the Council of Family and Child Caring Agencies (representing almost all foster care and preventive service agencies in New York State), and the Child Welfare Organizing Project (representing parent advocates) endorsed the change. I coordinated the effort, based at the Fund for Social Change, recommending the change in the regulations. No one opposed the change.

Even though OCFS promulgates the regulations, and there would be no cost implications for the change, it took more than a year and a half, until August 11, 2010, for the regulation to be implemented. [Letter from the parent advocates initiative, signed by David Tobis to Commissioner Carrion, February 11, 2009; § 441.2(o) and amendment of § 441.21(b)(1) and (2) of Title 18 of the NYCRR.]

ensure that the change benefits their organizations as much as possible or hurts them as little as possible. Reform in child welfare is generally a slow, incremental process of struggle and compromise among the forces that have shaped child welfare for the past century—these are primarily city, state, and federal government agencies that fund and regulate the system, and the religious and nonreligious agencies funded by government to deliver services. The yearly wave of approximately a 100,000 children, and their parents affected by the child welfare system—parents who were investigated by child protective services, whose families received services, or whose children were in foster care—were excluded from that process.[4]

The recent 20-year campaign of parents and their allies to gain a voice in child welfare decision making has begun to pay off. This chapter looks at the three centers of activity that cumulatively played the biggest role in shaping an environment that enabled parents and their allies to join the fray. These were the Child Welfare Fund (CWF), a small and, at the beginning of the 1990s, a very new foundation that focused its resources largely on increasing the power of parents in New York's child welfare system; the *Marisol v. Giuliani* class action lawsuit brought by Children's Rights Inc. (CRI), which led to the creation of the New York City Special Child Welfare Advisory Panel; and the Administration for Children's Services (ACS), the city's public child welfare agency created in 1996, which at first resisted listening to parents but then embraced meeting their needs, and more recently, championed their cause. These are not the only organizations and individuals that opened the way for parents, but they are the ones that had the largest and most sustained impact.[ii] They gave resources to parents and their allies, pushed the child welfare culture to see parents differently, and promoted an environment in which parents could organize and create a self-sustaining movement.

---

ii. Countless other organizations and individuals also tilled the soil. Other foundations provided resources for parents and their organizations including the wealthy and powerful—JPMorgan Global Foundations Group/Ira W. DeCamp Foundation, the network of Casey foundations, and the New York Community Trust—and the small and less powerful ones such as the New York Foundation, the Warner Fund and the Daphne Foundation. Many lawyers and law firms defended parents in court, helped train them, and hired them to work in their offices. The law firm of Lansner and Kubichek filed lawsuits defending parents who had their children removed. Bronx Defenders, the Brooklyn Family Defense Project, and the Center for Family Representation provided legal representation for parents. Foster care agency executive directors at St. Christopher's, Children's Village, Seamen's Society, JCCA, and New York Foundling hired parent advocates before it was popular to do so. Many of the other individuals and organizations who contributed to the movement are described throughout this book.

In 1991 a friend who was knowledgeable about children's programs received an inheritance and asked me to help her give it away to assist children. The donor remained anonymous, which gave me the extraordinary gift of shaping a new foundation with her and getting most of the thanks for the good work her money wrought.

Together we created the Child Welfare Fund, which operated as a small foundation, though it was never formally incorporated. In fact, it existed only on stationery letterhead. I worked at Hunter College at the time and met with potential grantees in my office there. Then I reviewed proposals and recommended grants for funding to the donor. She decided which grants would be funded, though in our 18 years of working together I think she rejected only one or two grants. However, she reshaped many others. Once she approved grants, she had checks issued from one or another of her various accounts. The Child Welfare Fund was an organizational fiction, though the $1 million a year it provided in grants was very real.

In the beginning, no one knew about us: We didn't have a website (no one had a website then), we weren't listed in foundation directories, and we didn't advertise. I would get ideas for a project and contact a person I knew or heard about and ask if he or she was interested in doing the project. Many people said it reminded them of the 1950s television show *The Millionaire* about an anonymous donor who each week selected an individual to receive $1 million, though our grants generally ranged between $25,000 and $50,000. For example, I thought it would be useful for children in foster care to have a publication in which they could write about their experiences before they entered care and while they were in it, and to present their ideas to improve the system in which they were living. I called Keith Hefner, a friend from the days when we were Revson Fellows at Columbia University, who was the editor of *New Youth Connections*, a publication for high school students.[iii] As so often happens when fertile ground is turned, he had had a similar idea. The Child Welfare Fund gave him a planning grant and then funded the paper for the next 15 years. The publication, originally called *Foster Care Youth United* but renamed *Represent* by the writers, is written by and for youth in foster care. It continues to be published quarterly, with a circulation of 8,200 but upward

iii. The Revson Fellows Program was created in 1979 by the Revson Foundation to recognize individuals who work to improve New York City. Every year it awards 8 to 10 individuals a stipend and access to the resources of Columbia University for a year to think about the next stage of their activism. Keith Hefner was a Revson Fellow in 1986–1987 and I was a Fellow the following year.

of 100,000 youth in care and people who work with them have read its articles reprinted in books and on websites.

Although in retrospect it may look as if the Child Welfare Fund had a well-developed grant-making strategy, we mostly had an idea and stumbled into a strategy to execute it through trial and many errors. First and foremost, the idea the donor and I shared was that the best way to improve the lives of children and families was to give them a greater role in decisions affecting their own lives. Otherwise the system, no matter how well intentioned its goals, would continue to break families apart rather than keep them together; it would punish rather than heal.

The strategy evolved from hit-and-miss grant making and from our different perspectives. Although the donor and I agreed that we wanted to help parents and youth gain power, we disagreed on how best to do that. She was a strong supporter of direct services because she believed that CWF grants should help people now. I thought that unless systems changed, the line of those in need would be just as long after we had expended all of CWF's resources. We reached a wise and useful compromise. Half the resources would go for direct services and half for system reform. The most important by-product of this agreement was that the direct service grants enabled us to see patterns of problems and focus our system-reform efforts where the problems surfaced. For example, we funded Green Chimney's Children's Services to train staff to work with gay and lesbian youth in foster care. As the extent of the neglect and maltreatment for lesbian, gay, bisexual, and transgender (LGBT) youth became clearer through that work, we funded the Urban Justice Center to bring a class action suit on their behalf.[iv]

One of the CWF's first projects was to find out what rights parents had to make decisions for their children while the youngsters were in care and to determine the extent to which parents could and did participate in program and policy decisions. The CWF provided a grant in 1994 to Terry Mizrahi, a professor at Hunter College School of Social Work, and to Beth Rosenthal, a consultant on community planning and organizing, to survey the rights of parents and to assess the extent to which those rights were respected.

Their findings confirmed what almost everyone knew anecdotally: Parents had almost no voice in child welfare decisions. Whereas New York

iv. It is ironic that the settlement of the *Marisol* lawsuit, which was supported by the Child Welfare Fund, precluded any other lawsuits in New York's child welfare system, including the Urban Justice Center's suit on behalf of LGBT youth, which was also supported by the Child Welfare Fund.

State law allowed parents to be involved in their own case decisions, foster care agencies rarely enabled parents to be heard.[5] For example, parents had the right to attend the case conference as part of the Service Plan Review of their case. This is the primary meeting for determining what parents must do to be reunited with their children. In 1994 the New York State Comptroller found that parents attended only 20.6% of these meetings, largely because agencies placed barriers in the parents' way, such as not being told of the conference, or scheduling meetings during the day for the convenience of caseworkers but during the time when most parents are at work.[6]

The study also found that parents were never involved in child welfare programs or policy decisions, though they had a right to be. None of the 60 or so foster care agencies that had contracts with the city at the time employed a parent who had been through the child welfare system, though legally they were allowed to do so;[7] none had a parent who had been embroiled in the system on its board of directors. And no city or state commissioner of child welfare had formally sought the advice of a parent who had experienced the child welfare system.[8]

Child welfare agencies believed that parents who had a child in foster care could not work with children and families. Martin Guggenheim, a professor at NYU Law School, prepared a legal opinion at the request of the Child Welfare Fund that concluded that parents who had had a child in foster care or who had been the subject of a confirmed case of abuse or neglect could legally work in a child welfare agency and have direct contact with children, so long as the executive director of the agency felt children's safety would not be compromised.[9] Guggenheim's opinion provided the legal documentation that agencies needed to hire parents who had been involved in the system.

The Child Welfare Fund set out to end the exclusion of parents from child welfare decision making. The donor and I developed three broad approaches to address this exclusion. First, CWF would create or support grassroots organizations to teach individual parents their rights, to train them to help other parents, and to instruct them in grassroots organizing. CWF operated on the principle that individuals bring about change but have far more power when they work through organizations. No organizations existed that both represented the interests of parents and included them in the decision-making process. We therefore had to create new organizations or nurture fledgling ones. CWF, unlike most foundations, was willing to give money to groups that had never been funded before.

In many cases, individuals with a good idea and a lot of passion came to the CWF seeking help to turn their ideas into a project and eventually into an organization that would fight for the rights of poor people in child welfare. More often than not, we funded them, though the initial grants to fragile organizations were small. But that was not always the case. For example, Susan Lob, a community organizer and long-time activist on behalf of women, wanted to create an organization of domestic violence survivors that would stand up to the Giuliani administration when existing domestic violence organizations were fearful of speaking out against his administration. The Child Welfare Fund provided a planning grant for Lob to design Voices of Women and then a grant to launch it.[v]

These groups both helped individual parents, accompanying them through the maze of child welfare hearings, and organized street demonstrations to draw attention to the system's shortcomings. A large rally outside Manhattan Family Court led to a meeting with the Supervising Judge of the Court. Another outside of St. Patrick's Cathedral focused on ACS and the deaths of children in Catholic foster care agencies. It led to more parents speaking out about the abuses they experienced. One candlelight vigil at the home of then commissioner Scoppetta on Thanksgiving Eve drew no press but got his attention, perhaps helping him listen to the more diplomatic criticisms from the Special Child Welfare Panel.

The second element of the Child Welfare Fund's strategy was to change the public's and professionals' perception of parents with a child welfare history. The media demonized these parents by sensationalizing and generalizing each horrible child death to be the norm for all parents whose children are placed into care, though most children are removed from their homes because they are neglected, often for reasons of poverty, not because of abuse.[10] Most child welfare workers, the press, and the public, whose views were shaped by the press, saw these parents as the primary cause of their own problems and failed to focus on the role played by poverty, unemployment, degraded communities, and racism. To change public and professional awareness, the Child Welfare Fund helped create three publications: the *Child Welfare Watch* for professionals, the aforementioned *Represent* magazine written by and for youth in care, and *Rise* magazine, written by and for

---

v. Many other nascent groups received their first financial support from the CWF including the Child Welfare Organizing Project, People United for Children, Concerned Citizens for Family Preservation, Legal Information for Families Today (LIFT), and the Welfare Rights Initiative (WRI). Starting new organizations, however, is filled with risks and failures, but the CWF believed that unless we had failures, we were not taking enough risks. Several groups that received their first funding from the CWF folded such as Birth Fathers Support Network, the Child Welfare Action Center, and Voices of Youth, crashing against the rocks of organizational conflicts, inexperience, and limited funding.

parents with children in foster care. The *Watch* is described below. *Rise* is described in Chapter 5.

The *Child Welfare Watch*, edited by Andrew White, now director of the Center for New York City Affairs at the New School University, began in 1997 as an eight-page report. It has since become the preeminent publication monitoring the child welfare system in New York City. It appears twice a year as a 24- to 40-page magazine that provides analysis and recommendations on different aspects of New York's child welfare system. Each issue of the *Watch* is then presented at a public forum hosted by the New School. The *Watch's* recommendations one year regularly turn into city policy in subsequent years. The shift from child removal to the provision of resources to help families, the provision of adequate legal representation of parents in Family Court, the creation of child welfare partnerships with communities, and extension of help to immigrant families were all recommendations of the *Watch* that eventually became ACS policy.

From the beginning, the *Watch* published articles sharply critical of ACS's oversight of the child welfare system and the performance of private foster care agencies. In fact, at the public forum presenting the findings of the first issue of the *Watch* in the spring of 1997, then Deputy ACS Commissioner William Bell, who participated on the panel discussing the findings, said that he had been unfairly attacked—"sandbagged," to use his phrase—and refused to participate in any subsequent *Watch* forums.

But the relationship changed with time: ACS improved and moved closer to the views and values of the people who produce the *Watch*, and the *Watch* became more understanding of the complications of reforming large systems. At a 2005 forum organized by *Watch* on redesigning the foster care system, ASC Commissioner John Mattingly said, "The *Child Welfare Watch* reports, I think, are the most thoughtful, balanced and detailed analysis of a particular set of issues in child welfare that I have ever seen anywhere."[11,vi]

vi. Two elements were important in creating the success of the *Watch* and its ability to influence public policy. The first is a talented investigative research team led by Andrew White, a seasoned journalist on the faculty of the New School. He walks the precarious line between academia and practice, between neutrality and advocacy, integrating the perspectives of parents and advocates, practitioners, and government. Each issue of the *Watch* is factually accurate and balanced. It is trusted by most of the players in the field.

The second essential element in the *Watch's* success is the Advisory Board, which guides it and presents the recommendations that accompany each issue. The Board was carefully selected to represent the most progressive, seasoned voices from the main child welfare constituencies. Members include former commissioners, legal advocates, current and former child welfare agency executive directors, parents who have been reunited with their children, and their advocates. For full disclosure, I have been the Chairman of the Advisory Board of the *Watch* since it began publishing.

Another CWF undertaking to change public and professional perception of the people served by the child welfare system was to create three annual awards programs: for youth in care who have overcome great difficulties and have helped others (begun in 1999), for parents who have been reunited with their children (begun in 2001), and for workers and parent advocates in the system who rise above the constraints of their jobs to meet the needs of children and families (begun in 2000). Hundreds of people in New York's child welfare system applied for these awards each year.[vii] The winners were profiled at public events, where their stories are told as they received a certificate and cash award, generally of $1000. The audiences who attended these ceremonies, the people who read about the ceremonies in the local press, the people who nominated the candidates for the awards, the judges who selected the winners, and the winners themselves all saw the people in the child welfare system differently as a result of the awards. The lives and the strengths of the recipients became real. Their exhausting battles to overcome addiction, abuse, or crushing caseloads make their accomplishments all the more moving.

Esmeralda Simmons is the director of the Center for Law and Social Justice and a judge for the Foster Care Youth Awards and the Family Unity Awards for Parents. She says about the ceremony for parents:

> We hear how parents, all for the love of their children, actually beat long-term drug addiction, debilitating mental illness and life cycles of violence. Listening to these parents' trials and ultimate victory restores one's faith in today's parents. In that room, on that day, hearing their stories, seeing these parents with their children, witnessing their hugging, kissing and tears of joy as they celebrate their family's being together evokes spontaneous cheers of support and admiration.[12]

The third element in the Child Welfare Fund's approach to increasing the influence of parents was to demonstrate the overwhelming benefit from having parents with child welfare experience directly helping families in distress and shaping service programs for them. CWF provided grants to foster care agencies to hire parent advocates. These are individuals who had children placed in foster care, changed their lives, learned the ins and outs of the child welfare system, and been trained in how to engage struggling parents and mentor them so they could reunite with their children. In 1994 CWF gave St. Christopher's, a large nondenominational foster care agency, a grant to hire one of the first two parents, if not the first

---

vii. The awards for parents ended in 2007. The awards for social workers and parent advocates continue. The awards for youth continue with other sources of funding.

such parent, with child welfare experience to be employed in a foster care agency. The parent advocate not only engaged and guided other parents struggling to be reunited with their children but also organized a parents' council at St. Christopher's to help shape the agency's programs and policies. CWF continued to provide seed funding to child welfare agencies to hire parent advocates, so that by the time of the March 16, 2011 forum there were about 100 parent advocates working in foster care, preventive service, and legal and advocacy organizations throughout New York City.

Another part of the Child Welfare Fund's effort to have parents with child welfare experience help struggling families and shape service programs was joining forces in 2000 with the Open Society Institute and other foundations to create a donors' collaborative.[viii] The project, called Bridge Builders, is located in the Highbridge section of the South Bronx, which had one of the highest number of children placed in foster care in the late 1990s.[13] Bridge Builders trains and hires parents from the community, some of whom have been involved in the child welfare system, to go door to door, asking their neighbors in housing projects, day care centers, and schools if they need help before their family problems become overwhelming. They refer the families to a network of service providers supported by the collaborative, including legal representation to ensure that their rights are protected and social service agencies to ensure that their needs are met. Bridge Builders is now administered by people from Highbridge and governed by a board of directors composed of members who live or work in that community.

When Bridge Builders began, Commissioner Scoppetta did not want ACS to be involved in the project because of his distrust of advocates, perhaps fueled by the Thanksgiving Eve demonstration outside his home. Four years later, Commissioner Bell who had his own doubts about advocates after having been "sandbagged" at the first forum of the *Child Welfare Watch*, embraced Bridge Builders and joined the collaborative.[ix] Three years later, Commissioner Mattingly became a champion of Bridge Builders, funding the program and using it as a model to promote community involvement in

viii. The foundations that were members of the donors' collaborative are as follows: Open Society Institute, the Child Welfare Fund, the New York Community Trust, JPMorgan/DeCamp, FAR Fund, Hechscher Foundation, Hagedorn Fund, Sills Family Foundation, A.E. Casey Foundation, Oak Foundation, United Way of New York City, Clark Foundation, Starr Foundation, Marguerite Casey Foundation/Casey Family Programs, New Yorkers for Children, and parallel funding from the Viola Bernard Foundation, the Rosenberg Foundation, and the Child Welfare Fund.

ix. As previously described, when Bell was deputy commissioner of ACS he felt "sandbagged" by the advocates; I was a prime culprit in his eyes. Our reconciliation and subsequent collaboration on Bridge Builders when he became commissioner are a reflection of his generosity and concern for children. He and I both were asked to

child welfare in the 11 highest risk communities in the city. The activities of parents in Bridge Builders and the collaborative's impact are described in greater detail in Chapter 5.

Although many other forces created the environment in which parents of children in foster care could be heard, the Child Welfare Fund was the first and most influential organization in New York City that had an explicit strategy focused on increasing the power of parents. Although its total grants were never more than $1 million a year, CWF's impact was far greater than its limited resources. As Bell said in 2004 in his speech at an event honoring the Child Welfare Fund and me for our work on behalf of parents:

> The New York City child welfare system has fundamentally changed over the last several years … because you have forced us to change, because you have said openly and loudly, "Things cannot continue to go the way they have been going." And we listened to that.[14]

It was unclear whether Bell's remarks referred to the parents in the audience who organized the event or to the Child Welfare Fund. Their activities had become so intertwined that it was hard to disentangle their impact.

After the anonymous donor and I worked together for 18 years, she decided to take the Child Welfare Fund in new directions, focusing eventually on mental health services for very young children. In April 2009 my involvement with the CWF ended, as did its primary focus on increasing the influence of parents in child welfare. The impact of this diminished focus on parents is discussed more fully in Chapter 8.

Children's Rights Inc., *Marisol v. Giuliani*, and the Special Child Welfare Advisory Panel

Marcia Lowry founded Children's Rights, Inc. (CRI) in 1995. By then she was already one of the most powerful, and to the state governments she

---

speak at the opening of the offices of Birth Fathers Support Network, an organization of men who had lost contact with or custody of their children, often as a result of prison. He spoke about his growing up in Mississippi, recounting that on the one night his father had come home to try to reconcile, unsuccessfully, with his mother, William was conceived. I was touched by his honesty, vulnerability, and his empathy for the people he was addressing, especially since I had lived in Mississippi as a civil rights worker in 1965. I wrote to him, telling him of my reaction to his presentation, and suggesting that we get together to talk. He agreed, we met, and slowly, in part through the creative bridging by his able deputy, Anne Williams Isom, he agreed to have ACS become a member of the Bridge Builders' steering committee.

sued, one of the most notorious forces for child welfare reform in the country. In her previous job, at the American Civil Liberties Union (1979–1995), she had brought class action lawsuits against dysfunctional child welfare systems in states across the country. She was known most prominently for the epic struggle she led to wrest control of New York's child welfare system from the religious agencies that dominated it for most of the twentieth century.

She filed *Wilder v. Bernstein* in 1973 when she was at the New York Civil Liberties Union (1973–1979), alleging that the New York child welfare system discriminated against black Protestant children (a violation of the fourteenth amendment of the U.S. Constitution), lacked separation of church and state (required by the first amendment), and placed children in institutions causing them cruel and unusual punishment (a violation of the eighth amendment).[15] The suit outraged New York's religious establishment that provided foster care and infuriated the governmental agencies that funded and oversaw their work.[x] The suit had dragged on for more than 20 years by the time she filed the *Marisol v. Giuliani* lawsuit at the end of 1995, soon after she founded CRI.

Lowry, a lawyer, is a fierce and relentless fighter for children's rights, which has often put her in conflict with the state governments and the voluntary agencies she sues and with the advocates who fight for the rights of parents and families. The lawsuits "have definitely focused people's attention and definitely generated some energy," says Bob McKeagney, vice-president of program operations for the Child Welfare League of America (an association of child welfare service providers) and former head of Maine's child welfare system. "But in most situations, they have proved to be debilitating and demoralizing to the departments themselves."[16] Some of her cases, including *Wilder*, became mired in the legal merry-go-round common to court-supervised settlements that often follow such lawsuits. The result is decades of litigation and little impact. By the mid-1990s, some supporters of her lawsuits had begun to question their value.[17] Among child and family advocates who abandoned her cause was Guggenheim, who enthusiastically had helped her early in the *Wilder* lawsuit.[18] In 2005, he wrote a scholarly book, *What's Wrong with Children's*

---

x. Particularly irritating to New York City's child welfare administrator at the time, Barbara Blum, was the fact that she had hired Lowry in 1972 to be her special assistant for program development at Special Services for Children (SSC), the city's child welfare agency at the time. In June 1973, only months after she left SSC, Lowry filed the Wilder lawsuit. "Outrage, fear, and a deep sense of betrayal overwhelmed general agreement [within SSC] with the substance of the suit." [Bernstein, *The Lost Children of Wilder*, 45.]

Rights, and intentionally did not mention her because of his anger at what he viewed as her betrayal of the rights of parents and families.[19]

Lowry filed *Marisol v. Giuliani* on December 13, 1995, less than a month after the death of Elisa Izquierdo exposed profound failings in New York's child welfare system. She brought the suit in the height of the pre-Christmas season for maximum visibility and public sympathy. In an overly simplified summary, Lowry said, "*Marisol* covered everything that was not covered in *Wilder*."[20] The lead plaintiff in the lawsuit, Marisol A., was a 5-year-old girl who had been returned to her mother from foster care. She was found locked in a closet by a housing inspector, malnourished, with a broken tibia, fractured teeth, and burns over her body. The suit charged that the city's child welfare agency repeatedly failed to investigate complaints of abuse against the mother and her boyfriend.

The lawsuit alleged that the city's child welfare agency, then known as the Child Welfare Administration, "was one of the most expensive and dysfunctional in the nation, persistently failing to care for and protect both the children in its custody and those reported to be in danger of abuse and neglect. Children were dying because of the city's neglect while others were being deprived of safe, stable and permanent childhoods." CRI filed *Marisol v. Giuliani* (No. 95-Civ-10533) in the U.S. District Court for the Southern District of New York on behalf of Marisol and more than 100,000 children whom the suit alleged had been subjected to the system's failings.[21]

Having been chastened by criticism of the limited impact of her previous lawsuits and disappointed by the long delays in effecting reforms, Lowry was amenable to a new approach for a court-supervised legal settlement in *Marisol*. That new approach was the brainchild of Tom Joe, the executive director of the Center for the Study of Social Policy (CSSP) in Washington, D.C., a policy and research center working with state governments to reform child welfare systems across the country. CSSP was very closely connected with, and heavily funded by, the newly expanded Annie E. Casey Foundation. Joe, blind and strategically brilliant, had been looking for a way to reduce the number of disruptive lawsuits that hampered efforts by CSSP and governments to reform child welfare without outside pressure.

Through Joe's long-standing connections with the Casey Foundation, Lowry, and ACS, on December 2, 1998 Marcia and the city and state defendants in *Marisol* signed agreements that established a new approach to court-supervised child welfare reform. Instead of having Lowry and her legal team oversee the reforms, as had been the case in her other lawsuits, the court established a Special Child Welfare Advisory Panel, which would have full access to ACS records and personnel, would assess various aspects of the child welfare system and make recommendations for reform, but would have no authority to force the city to implement anything. If the panel were to find that the city was failing to make a good faith effort at reform, plaintiffs could seek court-ordered injunctive relief. The settlement would allow Commissioner Scoppetta to work toward reform unfettered by the courts and advised by a well-respected group of outside child welfare professionals. As CSSP and the defendants wanted, the settlement also prohibited any other class-action lawsuit from being filed or going forward as long as the settlement agreement was in effect, forcing the shelving of a class-action lawsuit brought by the Urban Justice Center alleging mistreatment of gay and lesbian youth in New York City foster care.

The settlement was hailed widely as a fair compromise.[22] The Special Child Welfare Advisory Panel was seen by almost all members of the child welfare community in New York City as a group of the best and the brightest professionals in child welfare, though it was not without its shortcomings, specifically the absence of black or Latino panelists.[xi]

The panel was headed by Douglas Nelson, president, CEO, and member of the board of the Annie E. Casey Foundation, the largest foundation in the country focusing on child welfare. It then spent close to a quarter of a billion dollars a year to reform child welfare in targeted cities and states.[23] The five members were either Casey employees or consultants to Casey, including John Mattingly, the director of human services reforms at the Casey Foundation who would become the commissioner of ACS 4 years after the panel concluded its work in 2000. The panel's staff director was Steven Cohen, also employed by the Casey Foundation. He knew the system intimately, having previously worked in New York City's child welfare agency as well as at the Jewish Board of Family and Children's Services, a large and wealthy voluntary New York City child welfare agency.

---

xi. The Special Child Welfare Advisory Panel was initially composed of Douglas Nelson, president of the Annie E. Casey Foundation, John Mattingly, senior program associate of the Annie E. Casey Foundation, Judith Goodhand, former director of Cuyahoga County Department of Children and Family Services in Cleveland, and Paul Vincent, former director of the Division of Family and Children's Services of the Alabama Department of Human Resources. The omission of a person of color was subsequently addressed with the addition of Carol Williams Spigner to the Panel later in 1999. An African-American, she was former associate commissioner in the Children's Bureau of the Administration for Children and Families in the federal Department of Health and Human Services.

Parent participation in child welfare decisions was not raised in the *Marisol* complaint or in the remedies originally sought, though the lawsuit called for additional services to help families so their children would not have to be placed into foster care. Nevertheless, parent participation and the way parents were treated by the child welfare system became a focus of the panel's final report and a significant part of its recommendations. This change—placing parents' service needs, their right to participate in case decisions, and the utility of their views of the system at the center of child welfare reform—contributed greatly to the emergence of an environment in which parents and their allies would become respected voices in the child welfare debate.

How did *Marisol* come to play such an important role in paving the way for parent participation in child welfare reforms, though that participation was not part of Lowry's intent? It came about for three reasons. First, the panel members came to their work, according to Cohen, "with the belief entrenched in their thinking that you help children by helping their families." The panel believed, says Cohen, that "most of the families involved with the child welfare system are committed to their kids and are torn up by not being able to raise their kids safely and by confronting systems that hurt them rather than help them."[24] The panel members were therefore receptive to the idea that parents should be involved in case practice.

The panel initially spoke with the senior administrators of ACS, who were receptive to the panel's ideas for policy and practice reforms that would help families. The moment, however, the panel began to focus on practice in the field—reading case records, interviewing front-line workers and supervisors, seeing the interaction between workers and parents—"we saw that this was not a practice model that values families," says Cohen.[25]

That realization was the second factor that raised the prominence of parents in the panel's final report. The evidence of inadequate case practice encouraged the panel to focus on having the system engage more effectively with parents. "If there is something that I'd give the panel credit for in New York," says Cohen, "it would be helping the system understand that this [involving parents] is not solely a matter of justice or sympathy or a desire to be nice to parents, which is an ideological point of view that we can fight about. But we helped frame it as a critically important thing to do in order to help kids."

The third factor that raised the importance of parents was parents themselves, supported by their allies. Led by the Child Welfare Organizing

Project (CWOP), parents forcefully and repeatedly, between July 1999 and October 2000, met with and pushed the panel to focus on the rights of parents and the abuses they had endured from ACS and voluntary child welfare agencies. Representatives of various parent organizing groups, legal advocacy organizations, foundations, and other groups that worked with and advocated for parents met with the panel to critique its reports and press it to recognize the system's fundamental flaws.

Through meetings, letters, documents, and testimony from parents, CWOP made the needs of parents and the utility of involving them in policy decisions a focus of the panel's work. Half a dozen parents from CWOP and other organizations first met with the panel on July 8, 1999, after the panel had issued its second report, which focused on placement issues. CWOP's objections to that report were "not so much in its content, as in its omissions," said a written CWOP statement directed to the panel. Among other things, CWOP contended that the panel's report overlooked "the primary issue: when and why are children being removed to foster care in the first place." CWOP's statement to the panel used the analogy of a report on prison reform that didn't "say or do much about innocent men being sentenced to prison, but we can recommend that they be treated as well as possible while they're in custody."[26]

The panel acknowledged this omission. In an article 2 weeks later in the July 22 New York Times, Nelson[xii] wrote, "I'm afraid the report may reinforce the oversimplified view that we can protect at-risk kids in fragile families with an even more aggressive approach to removal. I feel the Mayor [Giuliani] in this city has overemphasized that."[27]

The second meeting between CWOP parents and the panel took place on November 30, 1999 and focused on the issue of front line practice. At the panel's request, CWOP parents prepared a set of questions to evaluate the performance of foster care providers. At the meeting parents spoke about their painful experiences with the child welfare system and reported that they were not being listened to by their case workers, their agencies, or by ACS.

Shortly after the November meeting, the panel recommended to Scoppetta that he meet with parents, listen to their opinions and concerns, and create a parents' advisory panel. Four months later a meeting

---

xii. Nelson was one of the most articulate spokespersons for child welfare reform in the country. His broad perspective and influence came from teaching history at the University of Wisconsin, serving as assistant secretary of the Wisconsin Department of Health and Social Services, and then working for 20 years as president of the Annie E. Casey Foundation, overseeing $3 billion in assets, providing $240 million to 900 grantees a year toward the end of his tenure at Casey.

between Scoppetta and parents from CWOP took place. It did not go well. According to CWOP executive director Mike Arsham, "We didn't want to be used just for information [for the commissioner]; we had our own agenda. ACS's expectation was that parents would tell their stories, limit their criticisms to contract agencies and not make any demands. We had a different idea."[28]

Scoppetta was unreceptive to the complaints of parents. After an exchange of charges and countercharges about lack of respect, trust, and collaboration by both ACS and CWOP, on June 5, 2000 Scoppetta wrote a letter to Arsham stating that ACS would no longer collaborate or communicate with CWOP. "For the present," he wrote, "ACS will pursue the initiatives we have begun with the partners we have."[29] CWOP became persona non grata at ACS. No one from ACS was allowed to meet or talk with anyone from CWOP.

The Special Child Welfare Advisory Panel, however, continued to be receptive to CWOP's concerns and reform agenda. A third panel meeting with parents from CWOP took place on October 17, shortly before the panel issued its final report containing its strong recommendations for ACS to involve parents more fully in their own cases and for them to have meaningful participation in program and policy decisions. In its written statement to the panel at the October meeting, CWOP acknowledged that the panel had "heard and internalized parents' concerns."

Nevertheless, CWOP criticized the panel for its endorsement of ACS's efforts to involve parents, since CWOP parents had been excluded from that process after CWOP's meeting with Scoppetta. The panel had written that "ACS has embraced the idea of gathering information from recipients of services."[30] According to CWOP, such enthusiasm for ACS's stance toward parents "is not simply inaccurate; it denies the reality and legitimacy of a group of parents who invested a lot of hope and energy in this doomed initiative."[31] In CWOP's written statement to the panel and during the October meeting, parents pressed for the creation of a public oversight body independent of ACS, comparable to the Civilian Complaint Review Board for the police, which would include parents and youth with direct personal experience with the child welfare system, a legally binding bill of rights for parents including prohibition of protective removals without a court order in nonemergency situations, meaningful parent participation in Service Plan Reviews, an increased proportion of ACS spending devoted to preventive services, and quality legal representation for indigent parents in the Family Court. Many of these recommendations were included in the panel's final report; the last three eventually became city policy.

Although parent participation in case work and policy decisions was not mentioned in the original *Marisol* complaint, the remedies recommended by the Special Child Welfare Advisory Panel put significant weight on improving parent participation and engagement in the system and even strongly promoted parent participation in policy decisions. One of the ultimate recommendations of the panel was that parents needed to have a more prominent voice in the system. The final report of the Special Child Welfare Advisory Panel issued in December 2000 talked about the significant changes that were still needed in the system. It concluded:

> We believe that the heart of a new system-wide approach to permanency is a re-thinking of the role of parents, around the primary themes of enhanced respect, engagement, and partnership.[32]

The final report proposed not only providing more services to families but expanding the role of parents in decision making on their own cases and developing a role for them in formulating public policy. The report said, "First, the *fundamental* intervention this system can make to improve the lives of most of the children it serves is to help make it possible for their parents to overcome the barriers that have kept them from providing a safe and nurturing home" (emphasis in the original).[33]

In discussing parent participation in their own cases, the panel's report criticized state regulations for merely *"inviting"* parents to attend case conferences and Service Plan Reviews (emphasis in original). "[W]e think it is telling. People are 'invited' to events at which their participation is optional, and which will go on whether they are present or not. No one is invited to go to court, or to vote, or to undergo a medical procedure." The report concludes:

> We believe that the system's success in meeting this larger challenge [of parent participation in case decisions] depends fundamentally on the kinds of relationships with parents it [ACS] pursues. When parents are expected, encouraged, and supported to play a key role in decisions about their children's futures (even when those children are in foster care)...they will be far more deeply involved than when these expectations are absent.[34]

In addition, the panel's report asserts that parents also should help shape public policy:

> Finally, we note that one measure of a system's effort to better engage parents is its willingness to hear from parents in roles other than that of recipient

of services. On those occasions when ACS engages parents in discussions of values, principles, policies, and procedures, it sends a powerful message that parents matter. We encourage ACS both to increase the number of occasions on which this kind of contact takes place and to broaden the range of parents who participate .... Similarly, we think the real challenge for ACS is in building relationships even with those parents who have significant complaints regarding the child welfare system.[35]

The panel's urging that ACS "broaden the range of parents who participate" and include "parents who have significant complaints" seems a direct response to Scoppetta's June 5 letter telling CWOP and its parents that they were unwelcome at ACS. The underlying values of the report and its explicit recommendations were what parents and advocates had been saying to members of the panel and fighting for in countless other venues. Over the next decade ACS increasingly embraced these recommendations and began not only to listen to parents and parent advocacy organizations, but also to implement their recommendations.

The force of *Marisol*, the meticulous, thoughtful, and balanced work of the Special Child Welfare Advisory Panel, the seminal role played by the Annie E. Casey Foundation on the panel, and the relentless pressure from parents planted the idea in ACS and the child welfare system as a whole that parents not only had a right to be heard but also had essential things to say that could improve frontline practice.

The panel ended its court-ordered role in December 2000 when it issued its final report that found ACS had acted in good faith in creating structural and policy reforms, but cautioned that a great deal of additional work would be required for those reforms to be fully implemented. Scoppetta's replacement in early 2002, William Bell, embraced the recommendations of the panel, and his replacement in July 2004, John Mattingly, who had been a member of the panel, implemented changes beyond the panel's recommendations. These two commissioners created an environment in ACS and the rest of the child welfare system that enabled the voice of parents and their allies to be heard and their recommendations to be implemented.

THE ADMINISTRATION FOR CHILDREN'S SERVICES

The Administration for Children's Services was slow to embrace parents as a legitimate voice in the debate to shape child welfare programs and policy because of Scoppetta's initial orientation, which changed during his tenure as commissioner. Once the agency changed further under Bell and Mattingly, ACS's impact on the role of parents was profound.

Scoppetta took charge of the newly created Administration for Children's Services in January 1996, inheriting a dysfunctional agency built on the remnants of its inept predecessor organizations. In the previous two decades public interest attorneys had filed 20 class-action lawsuits in state and federal courts against the city's child welfare agency because of the harm it was causing children and their families. ACS was operating under 11 court orders or stipulations from these suits in December 1996 when Scoppetta issued his Plan of Action to remedy the system's problems and to get the lawsuits off his back.[36]

Scoppetta's plan was thoughtful, comprehensive, and pointedly antiparent. It included the stark statement: "Any ambiguity regarding the safety of the child will be resolved in favor of removing the child from harm's way."[37] This led to 12,000 children being placed into foster care in 1998, a 51% increase from 7,949 children in 1995, the year before Scoppetta took office.[38] The plan also called for the criminalization of neglect. Rather than focusing on ameliorating the overwhelming stresses in the lives of poor families who had neglected their children, the city would not only place their children in foster care, but it would also arrest the mothers. Lamenting the fact that fewer than a third of the 25,328 abuse and neglect cases in 1995 that were eligible for referral to a District Attorney's Office for possible prosecution were so referred, the plan called for the creation of "instant response teams" composed of personnel from ACS, the Police Department, and the District Attorneys' Office who would be available on a 24-hour basis "to prosecute successfully all serious cases of abuse and neglect...."[39]

Scoppetta represented the old school of child welfare reform. He had spent 8 years in foster care, beginning in 1936 when he was 4 years old. At that time the system primarily served white children, often children of immigrant parents, as his were. Early in his career he served for 7 years as an assistant district attorney in the Manhattan DA's office, developing a prosecutorial perspective, which he brought to child welfare. Later in his career he served 16 years on the board of directors and 8 years as board chairman of the Children's Aid Society. As a result, when he became ACS commissioner, he saw the system from the eyes of a foster care agency that began in the middle of the nineteenth century with headquarters on Park Avenue. His view was that the best way to improve the child welfare system was through the three pillars of his plan: (1) "management, accountability and cultural change;" (2) clarity of mission, which was "to discover and report every instance of child abuse and neglect;" and (3) creating "a child-focused system that will protect all the children of New York."[40]

His old school view lacked recognition that 96% of the children in foster care while he was commissioner were African-American or Latino.[41] Nowhere in his 163-page Plan of Action, including a chapter diagnosing the culture of New York's child welfare system, are the words race or ethnicity mentioned, let alone a discussion of those issues or the role of parents in decision making.[42]

Parents protested against these policies, which they saw as clearly antiparent. Parents who had neglected their children mostly for reasons related to poverty, who had their children placed into foster care, and who felt abused by ACS demonstrated against the agency's policies. On Christmas morning in 1997 a dozen parents whose children had been swept into the child welfare system stood silently for hours across the street from St. Partick's Cathedral. One woman held a sign that read "BCW, SSC, CWA, ACS.[xiii] Everything is the same. Only the name is different." Another mother's sign bore the name of Caprice Reid, who was killed in foster care. The demonstration had been organized by People United for Children, a small but militant group of parents whose children had been in the child welfare or juvenile justice system. These mothers and one father thought it would be better to let the well-dressed St. Patrick's congregants know that the child welfare system had broken their families apart and violated their rights than to be at home without their children on Christmas morning.

Under pressure from parents and their allies—street demonstrations, parents in 1998 testifying for the first time at a city council hearing on child welfare, critical articles in the Child Welfare Watch, lobbying by advocacy groups to tighten the standards used to evaluate programs—and with guidance from the Special Child Welfare Panel, Scoppetta created modest policies and programs that inched the system toward involving parents in decision making and providing additional services to some. Under pressure from Citizens' Committee for Children, an advocacy organization founded in 1944, city council members, and others, he increased the number of preventive service slots.[43] He originally set a standard for evaluating foster care agencies that gave them credit for having children adopted but not for returning children to their families. Under pressure from the Child Welfare Action Center, a temporary coalition of advocacy groups, and other parent groups and their allies, in 1997 he made family reunification as important as adoption in evaluating agencies. Under pressure from lawyers for families and their allies, such as the Brooklyn Family Defense

---

xiii. The names over time of the city's child welfare agency included the following: Bureau of Child Welfare (1940–1974), Special Services for Children (1974–1989), Child Welfare Administration (1989–1996), and Administration for Children's Services (1996– present).

Project, he, in the city's system to evaluate agencies, "enhanced parent participation in permanency decision-making," which meant that agencies could be sanctioned if they failed to include parents in Service Plan Reviews, the meetings that determined the steps required of parents to reunify with their children.[44] Until then foster care agencies had discouraged, or at least had not encouraged or enabled, parents to attend these important meetings. As a result, few parents actually attended Service Plan Reviews.[45]

Toward the end of Scoppetta's tenure at ACS, in July 2001 the agency published a "Renewed Plan of Action," which proposed steps ACS should take to involve parents. After describing the progress the agency had made, the report concluded that "The areas still in need of improved performance are matters of front-line practice in permanency and parent engagement...to change the way the child welfare system works with families."[46] Parent engagement, that is, getting parents to be actively and cooperatively involved in their own case, is the first step for social workers to be able to work with a family. Parent engagement is a long way from genuine parent participation or leadership in shaping programs or policy. Yet under Scoppetta, ACS acknowledged that even engaging parents, let alone listening to their views, was a challenge.

Changing the culture of ACS and the foster care agencies so that they focused on the needs of parents and families, respected their rights, and valued their insights began in earnest with the appointment of William C. Bell as commissioner of ACS in January 2002, though Scoppetta and ACS began to change at the end of his tenure. As the number of children in foster care was decreasing, as he was leaving office Scoppetta said, "I am absolutely convinced that we have too many children in foster care."

Bell led what he referred to as "the second phase of reform."[47] Not until Giuliani and Scoppetta left office at the end of 2001 did ACS fully embrace the idea that parents should have a meaningful role in child welfare decisions.

At the outset, Bell, like Scoppetta, saw the child welfare system with the eyes of a foster care service provider, but a provider that was very different from the Children's Aid Society, which Scoppetta had headed. Before joining the city's child welfare agency in 1994, Bell had worked as associate executive director of Miracle Makers, a newly created African-American-run agency based in Brooklyn's Bedford-Stuyvesant, one of the poorest neighborhoods in the city. Miracle Makers began serving foster children in 1986 as one of very few minority-run foster care agencies in the city. These agencies had been set up with help from the city and state governments to be a small counterbalance to the white-run and white-controlled agencies that cared for almost all the children in foster care, almost all of whom were and are from ethnic minorities.[xiv]

Bell was born in Mississippi in 1957 to a single black mother when Jim Crow was the dominant culture in the South. Bell's upbringing and his time working at Miracle Makers contributed to his empathy for, and perhaps identification with, poor parents of color. While addressing a group of parents from the child welfare system in 2004 he said, "From about 1987–1989 I ran a parenting skills program in Brooklyn. That work left an indelible impression on me about what child welfare really should be all about."[48]

Very soon after becoming commissioner, Bell changed the mission statement of ACS. Investigating reports of abuse and neglect was still a central mission, but supporting families, rather than removing children, would be the agency's first response. "The First 100 Days," a report Bell released after his first 3 months of his commissionership, stated that "ACS's mission is to ensure the safety, permanency, and well-being of all the children of New York." The first way ACS would serve this mission would not be through investigation of reports of abuse and neglect, as had been the case under Scoppetta, but through "an extensive array of community based preventive and child care and Head Start services."[49]

To carry out this new mission, Bell significantly increased the number of children receiving preventive services so they could remain with their families. Whereas the number of families receiving preventive services fluctuated between 25,564 and 27,660 while Scoppetta ran ACS, the number grew by 16% to 31,692 by Bell's second year as commissioner.[50] One

xiv. Until 1969 no child welfare agency was located in a minority community and governed by people of color. In that year Harlem Dowling Children's Center was founded as a minority-governed agency that operated as a satellite of Spence-Chapin, a white-run child caring agency. In 1985 the Edwin Gould agency brought a "decisive number of Black leaders onto its board of directors," becoming a second minority-governed agency. In the late 1980s the New York State Legislature allocated funds to create several new minority-governed agencies and to transform small, existing agencies into foster care providers. Miracle Makers was a beneficiary of the later approach. The rapid rise and fall of Miracle Makers and the other minority-government foster care agencies is a long and painful story that was chronicled by Benjamin Weiser and Leslie Kaufman in the New York Times and the Task Force on Minority-Governed, Community-Based Foster Care Agencies. [Leslie Kaufman, "Foster Children at Risk, and an Opportunity Lost," New York Times, November 5, 2007; Benjamin Weiser, "City Is Slow to Limit Damage as a Hope for Children Fails," New York Times, November 6, 2007; Benjamin Weiser, "In Foster Care Reckoning, Vows of Help and Vigilance," New York Times, November 7, 2007; Task Force on Minority-Governed, Community-Based Foster Care Agencies, Report and Recommendations on the Status and Future of Minority-Governed, Community-Based Child Welfare Agencies (New York: Administration for Children's Services, November 2005).]

result of the policy change was a decrease from a high of 12,000 children removed from their families in FY 1998 under Scoppetta to 6,201 removed in FY 2004 under Bell.[51]

Bell also welcomed parents' participation in child welfare policy making. Early in his tenure he lifted the ban that Scoppetta had imposed on ACS contact with the Child Welfare Organizing Project. In 2003 he appointed Philomena Timmons, a parent with experience in child welfare who had been working with CWOP, to the Commissioner's Advisory Board.[xv] She was the first parent with a child who had been in foster care to serve on such a board. He also created a Parent Advocate/Specialist Consortium, which met regularly with ACS staff members to inform them about parents' experiences in the system.[52] He also implemented a client feedback system for foster boarding home programs, which interviewed foster parents, children in care, and 242 parents about the services they received. The information from the interviews was used to improve foster care programs and practices.[53]

Bell agreed in April 2004 to have ACS join the Bridge Builders collaborative in the South Bronx, another way he enabled parents to play a programmatic role in child welfare. Participation in Bridge Builders was a significant leap of faith for Bell since he had felt attacked by the leadership of Bridge Builders, John Courtney and me, who had been sharp critics of ACS. Bridge Builders was a community-run, foundation-supported project to involve parents with child welfare experience in helping their neighbors who were having problems with their children and with the child welfare system. He designated Deputy Commissioner for Community and Government Affairs Anne Williams Isom to represent ACS as a full partner in Bridge Builders.

Isom was an ideal person to link ACS with Bridge Builders and the South Bronx community. She was a pull-no-punches, Columbia University-trained black lawyer who talked back to commissioners when she disagreed with them, even in public meetings. She described herself as a passionate advocate for children but also an advocate for communities of color.

---

xv. Several years before, Philomena's 10-year-old son had been getting into trouble daily in school after his grandfather died. After his teacher called her to say that her son had cursed in class, Philomena hit him with a belt, leading to his removal from her custody for 2 years. Reading the Bible and realizing that she was out of control helped her control her anger. She went to the library to learn about her rights and read *The Family Act Book*, which she said armed her with knowledge of the system and her rights. She went to therapy and attended two parenting skills classes and began working with CWOP. She wrote: "Looking back, I did need help with my son because I felt out of control and it was affecting my relationship with him. But I don't believe that my children needed to be taken from me." [*Rise* 3 (Spring 2006): 1–3.]

Her honesty, skills, and connections with the black community (she lived in central Harlem) made her increasingly valuable to the three different commissioners she served and a powerful ally to Bridge Builders. Not only did she attend each quarterly meeting of Bridge Builders' funders, but she helped make the resources of ACS available to that organization. These resources included data analysis to assess the progress of the project in the community, open access to ACS's Bronx field office, and assigning an ACS staffer, Francis Ayuso, to be Bridge Builders' on-the-ground coordinator. Ayuso is a native of Belize, a social worker by training, and a community organizer in his soul. He was able to gain the trust of parents who had been mistreated by ACS and got ACS to listen to the views of parents and recognize the ways Bridge Builders could improve child welfare practice.

Although Bell focused on meeting parents' needs, he had to be pushed by the Child Welfare Organizing Project and other parent groups to fully embrace their cause. To his credit, and to the great benefit of parents, he allowed them to influence him and ACS. In June 2004, he was the keynote speaker at an event organized by parents of the Child Welfare Organizing Project to honor the Child Welfare Fund and my role helping to give parents a louder voice in the child welfare system.

In his opening remarks, he said, "I really believe that my being and speaking here tonight is historic." It was the first time that a commissioner had addressed and so fully embraced a group of parent advocates that had been fighting the city. Sharwline Nicholson, the named plaintiff in a victorious landmark lawsuit against ACS for illegally removing her children from her care, was chairwoman of CWOP. She was in the audience and stood proudly with Bell for a photograph after his speech.

Within a month of giving that speech, Bell resigned as commissioner of ACS to become executive vice-president of Casey Family Programs. The press release from Mayor Bloomberg's office was glowing: "William Bell has spent his career protecting New York's children and is leaving a legacy of excellence at ACS. He is a gifted administrator, a powerful advocate and a creative and talented policy maker."[54] As Bell tells the story, however, he had conflicts with the mayor regarding resources for ACS. Bell wanted to preserve and expand services for families; the mayor wanted budget cuts that would undermine Bell's efforts. Bloomberg made the cuts. Bell had also lost the support of the voluntary agencies who did not want to be evaluated and regulated as Bell had been doing.

John B. Mattingly replaced Bell as commissioner on July 6, 2004, leading to a third phase of child welfare reform that more fully promoted the rights and involvement of parents. Mattingly, as had Scoppetta and Bell, came to ACS with experience as a service provider. He had been executive director of the West Side Community House in Cleveland, a settlement house focusing on helping poor families in their community. Subsequently he was the executive director of Lucas County (Ohio) Children Services, the public child welfare agency serving the Toledo area. That job gave him experience in administering a public bureaucracy, albeit a small one compared to New York.

He also came with experience working on systemic reforms in child welfare from his years as director of human service reforms at the Annie E. Casey Foundation. As noted above, he served as a member of the New York City Special Child Welfare Advisory Panel from 1998 to 2000. By almost all accounts, his vast experience, his connection to the resources of the Annie E. Casey Foundation, his sensitivity to the various child welfare constituencies, and the trust the mayor had in him made him a most capable person for the job.

Mattingly changed ACS's mission statement, as had Scoppetta and Bell before him. His focus was based on the widely held belief that helping families is the best way to ensure the well-being of children. As his statement said, "ACS's mission is to ensure the safety, permanency and well-being of all New York City's children and to strengthen families."[55] ACS's primary goal was still to ensure child safety, but its mission was based on this core principle: "Whenever it is safe, children's birth and extended families should be strengthened and supported to provide a strong network of support for their children."[56]

In spite of this dedication to supporting families, ACS under Mattingly did not immediately increase the number of preventive service slots available to families experiencing difficulties, which perhaps reflected Bell's unsuccessful struggle to wrest more resources from the mayor. Under Mattingly, the number of children receiving preventive services annually between 2004 and 2007 was about 30,000, similar to the highpoint under Bell. Mattingly did not increase the number of preventive slots until 2008, when they reached 33,022 after a series of high profile deaths of children that occurred in late 2005 and early 2006. The number of preventive slots decreased again in subsequent years, reaching a low of 23,294 in June 2011.[57] The policy shift to "strengthen families" led to a continuous decrease in the number of children in foster care, which reached a low of 16,645 in 2006.[58] After a slight increase in 2006 and 2007, the numbers of children in care continued to decrease, reaching 13,781 in May 2012, the smallest number in at least the past 50 years.[59]

Mattingly maintained Bell's efforts to create a more parent-friendly environment in ACS. The Parents Advisory Work Group (PAWG), first begun by Bell as the Parent Advocate/Specialist Consortium, continues to meet, although the group is both a way to celebrate parents and a way for them to shape policy. Ten to 15 parents who have had experience in the child welfare system and work in advocacy, legal, or service agencies across the city attend meetings every other month. According to Dana Guyet, who headed the ACS Office of Advocacy from 2006 to 2011 that oversees the PAWG, the Group is not only a way for ACS to learn about problems in child welfare but is a way to "celebrate the work of parent advocates and of parents who succeed in reunifying with their children."[60] Family Fun Day, a PAWG project, is ACS's largest event of the year and is organized as a celebration for the children and families the agency serves. ACS held the first such celebration in Central Park in the early fall of 2005; food was served, games and music were played, and only a few speeches were delivered. The annual events make a small contribution to shifting the culture of ACS to a sharper focus on the strengths of families and to a greater emphasis on giving parents whose children were in foster care a feeling of greater respect from the agency that at times dominated their lives.

Mattingly met regularly with the Work Group to learn from the members' experience and to hear their ideas for reform. He says:

> Parents have a lot to say on the periphery of our policies. I don't think they've gotten into the heart of things. They are not systems change people. They are parents. They know what it's really like. That's why you bring them in.[61]

Mattingly also expanded the role parents play in ACS's work. Previously, neither ACS nor probably any other public child welfare agency in the country had employed a parent who had been embroiled in the child welfare system. In the fall of 2005 ACS began the unprecedented process of hiring such parents. ACS was wary of confronting civil service requirements and fearful of resistance from the Social Service Employees Union, until it could demonstrate that parents would be effective city employees and not a threat to the union. As a pilot program that would avoid such conflicts, ACS used a grant from the Child Welfare Fund[xvi] to employ three parents to work in ACS's Office of Advocacy. The parents, formally called Family Specialists/Parent Advocates, were hired to help parents who were having difficulties with foster care agencies and to help sensitize ACS staff to the perspective of parents. They also spoke to every graduating class of new child protective service workers and new ACS lawyers to increase

---

xvi. The grant was channeled through New Yorker's for Children (NYFC), ACS's nonprofit arm that could accept grants from foundations. NYFC was established by Commissioner Scoppetta in 1996.

their sensitivity to the perspective of parents. If the foundation-funded specialists were able to help families and operate effectively within ACS's daunting bureaucracy, ACS would hire them as full-time civil service employees.

The 2-year experiment was successful. In the fall of 2007 ACS created four civil service lines for Family Specialists, using the preexisting civil service title community associate. In January 2008 ACS hired three specialists who had had children in foster care as city employees, with all the benefits, rights, and responsibilities of full-time civil servants. It was the first time that parents whose children had been in foster care were employed by New York City to work with families.

Nevertheless, the transition to working in a large city bureaucracy on a civil service salary of $30,000 a year was not easy. While working on a salary provided by the foundation grant, the specialists continued to have Medicaid coverage and to receive other social services and Food Stamps. All that stopped when they became city employees. For some, their take-home pay decreased when they became city employees. Within a year one of them, Wanda Chambers (profiled above), left ACS to work as a parent advocate with the Brooklyn Family Defense Project. The job allowed her to have more contact with families and permitted her to go to court as their ally, which ACS did not let her do. The Brooklyn job also paid more. The following year a second Family Specialist left. With the city's hiring freeze and shifting priorities, as of 2011 only one Family Specialist was working at ACS.

One way Mattingly supported the rights of parents, beyond just listening to them, celebrating them, or hiring them, was by endorsing the decision of Bloomberg's criminal justice coordinator to underwrite improved legal representation for parents when ACS was going to remove their children from the parents' custody.[xvii] Previous coordinators had not supported institutional representation for parents, leaving them at the mercy of underpaid, underresourced 18B court-appointed lawyers working out of their briefcases without back-up offices, advocates, social workers, or investigators. The story of how adequate legal representation for parents came about is told in Chapter 7. It is one of the most important changes in the child welfare system in the past 15 years.

xvii. Before becoming commissioner, while employed at the Annie E. Casey Foundation and serving on the Marisol Special Child Welfare Panel, Mattingly actively supported legal representation for parents in New York City by providing a grant to create the Center for Family Representation, an institutional provider of quality legal representation for parents in Family Court, before city funding was available to fund institutional legal representation.

Mattingly considers the Improved Outcomes for Children program, which includes the use of Family Team Conferences (FTCs), to be one of the most important changes he made in the child welfare environment.[xviii] These case conferences are held at key decision points both before and during the time a child is in foster care. The conferences are held so that parents' views are heard and so that significant decisions are based on input from a variety of people who know the family. In the past, these decisions were generally made by one social worker with review by a supervisor. In FTCs decisions are made with input from the parents of the child, relatives of the child, the child care agency, community members (such as from a church group or a settlement house), and representatives of ACS. Eight to 10 people are typically involved in the decision to place a child, move a child to another foster home, or return the child to his or her parents. A significant difference from past practice is that the parent is present more often and regularly has an ally in the form of a parent advocate or community member. In principle, these conferences enable the opinions of parents, relatives, and community members to be heard, which can influence the outcome of the conference.[xix]

This excerpt from an article in *Rise* magazine by Bevanjae Kelley, a parent advocate working with CWOP, illustrates how FTCs work when a forceful, trained parent advocate is present.

Parents who are facing removal are allowed to bring friends, family and community members to the conference to talk with child welfare staff about their

---

xviii. Family Team Conferences are part of a larger reform initiative called Improved Outcomes for Children (IOC) that began as a pilot project in the fall of 2007. IOC represents a fundamental change in the way ACS works with the private child welfare agencies that provide direct services to families. In the pre-IOC model, private agencies did the case planning and the day-to-day work with families. The public agency was the case manager and held the ultimate authority for approving important decisions (e.g., case transfers and permanency goal changes). IOC redraws the boundaries between public and private sector responsibilities so that the individuals who have the most contact with children and families—the provider agencies—have the authority to make case decisions. In IOC, these case decisions are made in Family Team Conferences. The foster care providers liked the IOC approach because it gave them increased authority; the public sector union, Social Service Employees Union (SSEU), opposed the approach because it reduced the number of public sector jobs and diminished the nominal role of public sector employees in case decisions, though they mostly had functioned as a rubber stamp for decisions made by foster care agencies.

xix. Lawyers for the parent are not permitted to be in the Family Team Conference. Some argue that the absence of lawyers denies parents their right of legal representation in a proceeding that might lead to the removal of their children. Others, including Lauren Shapiro, a lawyer who is a strong advocate for parents' rights, argues that a forceful advocate who knows the child welfare system is the support parents need in a Family Team Conference. [Lauren Shapiro, remarks at a meeting of lawyers, advocates, and foundation officers supporting the Brooklyn Family Defense Project, November 3, 2010.]

family's strengths and needs. But many parents are overwhelmed. They don't know what to do or say at the meeting.

I work for an organization—the Child Welfare Organizing Project (CWOP)—that provides parents with trained Community Representatives to guide them. As a Community Rep, I help parents understand what they can ask for at the meeting. I help parents and child welfare staff work together to find a way to keep a child safe without placement in foster care, if possible.[62]

The actual operation of these conferences often differs from the principle. When the parent's only ally at the meeting is someone from the community who has not been trained as an advocate and whom the family probably doesn't know, "the outcome is often a rubber stamp of a pre-ordained decision to remove the child," according to Chris Gottlieb, a professor at New York University Law School who represents parents in Family Court. "Without a strong advocate, the conference can be Orwellian, with the government officials claiming that those present have reached a 'consensus' to remove the child when the parent's voice has not been meaningfully heard."[63] When a strong parent advocate trained by CWOP is present at a Family Team Conference, the decision tends to reflect the reasonable wishes of the parents, often allowing the child to remain with them, with a plan in place to ensure the child's safety.

The impact of FTCs is still limited. In conferences involving children in foster care, parents are present only half of the time.[64] This level of involvement, however, is a significant improvement from the 1990s, when parents were rarely present when Service Plan Review meetings, the analogous decision-making forum of that period, were held.

FTCs began as a pilot project in the fall of 2007 involving about a third of all foster care cases and half of all preventive service cases. In the spring of 2009 the city received approval from the New York State Office of Children and Family Services to expand the Improved Outcomes for Children Program, including Family Team Conferences, to all preventive and foster care cases beginning on June 15, 2009. As the process improves, as more parents are included in these decision-making conferences, and if enough parent advocates are available to cover all these conferences, parents will have an increasing say in case decisions affecting them and their families. At present, only a handful of trained parent advocates are available to attend a small proportion of FTCs because of lack of funding and because of concern from agencies and ACS that advocates may too aggressively side with parents.

According to Mattingly, these conferences, which engage parents and their advocates in decision-making processes, have been one of his most important reforms in child welfare practice. He believes that the FTCs and the restructured relationship between ACS and the voluntary child welfare agencies, which gives the agencies more independence and authority in individual cases, will be the foundation for sustained reform, ending the child welfare roller coaster ride. As he said in 2008:

> Remember, we are on a road. I can't say whether the reforms in child welfare will be permanent but we are close to breaking the cycle. But a crisis can start up again at any time with the *New York Post* out there. You need 10 years [to make a change permanent].[65]

***

The work of the Child Welfare Fund, *Marisol v. Giuliani*, the Special Child Welfare Advisory Panel, and the Administration for Children's Services itself promoted and expanded the meaningful participation of parents in New York's child welfare system. They enabled parents to work as advocates in foster care agencies, in preventive service programs, and in law firms representing parents in Family Court. They laid the foundation for parents to organize and to play a role in shaping child welfare policy, particularly pressing for fewer children to be removed from their families. For more than 10 years, from roughly the mid-1990s until the middle of the next decade, these forces within the city helped create an environment in which parents could organize, make their case loudly, and influence the direction of the city's child welfare system. It was an unprecedented moment in the struggle to reform child welfare.

Several lessons emerge. First, change needs to happen on many fronts. Activists can't be certain at the outset what activities will make a difference in the short-term and what will take root in the longer term. It is therefore important to work for reforms on many fronts—conducting research, improving service delivery, pressing for policy reform, carrying out grassroots organizing, demonstrating in the street, and filing law suits. These activities should be undertaken with many different partners both inside and outside of the system—activists, academics, administrators, and service providers. Since it is often unknown who will be allies and what will work, it is important to be experimental, to take risks, and to see what strategies gain traction with different parts of the community.

For a reform to be successful the entire environment needs to change, not just one element. Hiring parent advocates, for example, is not likely to succeed or to spread through the system and be successful unless the surrounding environment also changes. Often elements in the environment that must change include staff attitudes toward parents, resources for families that must increase, and caseload levels that must decrease.

CHAPTER 4

Parents Find Their Voice: The Child Welfare Organizing Project

O nce the organizations, events, and individuals described in the pre-vious chapter coalesced to create a more receptive environment for parent organizing, the Child Welfare Organizing Project (CWOP) became the preeminent group in New York for organizing parents to influence the child welfare system. CWOP was formed as a partnership between mothers whose children had been in foster care and professionals who had been struggling to reform child welfare. This chapter tells how CWOP started, almost collapsed, was a pariah, and then became a partner of the Administration for Children's Services (ACS).

ORIGIN OF THE CHILD WELFARE ORGANIZING PROJECT

In the early 1990s Terry Mizrahi was a tenured professor in the Hunter College School of Social Worker and director of the school's Education Center for Community Organizing. She talked fast and a lot but worked slowly and deliberately to create bridges between academia and community organizing groups that worked to improve the lives of social work's clients.

She undertook a study supported by the Child Welfare Fund that showed that parents in child welfare had few rights, that the rights they had were not enforced, and that they had almost no voice in shaping the programs and policies that affected their lives. For example, the report concluded that "the Advisory Board which oversees the CWA[i] programs and plans only includes one member who is not affiliated with a social service or educational institution.... Agencies are not *obligated* to have consumers on advisory boards, to obtain their evaluation of services..."[1] [emphasis in original].

She sought to change the situation by, in her words, "creating an organized client voice in child welfare."[2] As an activist herself, she realized that such activities would have to be organized by someone from the community, not by her. With another grant from the Child Welfare Fund, her first step in 1994 was to hire a fiery, seasoned Latina activist, Mabel Paulino, to be the executive director of the Child Welfare Organizing Project. Paulino lived in central Harlem, where the percentage of children removed from their families was among the highest in New York City. She had relatives and many friends who, from their perspective, had been tormented by child protective services. Switching from English to Spanish as her anger rose, she fought landlords, government, and just about anyone who crossed her many lines in the sand.

Paulino's first significant event as director of CWOP was a Client Summit in 1996 that brought together nearly 200 parents whose children were in foster care, youth who were in care, foster parents, and progressive social workers and other professionals who were the allies of parents. The summit took place in the cold institutional cafeteria of Wadleigh Junior High School in west Harlem, but the rhetoric was as fiery as Paulino and the energy was as white-hot as the anger of parents who felt abused by government. The summit energized parents, endorsed a platform for organizing, and spread the word about CWOP.

Paulino brought John Courtney into the ferment she was creating. As a white, middle-class, male social worker, he was an unusual partner for an activist who was hypersensitive to racism, particularly in child welfare. But John had values similar to Paulino's, had similarly strong criticisms of the child welfare system, and hardly anyone knew more about the inside baseball details of the child welfare system than he. John had been involved in child welfare for 25 years, working his way up through different parts of the city's bureaucracy before eventually becoming director of program planning for Special Services for Children (SSC), the city's child welfare agency at the time. In that role, he led SSC's efforts to create the Program

i. Child Welfare Administration, the name of New York City's child welfare agency from 1989 to 1996.

Assessment System that would hold foster care agencies accountable.[ii] He left SSC in the late 1980s and became associate executive director of Little Flower Children's Services, a large foster care agency with headquarters in Brooklyn, a residential facility on Long Island, and foster homes throughout the city. After half a dozen years at Little Flower he felt frustrated at being unable to reform the agency's antiquated practices. He left Little Flower in the mid-1990s to work outside the system as an advocate for families. By then he saw the child welfare system as "corrupt," though he meant that more in the spiritual sense than the financial one.

Paulino and Courtney, if not kindred spirits, saw the system similarly, as fostering cruel mistreatment of poor parents of color. Paulino recruited parents as volunteers. Courtney then trained the parents concerning their rights to visit their children while in care. Soon she asked him to be chairman of the board of CWOP, which he accepted. The board that they assembled consisted of professionals who worked in child welfare and parents who had been through the system. Courtney was the stabilizing force in CWOP's turbulent start-up years. His welcoming way of listening and nonconfrontational way of talking, the survival skills he had learned in government, his broad connections throughout the child welfare system, and the almost limitless time he devoted to CWOP kept the organization afloat.

At first CWOP's office bounced from one location to another, from a space in the Inwood section of upper Manhattan to a large industrial building in west Harlem that had once housed the early Manhattan Project. New York Foundling Hospital rented space in that building during the 1990s and provided a few rooms free of charge to CWOP.[iii] At a board meeting there in early 1997, Paulino stunned the board by announcing she was resigning. Her electric rhetoric and passionate advocacy crashed against the daily requirements

---

ii. In 1979 John Courtney had been working in SSC, developing a system to monitor the performance of foster care agencies. In that year I began working in the Office of City Council President Carol Bellamy, developing resolutions for the Board of Estimate that would require SSC to monitor foster care agencies and sanction those that performed poorly. Although he and I had similar goals, we were on opposite sides of the table in the negotiations pressing the mayor's office to endorse the resolutions. Through that clash, we became close friends, working together for the next 30 years to reform New York's child welfare system.

iii. At the time, New York Foundling, a Catholic foster care agency, had its first lay executive director in 150 years, Michael Garber. He was trying to bring the agency's practices into the twentieth century, in small part by including parents in shaping the Foundling's programs. He and his able deputy, Kathy McGlade, allowed CWOP to use the office space in west Harlem free of charge. Garber subsequently resigned from New York Foundling after a relatively short and frustrating tenure. Kathy McGlade left shortly thereafter, but not before she arranged for CWOP to move into other space used for training by New York Foundling in the Lehman Village Housing Project on 110th Street in East Harlem. CWOP has occupied that space ever since.

of administering an organization. She didn't want to play what she called the "organization game," fundraising, supervising, and keeping records. By the spring she was gone, leaving the fledgling and fragile CWOP in need of an administrator and an organizer. It was a difficult position to fill.

The board found another Latina for the job. But after a few months, according to Courtney, "It became painfully clear she was administratively incompetent. She could talk the talk, but she couldn't do anything. She was fired by the board after roughly six months." CWOP continued to limp along as the board looked for a new executive director.

Feeling disheartened about the prospects of finding the right person, discouraged by the mistake of their previous choice, and having no funding except a small grant from the Child Welfare Fund, the board discussed ending CWOP. Denise Williams, an African-American woman and an expert in nonprofit organizations who was then co-chair of the board, spoke to Courtney at the low point of CWOP. As he recalls the conversation: "Denise asked, 'Should we bother? Should we fold up our tent?' We concluded that the system needed CWOP. We decided to hang in and find another executive director."

The search turned up Mike Arsham, another white, middle-class male social worker. At the time, he was working as the head of preventive services for the Council of Family and Child Caring Agencies (COFCCA), the coordinating and lobbying organization for foster care agencies in New York State. COFCCA represented the core of the system that CWOP wanted to change. According to Courtney:

> Mike had the administrative experience Mabel [Paulino] lacked, but had commitment, fire and thought along the same political lines as we did. If we made another mistake, CWOP would not continue. We went for a proven administrator who had connections in the field.[3]

Hiring a white male to lead an organization of mostly black women and Latinas was, of course, controversial. Shortly after Mike joined CWOP several board members—both parents and professionals—resigned in protest. The board was left with Courtney, Williams, Mizrahi, Julia McGuire (a white parent), and Jeremy Kohomban (a professional of Sri Lanka and British origin).[iv] Arsham

---

iv. Jeremy Kohomban is unique. His mother is a Sephardic Jew and his father is a Sri Lankan Buddhist monk who converted to Christianity. At the time, he was a senior administrator of St. Christopher's, a large New York foster care agency. He is now president and CEO of Children's Village, a large foster care agency based in Dobbs Ferry, New York. He is one of the most parent-focused, reform-minded, and effective administrators in the field of child welfare.

began working as the executive director of CWOP in November 1998 and soon pulled CWOP "back from the brink," as Courtney says. Arsham brought administrative skills he had learned in the trenches at Rheedlen Centers for Children and Families, a community-based, multiservice center,[v] organizing skills he had learned in the struggle to preserve Family Rehabilitation Services for drug-involved parents, and an acute understanding of the power structure in child welfare that he had learned from being inside the system at COFCCA. He also brought his profound respect for parents and his uncompromising spirit to the process of nurturing CWOP back to health. Arsham, the board, a few staff members, and some parent volunteers, who had been both victimized and helped by the child welfare system, set about transforming CWOP into one of the most effective and uncompromising voices for parents in New York City and the nation.

HOW CWOP DID IT

Arsham, with the help of Courtney, the other board members, and the parents who were volunteering for or employed at CWOP, slowly built the organization from the shell that he inherited. More parents and professionals joined the board to expand CWOP's reach and solidify its direction. With the help of the Child Welfare Fund, Arsham raised money from other risk-taking foundations, such as the Daphne Foundation, New York Foundation, and the Ira W. DeCamp Foundation at JPMorgan Bank.

Working with Roger Green, a New York State Assemblyman from Brooklyn and chair of the Assembly's committee on children and families and the Black and Puerto Rican Legislative Caucus, Arsham and his colleagues helped draft language for a New York State Office of Children and Family Services budget appropriation for child welfare parent self-help and advisory councils. With the money it received from this appropriation, CWOP hired three parent organizers in July 2001.[4]

Arsham also arranged for parents to testify at city council hearings on the need to expand preventive services, to speak at conferences about problems in child welfare, and to present their perspective in social work classes to educate the next generation of child welfare professionals.

One of CWOP's first initiatives was to develop a curriculum to train parents to be advocates and organizers in child welfare. The idea for the training originated in discussions among the executive directors of some

---

v. Rheedlen became the Harlem Children's Zone, now directed by Geoffrey Canada.

agencies that had contracts with ACS. In 1999 six foster care and preventive service agencies calling themselves the Bushwick Managed Care Initiative (BMCI) operated in the impoverished northern Brooklyn neighborhood of Bushwick. They were preparing to respond to a request for proposals (RFP) from ACS that sought to induce contractors to be more involved with and responsive to the neighborhoods they served. Some of the agencies had significant ties to the Bushwick community; others did not. All wanted to improve their relationships with families as well as their image. They wanted CWOP's help to connect with families.

During the next 6 months, CWOP parents, as well as parents already working as advocates in several child welfare agencies, met with executives from the six foster care and preventive agencies. These discussions led to a partnership between CWOP and the agencies that produced CWOP's Parent Leadership Curriculum, a 6-month training program for parents with child welfare experience to learn about the child welfare system, to learn how to effectively advocate for themselves, and to learn how to help other parents advocate for themselves. The agencies would then hire the trained parents to engage and work with their hard-to-reach clients. Bernadette Blount, one of the trainees, described her experience:

> The information I received helped in my case: knowing what I can ask for—which is anything—what I can do, having that confidence makes you a little more steady! I'm a little less intimidated by "the professional." BMCI CWOP made that happen. By me taking the same courses as the professionals, there was less intimidation. We were learning the same things! My public speaking was rusty. But being put out there brushed a little of the rust off! It's helping me learn how to speak more effectively to professionals. I have made a friend or two. Offering support, being able to help others that are going through this fire, this terror, as I have, and are continuing, as I write. And to think, this experience just may help me get a job—or better yet, a career—making a living helping others help themselves.[5]

The development of a training program and the collaboration with foster and preventive agencies constituted a turning point for CWOP. The first class of six parent leaders graduated in 2001. Three of the graduates got full-time jobs as parent advocates; others worked directly with CWOP to bring the parent leadership training to CWOP's new offices in East Harlem.

A second CWOP initiative was to press the Special Child Welfare Advisory Panel to incorporate into its reports and recommendations the concerns of parents who had been victimized by the child welfare system.

The story of that campaign and the panel's favorable response to CWOP's well-documented complaints about child welfare's abuse and neglect of parents was told in Chapter 3. Among other things, the panel recommended that Scoppetta meet with CWOP so that he could learn directly about the problems encountered by parents. One parent had her children removed from her custody for lack of adequate housing, which is not legitimate grounds to remove a child. Another waited weeks before she knew where her children had been placed in foster care. Another had been investigated multiple times for neglecting her children because of malicious reports from a former boyfriend. The parents were very critical of ACS.

On March 9, 2000, Scoppetta met with Arsham and parents from CWOP who forcefully presented their complaints about ACS and the voluntary agencies. Mostly the parents talked. After charges and countercharges about lack of respect, trust, and collaboration by both ACS and CWOP, Scoppetta on June 5, 2000 wrote a letter to Arsham saying that ACS would no longer collaborate or communicate with CWOP. "For the present," he wrote, "ACS will pursue the initiatives we have begun with the partners we have."[6] CWOP became a pariah; no one from ACS could talk with anyone from CWOP. Although CWOP's mission statement called for it to work both "inside and independent of the system,"[7] during Scoppetta's term at ACS, CWOP worked independently of ACS, whose ban on collaborating with CWOP remained in effect until Bell became commissioner in January 2002. Bell welcomed CWOP as a partner in the family-focused reforms he made.

The next significant step in CWOP's work was becoming a partner with Bridge Builders in the South Bronx. Bridge Builders was just getting started in 2001 as a collaboration of foundations, service providers, and members of the Highbridge community. It was a demonstration project that hoped to show that people from a community could help their neighbors reduce the incidence of abuse and neglect and the need for foster care placement. CWOP became a central partner in the collaborative, both training parents from Highbridge to be advocates and then hiring them to help struggling parents.

Subsequently Bridge Builders began collaborating with ACS. ACS first provided data that allowed Bridge Builders to identify the blocks in the neighborhood from which most children were placed in foster care. This permitted Bridge Builders to better target its outreach and services. Under Bell, Bridge Builders began working directly with ACS's Bronx field office, which investigated families and determined if a child should be removed from his or her home. Bridge Builders partnered with the Bronx field office both to avert ACS from unnecessarily removing children from their homes but also to report families whose children had to be removed for their safety.

After several years of increasing collaboration between ACS and Bridge Builders, Frances Ayuso, an ACS community liaison, was deployed by ACS to be the coordinator of Bridge Builders. Frances's community organizing skills, the trust he engendered, and his easy access to ACS's resources linked parents in Highbridge with local service providers and connected all of them with ACS. This close relationship between ACS and Bridge Builders created conflicts in CWOP. Working behind the scenes with ACS to avert the removal of children was one thing; telling ACS that families might need to have a child removed was another. CWOP had some very contentious internal meetings about its relationship with ACS. Some staff and board members felt the relationship with ACS was an unholy alliance. Others felt ACS was acting in good faith and was trying to change how it worked with parents and families. After some board and staff members left CWOP because of misgivings about the arrangement with ACS, the relationship between ACS and CWOP continued and grew.

The next step in CWOP's growing collaboration with ACS occurred in 2007 when ACS created and underwrote the Community Partnership Initiative, which established collaborations between ACS, service providers, and residents of 11 high-risk neighborhoods, including Community District #4 in the South Bronx where Bridge Builders operated. ACS provided each collaborative with $150,000 a year to find more foster homes in its neighborhood, increase visiting between parents and their children in foster care, connect local preventive service programs with nearby daycare centers, and promote community involvement in Family Team Conferences. All of these activities were consistent with CWOP's agenda. After more internal debates, CWOP accepted a small part of these ACS funds through Bridge Builders.

The next step, and perhaps the most significant in CWOP's collaboration with ACS, was CWOP's decision in 2007 to participate in all meetings in East Harlem that determine whether a child would be placed in foster care. In East Harlem (Community District 11), where CWOP's headquarters are located, ACS signed an extraordinary agreement to have CWOP deploy a parent advocate to child safety conferences before any nonemergency child removal takes place in East Harlem. According to the memorandum of understanding between ACS and CWOP, "Children's Services will engage CWOP in all CD 11 CSCs [Child Safety Conferences]."[8,vi]

---

vi. CWOP's participation in East Harlem Child Safety Conferences is funded by the New York State Office of Children and Family Services through the Center for Family Representation, a law firm funded by the city to represent parents in Family Court.

CWOP's role would be to send a parent advocate to the conference to help "make the best safety decision for the child through in-home options, if such options can fully address the safety concern, or out of home placement, if necessary."[9]

WHAT CWOP HAS ACCOMPLISHED

As of 2010, CWOP employed 12 staff members; all but four have been embroiled in the child welfare system. Its 16-member board of directors is equally divided between professionals and parents. Its annual budget has grown to more than $600,000, about 20% of that coming from government. Since 2000, when it began courses for parents to become advocates, CWOP has trained 120 parents in 13 6-month sessions. These classes are now led and taught by parents who have been trained by CWOP. A lawyer who teaches about the Family Court and a social worker who teaches the history of child welfare in New York City are the only nonparents who do training. Half of the parents who have completed the CWOP course are now working in roughly 25 New York City child welfare or social service agencies helping parents with children in care or with other problems. Seventy percent of the parents who were trained by CWOP between 2000 and 2006 and who had children in foster care when the training began were reunited with their kids by the time the course was over.[10]

The outcomes of the Child Safety Conferences in East Harlem to ensure that children are not removed from their homes unnecessarily are also impressive. Since 2007 CWOP community representatives attended over 700 Child Safety Conferences. In two-thirds of the cases the child either remained with the parent or was placed with a relative.[11] A recent evaluation by the National Center on Permanency Planning of CWOP parent advocates' participation in Child Safety Conferences in East Harlem reported that 15.5% more children were remanded to foster care when CWOP's parent advocates were not present (42.9% vs. 58.4%).[12] CWOP's positive outcomes have contributed to it being added to the website of the California Evidence-Based Clearinghouse for Child Welfare.[13]

The memorandum of understanding requiring that a CWOP parent advocate be involved in all Child Safety Conferences in one district of the city and thus involved in all but emergency child removals in East Harlem is unprecedented in New York and the nation. Because of parent advocates' ability to help children remain safely at home, ACS is considering having trained parent advocates attend Child Safety Conferences throughout the city.[14]

Perhaps CWOP's greatest accomplishment has been to diminish the demonization of parents who have had child welfare involvement. CWOP parents have testified in government hearings, met with reporters to tell their stories, lectured regularly in social work and law school classes, and spoken on panels to child welfare professionals. People who have met these parents, heard them speak, read their stories, or read evaluations about their work have slowly begun to see them differently. Attitudes change very slowly, but parents with a history of having been involved in the child welfare system are increasingly seen as individuals with difficult lives who can change and have changed, whose ideas can improve child welfare practice, whose needs should be met, and whose rights should be protected.

New York City's child welfare system has improved dramatically during the past 18 years that CWOP has been organizing, speaking, and working on behalf of parents. CWOP has made the improvements deeper, broader, and probably longer-lasting as a result of its presence and pressure. How has CWOP been able to become a thriving organization with expanding activities, a solid budget in spite of the fiscal crisis, and increasing influence while other grassroots groups are struggling or have fallen by the wayside? Four factors seem most salient.

First, CWOP trained parents to be leaders. Women (and the few men who participate) who are poor, undereducated, and victims of racism and domestic violence need to be encouraged and supported to believe in themselves and to use their anger in ways that help rather than hobble them. They also need to learn the child welfare terrain—the system's rules and functioning—if they want to improve their own circumstances and to make broader change. And they need to learn how to bring about change, by learning to speak in public, identifying the right people to speak to, and having data and people to back them up.

When parents first begin to speak about their lives, they are often trapped in their own pain, desperately and endlessly telling their story to whomever will listen. As isolated individuals, it is very difficult for them to get beyond their own experience to understand the patterns and larger truths that need to be addressed. CWOP's training curriculum helps parents make the transition from the personal to the political.[vii]

vii. According to CWOP's training manual "...the child welfare system is experienced by parents as a vast, mystifying, internally inconsistent maze through which they may wander—confused and powerless—for years. The Parent Leadership Curriculum is a way for parents with child welfare involvement to negotiate that maze and to work to change it." [Child Welfare Organizing Project, *A Parent Leadership Curriculum* (New York: Child Welfare Organizing Project, 2006): 3.]

CWOP's training program has evolved into a 6-month, 10 hours a week course for parents who have been involved with the child welfare system. It consists of three parts: classroom training to give parents basic communication skills and knowledge about the child welfare system, experiential learning through internships that exposes trainees to experienced parent advocates as mentors, and a support group to provide a safe outlet for stress and to build camaraderie. CWOP's training program creates articulate, knowledgeable women who are able to harness their anger to become effective forces for change. Some of these parents now advocate on behalf of other parents or sit at policy tables.

These parents are paid both while in training and on the job. CWOP provides stipends to parents who participate in its training classes, $10 an hour for 10 hours a week during its 6-month course. When the parents are employed full-time by, for example, a foster care agency, they receive a salary, usually about $30,000 a year. When they are volunteers, CWOP requires that when they attended meetings or speak in forums in which their advice is sought, they be paid about $10–$15 an hour, since agency representatives are paid to attend the same meetings.

The second factor that enabled CWOP to flourish is its culture of inclusion. It has created a community for child welfare survivors. CWOP encourages but does not require parents to participate in a weekly support group to deal with the wide range of their strong feelings. As described in the CWOP training manual:

> The support group is a pressure valve. It is a weekly meeting without an agenda in which parents are free to rage, cry, whine, and vent with impunity. The group is led by parent organizers. Therefore, the person sitting across the table from you is unlikely to say "you shouldn't act that way," or "you shouldn't feel that way," or "that is damaging or counterproductive." They are more likely to say, "I remember when I felt exactly that same way. If you like, I can tell you how I lived through it and stayed focused on my goals."[15]

Contributing to the culture of inclusion are the facts, previously noted, that two-thirds of CWOP staff members are parents who were involved with the child welfare system and that half of CWOP's board are parents who have had children in foster care. In 2006, to strengthen the culture of inclusion, Courtney stepped down as chairman of the board. Sharwline Nicholson, the named plaintiff in the successful class action lawsuit against the city's child welfare administration for unlawfully removing her children, became chairman of the board.

While these staff and board structures are important in sustaining the atmosphere of inclusion, of equal importance in achieving this atmosphere is the culture of the organization. No significant CWOP decision is made without the involvement of parents who have been through the child welfare system. All trainings and the support groups are led by such parents. Fundraising is still primarily the responsibility of the executive director who also develops the long-term plan for CWOP, but parents review and vote on the organization's new programs and long-term direction.

A third factor that enabled CWOP to thrive is that it has been able to give parents something that for some of them may be even more important than having gotten their kids back. According to Arsham:

> Parents come to CWOP because they want to get their kids back, but they get more than that. They get a sense of their own value and worth. They say, "I can use my own experience to help. I realize my problems are happening to others. It makes me feel part of a larger phenomenon, less isolated. I took a horrible event in my life and turned it into something positive, into a job that matters, that I do well." CWOP enables parents to fight back and not just be a victim.[16]

The fourth factor is that CWOP has changed as the situation has changed. The board, the parents, the staff, and particularly Arsham at the outset were uncompromising in their positions. When government allocated more funds for preventive services, CWOP focused on the inadequate quality of services that were provided. When ACS reported the dramatic decline in the number of children in foster care, CWOP cited examples of children who did not have to be in care. Although CWOP praised the reformers who are leading ACS, it has complained that members of the line staff have the same punitive attitudes as their predecessors decades ago.

As CWOP became more secure as an organization, as its parents became respected in the field, and as ACS and the foster care agencies became more responsive to CWOP's concerns and demands, CWOP began to collaborate with the most progressive of the child welfare agencies and then with ACS. CWOP still fights for the same reforms, but it has become flexible in its strategies and formed alliances with former foes. CWOP has shifted from having an exclusively outside strategy—agitating, criticizing, demonstrating on the streets, denouncing ACS, and demanding change—to an inside and outside strategy. Arsham sat on Mattingly's advisory board. As noted earlier, CWOP signed the memorandum of understanding with ACS that requires, in effect, that any time ACS is contemplating the removal of an East Harlem child from his or her family it will first call CWOP to dispatch a parent advocate to participate in the Child Safety Conference that will decide if removal is necessary. In 2007 ACS began funding CWOP through its Community Partnership Initiative to strengthen the role of the Highbridge community in child welfare decision making.

As ACS and the child welfare system have improved, CWOP has become more comfortable with the changes that have come about and has been less critical of ACS, at least until recently. But the alliances between ACS and CWOP are complicated and are not without pitfalls. Does this shift take the edge off of the reform movement? According to Arsham:

> There is no easy answer. It's a struggle. We walk a fine line between being too radical for ACS to work with us and too co-opted for parents to trust us. At times we will be co-opted. The only thing worse than having ACS as an enemy is having ACS as a friend.[17]

In CWOP's continuing drive to have the organization reflect its constituency, in the summer of 2012 Mike Arsham decided to step down as executive director after 14 years. He will likely remain until the spring of 2013 by which time a replacement will probably be found. The two would overlap for several months for a smooth transition.

The following stories of three people at the heart of CWOP give a more robust view of the organization, its culture, and its accomplishments. They are Arsham, CWOP's executive director for the past 14 years; Tracey Carter, a parent advocate working with Bridge Builders in the South Bronx; and Sharwline Nicholson, chair of CWOP's board of directors for 5 years until 2011 and the named plaintiff in the historic and successful *Nicholson v. Scoppetta* suit against ACS.

MIKE ARSHAM'S STORY

Mike Arsham has a master's degree in social work from the University of Pennsylvania and has worked in child welfare for 30 years. He spent the first part of his career helping children who were in residential care, providing services to families so their children would not have go into care, and trying to improve child welfare policies. In 1998, when the Child Welfare Organizing Project was on the verge of collapse, he became its executive director. He helped turn CWOP into the most effective grassroots organization of child welfare parents in the city or the country.

Arsham is the grandson on his father's side of Jewish immigrants who left Russia, according to their grandson, "one step ahead of the Czar." Grandpa Jacob Arsham began with a pushcart on the teeming Lower East

Side of New York City and eventually created a trimmings business that some of the time did a little better than break even. "It was both a beautiful and a terrible legacy," says Mike Arsham. "I grew up with the value of hard work, lack of self-pity, and grateful to be alive. My dad grew up poor but didn't see himself that way. He worked all the time, mostly in the security division of Paramount pictures, checking if theater owners were cheating on their receipts. It wasn't a glamorous position.

"My dad never went to college but was a frustrated social worker. He did it naturally. His close friend who came on family outings was bipolar. Someone else was developmentally disabled. His heart went out to the underdog because he was an underdog himself. He wore thick bottle-bottom glasses and was legally blind. He was picked on a lot and couldn't stand a bully or abuse of power. That's where I got a lot of my values.

"My father told me, 'It's a lie that anyone can grow up to be President. You'll have to work harder and be better. There was an effort to wipe us off the face of the earth.' As a result of growing up that way, there are Jewish people of my generation who know what it is to be the target of discrimination."

Arsham matriculated at New York University's University Heights (Bronx) campus in the 1970s and lived in the dorm there for 2 years. When NYU closed that campus he transferred to the State University at Buffalo because he didn't want to return to lower Manhattan.

To pay his college expenses, he took a job at a residential treatment center in Buffalo, the Conners Children's Center, a unit of the Erie County foster care system. "It was small, with fewer than 30 kids in four cottages," Arsham says. "They were warm and home-like. It was not an awful place, but the kids had disturbing case histories. One boy, when he was 4 years old, watched his father stab his mother to death. The father was in jail, and there were very few options for the kid. He had night terrors and violent tantrums. Another kid when he was 7 burned down two houses. These fires were not accidents; he spread accelerants. They were well thought out, so the houses would burn to the ground. One 7-year-old boy, whose mother was psychotic and obsessed with feeding him, weighed 250 pounds."

"When I graduated college at 21, I was aimless and rootless. Being with these kids was a transformative experience for me. Having them look up to me came as a wakeup call. I realized I needed to start being a role model. I liked helping those kids and being part of a family for them. I stayed at Conners for 3 years and moved up to be a counselor in charge of a cottage. But I saw there was a real limit to how far I could go with only a B.A. Some people I worked with then are still there 30 years later, doing the same thing. For them it was a job they could hold on to in a dying city."

In 1978, at age 24, Arsham was homesick. He had broken up with his girlfriend and was sick of the bitter cold Buffalo weather. He moved back to New York City and tried to find similar work. He knew Frank Modica, head of Hamilton-Madison House, a settlement house on Manhattan's Lower East Side. Modica called Emory Brooks on Arsham's behalf. Brooks worked at Hawthorne Cedar Knolls, a residential treatment center in Westchester County, just north of New York City. The program served difficult-to-handle adolescents. Concerned about safety at the school, Brooks asked about Arsham, "How big is he?" Although he is not big, Arsham got the job.

"Hawthorne is not as benign a place as Conners was," Arsham says. "At 16 to 21 years old, they're not really kids. The ratio of staff to residents was horrible. It was a tough job. Some kids were in foster care, some were from the mental health system, and some were from juvenile justice. These were the most difficult kids from the most difficult neighborhoods, with all of them confined together. You were expected to keep a lid on it, to run a quiet cottage, to keep to a bare minimum the number of runaways, the number of rapes and assaults on staff. They didn't really care how you did it. I did it by befriending the kids who everyone else was terrified of. Not in a sleazy way, but by showing mutual respect."

"At Hawthorne there were more kids who caused me to ask myself: Why were they there? Why didn't someone intervene earlier? I met parents who were involved with their kids' lives. Why weren't parents given supports in the community? Why did it have to come to this?"

Frustrated that Hawthorne wasn't more effective in its treatment of kids and eager to improve his professional credentials, Arsham applied to 15 schools of social work. He went to the University of Pennsylvania because it gave him the biggest scholarship. At Penn Arsham met a social work professor, Louis Carter, a former U.S. Marines sergeant and the son of a black sharecropper, who became his mentor. "He had a profound impact on me," Arsham says. "He taught me how racism works. He had run a juvenile lock up facility and had kids from it talk to the students in our class. He said, 'They are your teachers today. Learn from them.'"

In 1981 Arsham returned to New York City and interviewed for a job with John Courtney, who was working at Special Services for Children, the city's child welfare agency. Courtney was hiring staff to work on the city's newly developed monitoring system, mandated by the Board of Estimate, to assess the performance of voluntary agencies with whom the city contracted to provide foster care services. Arsham told Courtney about the poor treatment the young men at Hawthorne Cedar Knolls received, saying that agencies like that needed more public scrutiny. Courtney asked,

"What did you do to improve the situation while you were there?" Arsham didn't have a very good answer. He didn't get the job.

Shortly thereafter Arsham interviewed for a job at a drug treatment program in Chinatown that was providing in-depth, long-term individual psychotherapy to heroin addicts and other drug users. Arsham bridled, saying, "These clients are not sick. They're oppressed." He did not get that job either.

He eventually went to work for the innovative, larger-than-life Richard Murphy at the Rheedlen Foundation, a small, struggling preventive service agency that was part of the new class of programs focused on keeping children out of foster care. Murphy had big plans—in 1990 he became New York City Commissioner of Youth Services under Mayor David Dinkins—and saw Arsham as someone who could help Rheedlen grow.

Arsham became the director of Rheedlen's satellite program at PS 207 on 117th Street in Harlem. Although he was called the director, he was Rheedlen's only staff person at the school. His job was to help families who were having problems that affected their children's school performance or who put their children at risk of being placed into foster care.

Under Arsham's skilled and caring social work with families and Murphy's seasoned and well-connected fundraising, the program expanded. Arsham was promoted to intake coordinator for the entire agency, the first point of contact for hundreds of young people and their families receiving services from Rheedlen. "It was an intense position, serving people who were in a crisis," Arsham says. "I began to experience vicarious trauma." He also became frustrated at having to deal with the bureaucratic strains of a rapidly expanding agency in which he and other staff members were pulled from their primary responsibilities to raise funds for expansion. To reduce his growing conflict with people in other branches of the agency, he became the head of Rheedlen Place, a self-contained preventive service program in Hell's Kitchen in Manhattan. He stayed in that position for 7 years. Arsham says, "Through that position, I learned the nuts and bolts of managing, supervising, finding and nurturing good staff and compensating for the talent that wasn't there. Some years we provided good preventive services, some years we didn't."

In 1994 he left Rheedlen, he says, "because preventive services is a difficult field. I was tired of being in the trenches. You are constantly defending the ground you stand on. You have to justify why overwhelmed families deserve the help they get. I wanted to have a broader view. I wanted to see who was passing the laws, so I wouldn't be a perpetual victim of them."

Arsham went to work for the Council of Family and Child Caring Agencies (COFCCA), the statewide association of voluntary foster care and preventive service providers that lobbies for the interests of service providers. "I saw COFCCA as a way to have the broader view and the influence that I wanted," Arsham says. "After working there as head of preventive services, I saw that the foster care agencies were more concerned about their bottom lines than with preventing children from coming into foster care. I saw some prominent agency directors play both sides of the fence shamelessly."

Arsham stayed at COFCCA for 5 years. "I learned how budgets are made," he says. "I learned about the self-interest that professional groups have. I learned about the deep political connections of 150-year-old child welfare institutions and how entrenched those special interests have become. I learned why preventive services get short shrift since they bring in so much less money per child than foster care brings in to the big agencies. I learned about the crazy ambivalence these agencies have: Do they want to help these families or punish them?"

Arsham was able to use his position at COFCCA, with the protection of its honorable but shackled executive director, Fred Brancato, to lead a successful campaign to preserve Family Rehabilitation Programs (FRP). Those programs were set up during the crack epidemic in the late 1980s to help recovering black and Latino mothers. In October 1994 Mayor Rudolph Giuliani, who believed that the poor are responsible for their problems and should solve them by themselves, proposed eliminating all the FRP programs. The mothers who were served by those programs mobilized to preserve them. Mike, who was able to get COFCCA to support their efforts, was at the center of a coalition consisting of agencies that provided the services, the mothers and families that were helped by the programs, advocacy groups, and COFCCA. Arsham says: "The Family Rehabilitation Programs use a group approach, and at its best the moms take ownership of the program. It is a program for poor people, but to them it is all they have. It is their Betty Ford Clinic. It is their only hope for keeping their kids and for getting clean. The mothers said, 'Without these programs, we have no future and our kids have no future.'"

"Everyone but the mayor was for the FRP. We held rallies and filled City Hall Park. We had a letter-writing campaign, a petition drive and met with members of the City Council. The FRP was a parent-professional model, and the campaign to preserve the programs was a parent-professional coalition. That campaign was a big part of what drove me to the Child Welfare Organizing Project."

The coalition won a mixed but important victory. When the city budget was passed in June 1995, the FRP programs were saved, but their capacity was cut in half. "Fortunately there was enough of the program left for it to become a core, ongoing child welfare service," Arsham says.

"The campaign to preserve the FRP programs was a bruising experience, especially without the full backing of my employers. After we won, I felt tired, burned out, and didn't know what to do next." At about that time the Child Welfare Organizing Project was getting off the ground, led by the magnetic, fiery organizer Mabel Paulino. "Feeling burned out in Mabel's presence was not an option. And she knew how to bring people into her orbit."

Arsham had met Paulino at Hunter College, at a focus group of child welfare-involved parents, professionals, and policy makers. "I had just seen the overwhelming power of parents organizing themselves in the FRP campaign," Arsham says. "At the meeting with Mabel, I saw the potential of CWOP, an organization of angry parents wanting to change the child welfare system. I was very invested in CWOP from the moment I saw it. It was revolutionary, the missing link in child welfare reform."

Arsham brought Paulino to meetings of the COFCCA preventive service agencies and to meetings with Shirley Whitney, who oversaw preventive services at the city's child welfare agency. "I gave Mabel access to the people I had access to," he says. "We at COFCCA had opinions on everything, but we never talked with kids or parents to find out what they thought. When people at COFCCA did hear what parents had to say, most didn't like what they heard."

Arsham helped connect CWOP and Paulino to the mainstream child welfare groups. After Paulino resigned and CWOP was struggling, he offered to help solve CWOP's problems. When CWOP was adrift after Paulino's replacement was fired, he continued to offer his help, but he had no desire to become CWOP's executive director. "The job was kind of thrust upon me," he says. "I thought I was inappropriate for it."

Nevertheless Arsham took the job, helping to create a culture of inclusion so that parents and Mike himself would feel part of something larger than themselves. "My role and ideas come from the people around me. I'm always forced to think about what would Bernie or Teresa or Shawrline think about this or that. I'm surrounded by people who are inflexible in a good way. We found each other."

And so white, middle-class Mike Arsham became the executive director of an agency serving and led by poor black and Latino women who had experienced the trauma of having their children taken from them. He has forged their experiences, their skills, and their righteous anger into a powerful force that has pushed the city's child welfare system to change more in the past 15 years than at any other time in recent history. He has helped to create an environment in CWOP that allowed parents and him to become their best selves. It is likely that in the future CWOP will have an executive director who more closely resembles its constituents. It is hard to imagine, though, anyone else who could have brought CWOP back from the brink and into the mainstream.

TRACEY CARTER'S STORY[VIII]

The deaths of Tracey Carter's parents plunged her middle-class life into drug addiction, homelessness, and the loss of her children to foster care and adoption. After several drug treatment programs were unsuccessful, she and her husband became sober in 2002. She has remained clean ever since. Her two youngest children returned to her from foster care later that year. Since then she has been trained as a parent advocate and now works with CWOP helping other parents to become sober and reunite with their children.

Tracey Carter is an attractive, middle-aged, hardworking mom. She wears jeans, small gold hoops in her ears, and a bright blue slicker with *Bridge Builders* in large white letters on the back. To look at her, you would not imagine that six of her 11 children have been in foster care, five other children were adopted, and she spent 13 years on the streets smoking crack.

Today Carter is a parent organizer, working in the storefront office of Bridge Builders on Ogden Avenue and 164th Street in the Highbridge section of the Bronx. She helps parents who are struggling to come back "from the other side," as she describes her former life.

Marjorie, a young African-American woman, walked into the storefront looking for Carter. Her son, who had 3 months left to finish high school, had been killed a few weeks before in Boston. He'd moved there to escape the streets of the South Bronx. Marjorie was still grieving, and she knew that talking to Carter would bring her comfort.

One of Carter's proudest moments as a parent organizer for Bridge Builders involved helping Marjorie. At 11:00 p.m. one evening, when Carter was asleep at home, Marjorie called. Although Carter gives out her home phone number to each of her clients in case the client has an emergency, a call this late was unusual. Marjorie was about to relapse into drug use. Carter spent 2 hours on the phone with her. "I let her vent," Carter says. "The next day she enrolled in Success Counseling, a drug treatment program that is part of Bridge Builders. She graduated and is still clean."

viii. I interviewed Tracey in January 2007 and again in December 2011.

Working with parents like Marjorie is part of Carter's job as a parent organizer for CWOP, which is working with Bridge Builders, a community-service program in the South Bronx. CWOP employs parents from the neighborhood to reduce abuse and neglect and help families keep their children out of foster care. Another aspect of her job is co-leading a weekly support group for parents who have lost their children to foster care. "Sometimes I have to contain myself when parents talk about their lives," Carter says. "I want to cry remembering my life and hearing about the same things they are going through."

Along with her colleagues at CWOP, Carter has also worked to change child welfare policy. The goal is to ensure that the system helps rather than punishes parents. In one campaign, CWOP pressed the New York City Council to write and pass legislation to create a parent advisory board to the city's Administration for Children's Services (ACS). The board would advise the ACS commissioner on policy and promote the education and employment of parents as peer advocates in the system. Parents and consumers in other social service areas—mental health and developmental disabilities, to cite two examples—participate in advisory and advocacy councils.[18] Why not in child welfare?

On December 9, 2004, the general welfare committee of the city council held a public hearing on Intro 492, legislation promoted by CWOP and introduced by council member Tracy Boyland. The legislation would create a 14-member parent advisory board for the ACS commissioner. The hearing took place in the august council chamber, whose towering walls are covered with large portraits of city fathers. Almost 200 people attended and dozens spoke. ACS commissioner John Mattingly was the first to testify. Although he was an ally of parents who have become embroiled in the child welfare system, he cautioned that the bill was not necessary because ACS already had a means for parents to have their voices heard. New York State assemblyman Roger Green, also an ally of parents, spoke passionately in favor of the bill. Four black and Latino mothers from CWOP testified about their painful experiences in the child welfare system and argued for the bill's passage.

Carter came to the hearing but didn't speak. "It was the most surprising experience for me," she says. "I had never been at City Hall, and now I was inside and we had a voice. The city council people were actually listening to what the parents had to say." It took months of negotiating between CWOP and ACS before an agreement was reached that resulted in the bill's being passed unanimously in December 2005 and signed by the mayor.

Carter did speak several months later at a conference of 300 social workers from different child welfare agencies who meet regularly in support of the Family Rehabilitation Programs for drug-addicted parents. She speaks powerfully about the dangers of drugs, the pain of losing children to foster care, and the child welfare system's abuse of parents' rights. "Talking about myself, I had people crying and laughing," Carter says. "One of the ironies was that staff from Child Development Support Corporation, the agency that had my children in foster care, were at the presentation. They were very proud of me speaking, even though I gave them a hard time when my kids were in care."

The story of how six of Tracey's 11 children ended up in foster care, five others were adopted, and how she extricated herself from a life of crack and homelessness is painful and inspiring.

Tracey was a quiet child, the 12th of 13 children. "I grew up in a house that my parents owned in St. Albans, Queens. My mother was a teacher's aide at PS 36, and my father drove an 18-wheeler. I grew up in a nice, loving home. We went to Calvary Baptist Church on Sundays where my dad was a deacon. There was always something to eat, clothes on my back. We went on picnics and trips to Palisades Park, Bear Mountain, on the Circle Line. Once in a while we went to my grandfather's farm in Rice, Virginia. I didn't want for nothing as a child."

In 1972, when Tracey was 10, her mother died from cancer. Two weeks later, her father "died of a broken heart," she says. Her father's mother moved into the house and took care of Tracey and her nonadult siblings. When raising grandchildren became too difficult for her grandmother, Tracey moved to Far Rockaway, Queens, to live with her oldest sister, Marilyn.

At 19, she hooked up with James Smith, who was twice her age. She moved in with him in South Jamaica, Queens, became pregnant quickly, had a miscarriage, and became pregnant again with her first child, Gary. Ten and a half months later, she gave birth to her second child, James. They had two other children, Jennifer and Geneen.

"We were living on welfare, and things started going downhill with me and James. Slowly but surely James started disappearing. He left us living in an abandoned house that the police had raided and destroyed. We stayed there a couple of months. We had no heat, and we were running wires from outside, tapping electricity from the street."

Tracey moved in with her older sister Jean. She began hanging out on weekends with her younger sister Kim, who introduced her to freebasing (smoking crack). "Weekends of using became week days and started turning to months," Tracey says. Tracey took to the streets and gave her food stamp and welfare cards to her sister so her kids could eat.

On the streets, Carter met Joshua, a construction worker who got high on crack with her. Their child, Carter's fifth, was born the next year with cocaine in her blood. ACS took the child, Pamela, directly from the hospital and placed her in foster care. Jean pulled Pamela out of foster care and adopted her and Tracey's other four children. Jean then moved with all the kids to Virginia Beach, Virginia.

Tracey and Josh had two more children together: David and Nicole. Like Pamela, they were taken directly from the hospital and placed in foster care. Tracey's parental rights to David and Nicole were terminated; they were adopted by their foster mother.

In 1993, Carter enrolled in a drug treatment program. Not only had she lost custody of seven children, but she was being physically abused by Josh. "He broke my ribs," she says. "He made me do unthinkable things to him. But I stayed because it was a roof over my head." A neighbor helped her get into Phoenix House, a residential drug program. While at Phoenix House from February to September 1993, Carter met her husband-to-be, Theodore, whom she calls T. Soon after they both graduated from the program, on November 17, 1993, they were married at City Hall. "Just the two of us," Carter says. "Some others who were getting married were our witnesses. We've been together ever since."

Soon she was pregnant, and she and T moved into a shelter in East New York, Brooklyn, for pregnant women and their husbands. That shelter didn't accommodate children, so when Jason was born in June 1994, the family moved to a shelter in Brownsville, Brooklyn. Though Carter had relapsed and Jason was born with cocaine in his blood, the social worker let the infant go home with Carter since she was in an outpatient drug program at Daytop Village. The family stayed in the Brownsville shelter for a few more months before moving into a subsidized three-bedroom apartment in East New York.

Carter's relapses continued. T had also relapsed and they began using crack together. "We smoked up welfare, buying less food and smoking more," Carter says. She stopped going to her aftercare program at Daytop, and officials there called protective services. ACS went to court and gained custody of Jason. "I left court with an empty stroller."

Carter became pregnant again. Her baby, Anton, received no prenatal care since Carter was smoking crack every day. She went into labor at home on Christmas Eve 1994. "The fire department came, and he was coming out," Carter says. "It was the first time I had seen a child born." Anton went straight into the system from the hospital.

Carter never stopped using and lost the apartment, though she and T saw the kids. "The foster mother was nice. She took baby pictures, so I could see them. Visiting them was an off and on thing because my drug habit became worse. We wound up on the street, sleeping on trains. It was a mess. But I never sold drugs."

Carter and T got another apartment, this time in the Bronx. They were panhandling, holding doors, holding cups, getting enough to get by. "I had two miscarriages during that time because I was smoking real heavy," Carter says.

Then she got pregnant again, with her 10th child, a girl named Tahjai. According to Carter, one day she and T simply stopped smoking crack so T could have the daughter he always wanted and she could bring the baby home from the hospital. For 6 months she was clean.

But a few months after Tahjai was born, Carter relapsed. T did the same as soon as he found out that she was using. They lived in the Bronx and panhandled on 6th Avenue and 9th Street, right near the Path Train in Manhattan, Carter says. They lived on Field Place and 183rd Street in the Bronx while they were panhandling in Manhattan. Carter became pregnant once more, and again she and T stopped using crack because they wanted to keep the child. But Carter relapsed in 2000, the day Tyrek was born. Staff members at St. Barnabas Hospital, where the baby was born, called ACS, and Tyrek was placed in foster care.

"A couple of days later, July 3rd, I never will forget it, we were planning to take Tahjai the next day to see the Macy's fireworks for the fourth of July," Carter says. A worker from the Bronx field office of ACS came to Tracey's and T's apartment at midnight with two policemen to remove 17-month-old Tahjai. "This one slipped through the cracks," Carter remembers the social worker saying.

"It took me a long time to let go of her," Carter says. "The ACS worker was getting impatient, and she started pulling Tahjai out of my arms, so we had a tug of war. One of the police officers was sympathetic and said to the protective service worker, 'She's very emotional now, give her time.' But she just saw me as an unfit mother. I finally let Tahjai go, and they walked out the door." Carter broke down, crying and screaming. It would take her a month to find out where her two children were in foster care and to see them.

Sabrina, a neighbor who Tracey trusted, heard her screams and came over to her apartment. She urged Carter to get help for her drug use and arranged for her to get into the Neighborhood Youth and Family Services program for mothers using drugs. Carter stayed in the program for 18 months, graduating in April 2002. She says she has been clean ever since.

A Family Court judge decided that after Carter's graduation from the drug program her youngest two children could come home from foster care on a trial discharge. But the Child Development Support Corporation (CDSC), the foster care agency that had custody of the two children, refused to discharge them to Carter and her husband because they were living with T's sister on the Lower East Side of Manhattan in an apartment that CDSC felt was inadequate. Carter and T, desperately wanting to be with their children, left his sister's apartment. That meant they would be defined as homeless and, they thought, be eligible for an apartment that was large enough for their four-member family. "We had Mother's Day at T's sister's house with the kids," Carter says. "The next weekend we left for the city's Emergency Assistance Unit [EAU]." The EAU found that they qualified for homeless housing. However, they were victims of one of poverty's Catch-22s. A homeless person is eligible only for an apartment large enough to house the people who are with him or her upon arrival at the shelter. Since the children weren't with Carter and T, Homeless Services would provide an apartment large enough for just two people.

Instead, after living in a series of shelters, Carter and T were sent to the Park View Hotel at 110th Street and Lenox Avenue in Manhattan, which didn't allow children. As a result, Tracey and T could not have overnight or weekend visits with their kids. They were limited to daytime visits on Saturday. They picked the kids up at the agency in Brooklyn, came back to Manhattan, and brought them back to Brooklyn by 6:00 p.m. This back and forth to Brooklyn with no overnight visits went on from April until September. "I started to get frustrated, not to the point that I wanted to use again, but I was depressed because I wanted my kids home. The kids had a good foster mother. They still call her Grandma and they still talk to her on the phone, but we wanted to be together as a family."

After the judge's decision in 2002, Carter learned about Jessica Marcus at South Brooklyn Legal Services. When Carter arrived in Jessica's office in September 2002, her large case file was on Jessica's desk. "I was very impressed," Carter says.

Housing was the only barrier to reuniting Carter and T with their children. They completed the drug treatment program, were both clean, and T had a part-time job. The lack of housing was not a reason to keep children in foster care. Early in October, Carter and Marcus appeared before a referee who said Carter and T's children could come home. "It was the happiest day of my life. If it wasn't for Jessica, I might still be fighting for my kids to come home," Carter says.

The next day Carter and T picked up 3-year-old Tahjai and 2-year-old Tyrek from the foster care agency in Brooklyn. "We were four people and the kids had so many things stuffed into plastic bags that we had to take two cabs from Brooklyn back to the EAU to add the kids to our case," Carter says. They took them to Brooklyn HELP I,[ix] in East New York.

ix. HELP I is a Tier II shelter. It is a nonprofit agency that provides apartments in a building that provides on-site social services such as daycare and job training.

"As soon as we got there, I knew this wasn't going to work. People were getting high, smoking weed, drinking. My daughter got bit in the face by a roach that shut her eye. I was scared to death because she had just come home."

The next day Carter told her social worker that they wanted to be transferred to another apartment. "This wasn't a safe environment," she says. "The social worker said it was on us. If we leave, we'll be marked AWOL." But she decided to chance it and called her brother who took them back to the EAU. After spending a couple of days there with the kids, they were sent to a scatter-site apartment[x] on Ocean Avenue in Brooklyn. "The place was a dump. The bathroom ceiling had collapsed and was inside the bathtub. They gave us dirty sheets that another family left behind. So we ended up sleeping in our clothes. My daughter started crying. I was crying. My husband went downstairs and called the social worker at the EAU. She came and inspected the apartment and apologized and sent us back to the EAU. That night we were back on the train, back to the EAU to start all over again. They were frustrated with us. They said we can't keep turning down places."

Carter called Jessica and explained what had been going on since the kids had come home. She made some calls and 2 days later the EAU found them an apartment on Walton Avenue in the Highbridge section of the Bronx. It was a fifth floor walk-up with two bedrooms. "Okay, I said. Now I can see we're home."

Things then settled down. After living on Walton Avenue for 3 years Carter, T, and their two children Tahjai and Tyrek moved to a New York City Housing Authority (NYCHA) three bedroom apartment where they now live. Tyrek and Tahjai were in school, and T got a job with the parks department. Tracey finally had a little free time and called Marcus at South Brooklyn Legal Services to see if she could help her get a job. Marcus told her about CWOP, whose office in Highbridge was near where Carter lived. Carter started going to a CWOP support group and then enrolled in CWOP's 6-month training program for parent advocates. She graduated in June 2004.

"When my kids were in the system, I didn't know my rights," Carter says. "I wish I had known them back then. Hearing the stories of other parents I realized I'm not the only one who went through hard times trying to get my kids out. Some of the parents had it worse than I did. Their kids didn't have to be placed into the system."

x. Rental apartments in different locations administered by a nonprofit agency that also provides tenants with an array of supportive services.

One month after Carter graduated from training, she was hired by CWOP as a parent advocate to work with Bridge Builders. After a year of working with families, going to case conferences and court with parents, training ACS staff, leading a parent support group, and speaking at conferences, Tracey became the parent trainer in the CWOP class. And so the little ripples in Carter's life that were set in motion by dogged and skilled legal work and by nurturing and informed training have started to cause ripples of their own.

But Carter's life is challenging. T fell off a scaffold at his job and can't work because of his injuries. Tracey had a scare with cancer but at the moment her health is okay. Tyrek is in a special education program in a public school. When he is disruptive in school, which is often, the school calls Carter to get him, threatening Tyrek's suspension or a call to ACS for educational neglect if she doesn't. As the person responsible for the family's children, Tracey has to drop everything to get him, undermining her dependability for Bridge Builders and CWOP. Nevertheless, according to Arsham, "Her great smarts and great courage make it worth it for us."

However, the funding for Bridge Builders has been continuously reduced over the last few years, so that she is now the only parent advocate in the Storefront where once there were eight. She works 17.5 hours a week, spread out over 5 days, but receives no benefits and often puts in many unpaid hours sitting in court or visiting parents in their homes. "Saturday is my day with my kids, and Sunday I try to get some rest."

SHARWLINE NICHOLSON'S STORY

Sharwline Nicholson was an immigrant from Jamaica. When her enraged boyfriend beat her in front of her daughter, her two children were placed in foster care. She was the named plaintiff in the class action lawsuit against what she felt was the illegal removal of her children and won. She became a national leader in the movements for child welfare reform and for the rights of domestic violence survivors. In 2002 she joined the board of directors of Child Welfare Organizing Project and became its chairperson in 2006. She has worked as a supervisor at Home Depot since 1999.

Sharwline Nicholson grew up in the town of Ocho Rios on the island of Jamaica with her father and his large extended family. When Sharwline was two, her mother moved to North Plainfield, New Jersey. "When you are in a third world country, you are always looking for something better," Nicholson explains without referring to the possibility that the relationship between her mother and father might have contributed to the mother's decision to leave Jamaica.

"My dad worked as a taxi driver. My aunt was a domestic worker, and my grandfather had a small farm where we had goats and exported tomatoes, pineapples and oranges. We could afford to live a decent life," Nicholson says.

When Sharwline was almost 12 she went to an all-girls boarding high school in the countryside where she developed many of her personal skills. She was an organizer of the Extravaganza Fair to raise money for the school, was Key Club President, and led a magazine group. "I've been an organizer from early on."

When she graduated from high school, her father wanted her to go to college, but she wanted to experience work. She found a job that quickly became tedious and went to the United States to live with her mother within 2 years of finishing high school. "Living with my mother was horrible," she says. "I believe in signs. She did not grow me, we did not grow up together. I had my own personality, and we weren't on the same page. I moved out in 6 months. I got a job taking care of children and then taking care of the elderly. I did that for 5 years, but that was not me."

While living in New Jersey, Nicholson met Kendell. "He was a no good guy. He wasn't physically abusive in any way, but he wasn't the best character. He was in and out of jail. I wouldn't choose him again." They were together for 3 years, and had a son named Kendell.

Eventually she left Kendell the father and moved with Kendell the son to Flatbush in Brooklyn, where she says almost all Jamaican immigrants live. "I had it rough then. I was on public assistance for 3 or 4 years while I took care of Kendell." During that time she met Claude, another man who could never keep a job. With Claude she had a second child, Destinee.

"After you have a child you start thinking you have potential and you want to do something more," Nicholson says. "I wanted to get off public assistance. I had Destinee in March 1998 and enrolled in Mercy College. I finished one semester in December. The next month, January 1999, the new semester was going to start when the drama with child welfare began. I had to quit school."

Before Nicholson gave birth to Destinee, Claude went to South Carolina to find work, returning every month or so to see Nicholson and the new baby. While living apart, both Claude and Nicholson heard through their respective grapevines that the other was seeing someone else. Claude returned to New York City in January 1999. Destinee was in the bedroom; Kendell was in school. Claude confronted Nicholson with the story he had heard about her and another man. He became enraged when she would not deny his accusations. For the first time in their relationship he hit her. "He started throwing things," Nicholson says. "I was blocking things with my arm and ended up with a broken arm. I was on the floor. He kicked me. My ribs were broken, and my head was injured. He was a crazy man. I was screaming, which scared him. He ran out the door, and I called 911."

Neighbors also called the police who came quickly. Nicholson left her daughter with a trusted neighbor with whom she had previously exchanged babysitting. The neighbor also agreed to take care of Kendell when he came home from school. The police took Nicholson to the emergency room at Kings County Hospital. She stayed overnight because the doctors feared that she might have internal bleeding, which turned out not to be the case. "ACS called me in the hospital the next morning," Nicholson says. "They said, 'If you want to see your kids, you have to come to court.' They didn't tell me anything. It was very confusing."

ACS charged that Nicholson had "engaged in domestic violence" and petitioned Family Court to place the children in foster care. Although Nicholson had given ACS the name of a cousin in New Jersey who would take her children, ACS placed her children with strangers in a foster home that was part of the New York Foundling Hospital system. She did not see her children for several weeks.

According to Nicholson, "The foster care placement was horrible. My son had a black eye. My daughter, who was 9 months old, had fingernails that were longer than mine. Her face had scratches caused by the long nails. She had a cold with mucus crusted on her face. You just wonder, 'What happened here?' You're just lost."

When she appeared in Family Court in February, the case was adjourned because she did not have a lawyer to represent her. She was assigned a court-appointed attorney who represented her at her next hearing. The judge ordered the children returned to her, but ACS and New York Foundling took another 3 weeks to return the children. They said she could not go back to living in her Brooklyn apartment because Claude might return. She found a suitable place with a relative, but once she did, Foundling had other requirements, like demanding that she prove that she had adequate home furnishings such as sheets for the children's beds. And so it went for 3 weeks.

After her children were returned to her, Nicholson was nervous about ACS's continued and, from her perspective, unfair involvement in her life. She took the children to New Jersey where she was when ACS made unannounced visits to her Brooklyn apartment. ACS said they needed to see the children. Frightened that she might lose her children again, she sent them to her family in Jamaica. ACS issued a warrant for Nicholson's arrest. She was apprehended when she went to the post office. She was assigned a different court-appointed lawyer. The judge said she had 2 weeks to return the children to ACS.

During this time, Nicholson began studying the law. She had no kids, and had time. She went to Victims' Rights Services, to Criminal Court, and to Family Court. She went to the law library to learn about Article 10 of the Family Court Act that governs abuse and neglect proceedings. She got a list of lawyers from her neighbor and by chance selected the law firm of Lansner and Kubitschek from the list. "I paid $25 for a consultation. It was the best $25 I ever spent."

She contacted Sanctuary for Families, an agency that serves victims of domestic violence. "I used all the services that Sanctuary had to offer," she says. She started therapy, went back into school, and in August 1999 got herself a job at Home Depot. She began as a cashier and now works as a supervisor for contracted services. She's been there for 13 years. "I love Home Depot. They let me start anew."

Jill Zuccardy at Sanctuary for Families joined forces with Lansner and Kubitschek to bring a federal lawsuit in January 2001 against the city and state of New York with Nicholson as the lead plaintiff. The suit alleged that ACS removed children from their mothers' custody without the court orders required by ACS's own regulations merely because of the mothers' "failure to protect" their children when the mothers were being battered. This, the suit charged, violated both mothers' and children's rights.[19]

After a 2-month trial that included 44 witnesses, including Nicholson, nine other mothers in similar situations, and numerous experts, District Court Judge Jack Weinstein issued his landmark decision on March 11, 2002. In his 188 page decision, he found, among other things, that ACS often alleged neglect by mothers simply because the mothers were battered and that ACS had removed children unnecessarily. He cited ACS's violation of the Ninth, Thirteenth, and Fourteenth Amendments of the U.S. Constitution, comparing the mothers' "stigmatization and loss of control to slavery."[20]

The child welfare system changed as a result of Weinstein's ruling. Zuccardy, who filed the suit, wrote that "The most important change is that ACS can't, as a matter of policy, remove children from victims of domestic violence solely because they're victims.[xi] Obviously that doesn't

---

xi. Professor Martin Guggenheim argues that the most important outcome of the lawsuit is that Judge Weinstein ordered compensation for 18B attorneys representing parents to be raised to $90 an hour for both in and out of court work. His ruling could never have been enforced, but it was the catalyst for the New York State

mean that it never happens. Some caseworkers make threats of removal inappropriately, now it's the exception and it's against the law."[21]

The leadership of CWOP heard about the Nicholson lawsuit and attended the court proceedings. They invited Nicholson to speak at a CWOP meeting. About 50 people attended. "Each of us was taken with the other," according to Arsham. Nicholson felt she was really needed at CWOP, and when she was asked to join CWOP's board of directors in 2002, she agreed. After 4 years on the board, she became chairperson when John Courtney stepped down so that a person with child welfare experience could fill the role.

In 2011, after serving for 9 years on CWOP's board, most of them as chairperson, she left the board. "I love CWOP and the work they do," Sharwline says. "But I spent a long time there. If I stayed, I would not be giving it my all. At some point you realize you have to let go. It was time for me to do something else."

Her son, Kendell, is getting ready for college; he's already been accepted at two CUNY schools, though neither is his first choice. Her daughter, Destinee, is doing well in junior high and is applying for a scholarship to go to a boarding school. As Sharwline says, "I am the mother eagle with my two little eagles. I flew down a little to get my babies on top."

Sharwline continues to work as a supervisor at Home Depot and attends college at night in hope of becoming a social worker. Child welfare is beginning to be in her past. She hasn't spoken to audiences across the country about her case or about child welfare in almost 2 years. Every 3 months, though, she is a presenter in a training session for organizations that work with survivors of domestic violence. Domestic Violence 101 is what she calls her section of the course. "I am reexamining my life now. My passion is with CWOP and what it does. I want to advocate for families and children and empower young girls. But I want to go back to school to be equipped." Sharwline is a few credits away from completing a bachelor's degree, is thinking about completing college in 2012, and is considering a master's degree after that. ACS has not been in her life, nor has the man who beat her. Have there been any big problems in her life in the past few years? "Only money issues. I'm sure there have been other big problems but I can't think of any now."

***

legislature to raise the compensation for 18B attorneys and eventually for the city to create institutional representation for parents in family court. How this ruling by Judge Weinstein transformed parent representation in family court is recounted in detail by Professor Guggenheim in Chapter 7.

The story of CWOP is larger than the stories of Arsham, Carter, or Nicholson. The organization and the movement it spawned were built by dozens of parent who are trained as advocates and leaders and who work tirelessly to be reunited with their children. Some now work to help others; other parents have moved on in their lives after working at CWOP. They include parents like the following:

Teresa Bachiller has worked with CWOP since 2002 when she was a member of the first training class at the East Harlem headquarters. The city's child welfare system has been a presence in her family's life for four generations. It has been in her life from the time she was a defiant teenager and was placed by the city's child welfare agency into a group care facility. "I felt there should have been a better solution, but my feelings were not respected or valued," Bachiller says. Later, after she became a parent and her oldest child became a defiant teenager and ran away to a godparent's home, all of her children, including her 6-year old daughter, were removed by ACS. "I was devastated. Why had no one talked to me before making such a life-altering call? Why had ACS taken my children with so little explanation or proof? Eventually ACS conceded that the allegations were false and returned my children, but permanent emotional damage had been done to my family....Later, my grandson was taken away from my adult daughter. I was able to gain custody, but I could not become a kinship foster parent due to my own history with ACS, even though the allegations that began that history were false."[22]

Bachiller now leads CWOP's leadership training programs and support groups, and has testified at city council hearings. She lives in East Harlem as she has her entire life.

When **Carlos Boyet** was in his mid-teens, he and his estranged girlfriend, Jasmine, had a son named Jeremy. Three years later, when a court contacted Boyet to pay child support, he denied that he was Jeremy's father. "I had all the reactions of a deadbeat father in those days," he says. When an ACS caseworker subsequently contacted him to say that Jasmine was using drugs and that Jeremy had been put in foster care, Carlos took custody of his son. In the 4 years Jeremy had been in foster care, he had been in nine different homes, due in large part to behavioral problems variously identified as cerebral palsy, learning disabilities, attention deficit disorder, mental illness, and autism.

While in his father's care, Jeremy was placed in several unsatisfactory schools for children with learning disabilities. "I got pissed off and took him out of school," Boyet says. Upon learning from Jeremy's school that the boy wasn't attending classes, ACS tried to have him removed from his father's custody. At about that time, Boyet ran into India Echevarria, whom he knew slightly from his Bronx neighborhood. The meeting would change his life. India was working as a family support worker at Bridge Builders, a collaborative in which CWOP participated.

At Echevarria's suggestion, Boyet enrolled in a parenting class offered by Highbridge Community Life Center and participated in a fathers' support group run by CWOP. Eventually he took CWOP's 6-month training program and was later hired by CWOP to lead the fathers' support group and to work as a community organizer. His dedication to his son, his leadership skills, and his cooperative manner led him to become co-chair of Bridge Builders' steering committee that guided the community collaborative.

But his son's problems became overwhelming. While Carlos and Jeremy were visiting relatives in Pennsylvania, Jeremy was arrested. Carlos at first took a leave of absence from Bridge Builders and CWOP, but then left his life in the Bronx to take care of his son and to begin again.

Carmen Caban was abused as a child. She is now a 46-year-old grandmother and parent advocate, trained by CWOP and employed by it. She attends Child Safety Conferences as an ally of parents who might have their children placed in foster care. Her four children were removed from her custody. The state terminated her parental rights to her two youngest children more than 15 years ago because of her drug addiction. After they were put in care, she successfully completed drug treatment and parenting and anger management classes that were obligatory if she ever wanted to regain custody of her kids. Today three of her four children live with her, and the fourth visits, though their relationship continues to be stormy. In 2012 because of budget cuts, CWOP had to eliminate all of its community representatives. Carmen was among the five who were let go, though two were rehired. She is out of work, planning to get married, and is involved in her church.

Julia McGuire's depression led her to voluntarily place her three children in foster care. She then couldn't get them back until they were old enough to leave foster care on their own. While they were in care she traveled every other week from her apartment in the Roberto Clemente Houses in the Bronx, by bus, subway, commuter rail, and cab to St. Mary's, a foster care agency in the suburban Long Island town of Syosset, and back for most of 10 years to visit her children. All are now adults and living at home with her. After serving on CWOP's board of directors for many years, she now works in a school cafeteria and is taking college classes to become a teacher's aide.

These are some of the heroines and heroes who have created and sustain CWOP. They have helped transform how ACS and foster care agencies treat parents and how parents see themselves. The changes they helped bring about in the city's child welfare system were not made by themselves alone. They had allies in high places, most importantly ACS commissioners Bell and Mattingly, who listened to their complaints, encouraged their activities, and eventually funded their work. Bell and Mattingly brought parents and CWOP into child welfare's mainstream after parents had pushed their way through the door. As previously noted, the parents had other allies as well—lawyers, social workers, foundation officers, academics, and the progressive leadership of several foster care agencies. They also had allies in other grassroots parent organizations that added strength to the parents' movement. In a moment we turn to the story of four of those grassroots groups, but first, three lessons have been learned from CWOP's experience.

First, social movements thrive when participants feel part of something larger than themselves. They come to recognize that their personal problems are shaped in large part by forces beyond their individual control. They can see that those forces can be influenced by the mutual aid, compassion, and collective action from their movement, "collective efficacy," as described by Harvard sociologist Felton Earls.[23] In the process, people develop a sense of their own self-worth and a sense of a shared identity that can energize and sustain them. CWOP, and the parents' movement, created that shared identity.

Second, in CWOP's case, organization trumped philosophy. Initially, CWOP's fiery leadership had the right beliefs and a winning program, but lacked the ability to administer the organization or to carry out a successful campaign to reform child welfare. CWOP thrived when it found an individual with the organizational skills to carry its platform forward. Certainly philosophy is important, but without an organization to implement the mission, the efforts are likely to founder.

And third, whether one chooses an inside strategy—collaborating with the establishment—or an outside strategy—agitating from the streets or bringing a lawsuit in the courts—the key to success is power. Without power, either an inside or an outside strategy will falter. Power comes from different sources—money, information, people, and connections. Before choosing whether to collaborate or to agitate, it is wise to build and assess your strength in each of those areas.

CHAPTER 5

Other New York City Parent-Led Grassroots Organizations

The parents who had become embroiled in the child welfare system and their allies did not rely solely on the Child Welfare Organizing Project (CWOP) to shape child welfare programs and influence policy. Once a more welcoming environment for parent participation was created in the 1990s, other grassroots organizations sprouted. Some of them were led by parents; others were launched by professionals in partnership with parents.

These groups reached the peak of their organizational strength and influence on the child welfare system around the middle of the first decade of the twenty-first century. In their heyday they were highly active both outside and inside the child welfare system. Outside they filed law suits against the New York City Administration for Children's Services (ACS), organized street demonstrations of survivors of domestic violence and victims of the bureaucracy and foster care agencies, conducted research on Family Court, published the writings of child welfare-involved parents, testified at city council hearings; spoke regularly at forums on child welfare policy and practices and to classes of law and social work, appeared on television and radio, and were interviewed for newspaper articles. Inside they advised the ASC commissioner, worked as parent mentors in preventive service and foster care programs, and coached parents in case conferences. The organizations' work enabled parents and their allies to play an unprecedented role in shaping the child welfare system.

Many of these activities continue today, but by the end of 2010 the strength of several of these other organizations had diminished, which was a reflection in part of the inherent difficulty of organizing child welfare parents but, more important, the less supportive environment exacerbated by the fiscal crisis that began in 2008.

This chapter profiles four organizations that represent the range of parent-led groups that began between the mid-1990s and 2005. As of now, three had survived and one had folded. But even the ones that survived were struggling, though they continued to play a role in the movement to reform New York's child welfare system. *Rise,* a publication written by and for parents who have encountered the child welfare system, was created in 2005. It reconfigured itself and was able to survive and even grow, expanding its influence. Bridge Builders began in 2002 as a collaboration of foundations, service providers, and South Bronx residents, including parents with child welfare involvement. By 2011 the program was administered by the community but struggled to survive with a budget half as large as it was when Bridge Builders started. The Voices of Women Organizing Project (VOW), created in 2000, organizes survivors of domestic violence for self-help and to reform child welfare and the Family Court. When its founding director left, VOW stumbled but was again providing self-help to survivors and trying to have an influence by collaborating with ACS and working to reform Family Court. People United for Children (PUC) was created in the early 1990s by one of the parents whose son was falsely accused, convicted, and jailed in the Central Park Jogger case (details of that case appear below). The organization soon shifted its focus to child welfare as a pathway to the juvenile justice system. PUC folded in 2009 because of lack of funding and organizational depth.

RISE MAGAZINE

Four women sit around a table in a small room at CWOP's office in the Lehman Housing Project on 110th street in East Harlem. The walls of the room are covered with posters about Puerto Rico, a photo of Mississippi civil rights leader Fannie Lou Hammer, recent news articles about foster care, and poems by parents. The sound and sight of a Metro North train, passing on the adjacent elevated railway, periodically punctuate the conversation. Before the women begin to write they talk back and forth about their lives. "My daughter Nelly said she couldn't depend on me," Youshell says. "I used to get angry when she said things like that, but I realize she's got feelings behind those words." Pamela talked about her daughter Nadairee, who was adopted at birth by Pamela's sister. Eight months ago, when Nadairee was 17, she was killed at a party in the Bronx. "It broke my heart that I never told her that I loved her or that I was finally clean," Pamela says. Slowly, seamlessly Nora McCarthy, the writing teacher for the group, starts to comment on the stories the women have written at home and brought in to discuss with her and the other parents.

These women are writers for *Rise*, a magazine, according to its masthead, "by and for parents who have been involved with the New York City child welfare system." Its mission is to help parents advocate for themselves and their children."[1] The magazine began in 2005 as an eight-page newsletter with a circulation of 2,000. By 2011 it had become a 12-page magazine, published three times a year, with a circulation of 14,000. It is read by parents, child welfare professionals, and policy makers throughout the country. The *Los Angeles Times* ran a feature article profiling several of the parents whose stories appeared in *Rise*.[2] About half of the subscribers are in New York City (ACS buys 3,300 copies of each issue) and half are distributed in other states. Most of the readers of the print version of *Rise* are parents who have been embroiled in the child welfare system. *Rise* also publishes an online edition (www.risemagazine.org) in English and in Spanish with new stories posted monthly. Fifteen hundred people visit the *Rise* website each month, and 1,000 people, mostly child welfare professionals, receive articles by email every month.

The driving force behind *Rise* is Nora McCarthy, a journalist with a gift for getting people to feel comfortable enough to tell their painful stories. She had been working at *Represent* magazine, a New York City publication written by youth in foster care, and had been running a workshop to produce stories by parents with children in foster care for *Represent*. In 2005 she created *Rise*, as a project nested in Youth Communication, which publishes *Represent*, but after a year *Rise* became an independent publication with child welfare-involved parents and professionals on both the editorial board and the governing board. Youth Communication became its fiscal sponsor in 2008. Nothing like *Rise* exists elsewhere in the United States, except perhaps small newsletters published by a foster care agency or local parent organization that periodically tells the story of a parent's struggles. Such articles are usually written by a social service professional.

Each issue of *Rise* focuses on a different aspect of child welfare such as staying connected with your kids, addiction and recovery, how families reunite, and how parents have changed the system. Most of the articles are written by parents. One or two articles in each issue are interviews conducted by parents of a professional providing legal advice, social work guidance, or information about a resource that might be useful to a parent with a child in foster care.

Rise's strength is the process by which each article is written. McCarthy meets with each group of parent-writers in an office familiar to the women or where they are living—at CWOP, Voices of Women, the Center for Family Life, Bedford Hills Correctional Facility, or Sing Sing Correctional Facility. The mothers and fathers write their stories during 12 weekly sessions. As Nora describes the process[i]:

> They are a distrustful group, and I don't have clear overlaps with them. I'm white and I never had a child in foster care. I'm clear that they are the experts, but that I do know how to help them write a painful and difficult story. I give a lot of feedback on their drafts. I ask a ton of questions, perhaps 100 for a very short piece, especially at the beginning. I provide empathy and support, and I show them what their strengths are as writers and as people. They feel appreciated.

Writing their stories profoundly affects the writers as well as other parents who read the stories. According to Youshell Williams, who has written several articles for *Rise,* "Nora came to the CWOP parent training I was taking. I didn't want to write at all. But she's pushy. You can't hide from Nora. She has these x-ray eyes."[3]

According to Bevanjae Kelley, a writer for *Rise:*

> Nora came weekly to tell us about writing and to encourage us to write our stories. At first I was a little resistant. I didn't know how to start my story. Once I was encouraged, it took me a little long, but I got my story out.

> Even though I had told my story many times in support groups, writing my story enabled me to think more about my experiences, and it made me feel a sense of relief. My whole initial thought of how everything went down with me was that I felt that I failed as a mother to my own child, my daughter. My daughter was sexually assaulted when she was a teenager, and it changed her life. When she had children, she was unable to care for them and I became the custodial parent to my grandchildren, my daughter's children. Through my

i. The quotes in this section are from interviews with Nora McCarthy by the author on January 29, 2009 and March 7, 2011.

writing, I realized I wasn't really at fault. When I saw my story published, I felt good. I felt that maybe someone wouldn't have the exact story that I had, but maybe they had a similar story and my story could help them. Also, it would help someone else understand me.[4]

McCarthy says, "Writing has been a way for parents to build a narrative of their lives." In the workshops for first-time writers, parents begin slowly and fearfully, leaving out the rich details of their lives and the underlying reasons that explain their paths. After weeks of talking, writing, listening, and hearing McCarthy's respectful but honest questions, parents gradually feel comfortable enough to write the vivid, painful details of their stories, and to begin to feel proud of who they are, what they've come through, and what they've written. Often one parent, at times two, in a writing group is unable to finish her story. The stories of those who finish are moving, first-person accounts of the lives of people who are coming back "from the other side": homeless, addicted, battered by their partners, or abused by the system. Many have neglected their children. A few have abused their children. Almost all have had their children removed from their custody; some had their children taken from them unnecessarily or illegally. They have been investigated and demonized and are struggling to change their lives.

When other parents who are struggling with the child welfare system read the stories, they are moved by their honesty and feel inspired. Jennifer Wade, a social worker with ACS, incorporated stories from *Rise* magazine into parenting classes she teaches to women imprisoned on Riker's Island, the site of New York City jails, on charges related to drugs or domestic violence. She writes:

> When the mothers first came to the class, they acted negatively. They'd say, "I have to do this because the judge said so." Many of them didn't want to be there. At graduation, they were all crying and saying how great it was and how they felt listened to and cared about. The stories are complex but written on a simple, basic level. The biggest impact of the *Rise* stories was that they gave the mothers a sense of hope.

Professionals who read the stories are also affected. Some agencies— family support programs, foster care agencies, drug treatment programs, legal services providers, ACS's Satterwhite Training Academy—use the stories to train their staff and foster parents. According to McCarthy:

> Some workers just read the stories. The stories give them background and help them see parents in a more empathetic light. They already feel sympathy for

the kids, but the kids in foster care will grow to be parents for whom the workers have no sympathy. The stories also create empathy.

The following excerpts from articles in *Rise* show the range of the parents' stories, the difficulties of their lives, and the changes they have made.

Erica Harrigan describes her depression and need for help:[5]

When I found out I was expecting, I didn't feel like I was mentally ready to care for a baby. I had just aged out of foster care and was only beginning to learn how to handle life without the system. I also have a mood disorder and I wasn't taking my medication on a regular basis. I'd seen stories on the news about mentally ill mothers harming their children and I was afraid that I might end up on the news too.

My boyfriend, Michael, and I both grew up in foster care. We hoped to give our baby all the things we longed for—a stable home and a loving mother and father to guide her and help her with whatever she might need. So during my pregnancy, I took many steps to set up a safe home for our child. I got a referral to speak with a therapist who is experienced in supporting mothers. She talked with me about how to build the connection between mother and child. She said that breastfeeding is the best way to bond. I thought, "She is crazy!" I thought breastfeeding was gross until I learned that breast milk is the best milk for a baby. I also started attending parenting classes and support groups for first-time mothers. I learned mother-to-be tools, like how to bathe a baby, create bedtime routines and set feeding times. I was glad to be armed with the knowledge.

As I hit the sixth month of my pregnancy, I began to catch overwhelming ups and downs. I tend to melt down when things don't go as planned. At those times, I walked myself to the pysch ER. I was losing my mind slowly. After about five hospital visits in a month, the doctors suggested I seek more treatment. I talked it over with the hospital's social worker, and she suggested I sign up for day treatment. I had my doubts, but I agreed to take a 3-day trial. I found out that I felt safe and secure there. In the morning I had 45 minutes of counseling with a therapist I came to adore, and after that I had groups. I learned more about coping when things don't go my way. Usually I don't stick with treatment because I don't think it will work, or I find it overwhelming. My therapists are mostly interns and I get a new one just as I begin to trust the one I had. But this time, I found that my treatment program felt like a family and I love to be in a family setting.

When my baby girl, Emmanuella, came into this world, I loved her from holding her the very first time. That day, Emma made me feel like the happiest person on this earth. Still, the first few weeks after we came home from the hospital, I felt distant and overwhelmed. I was afraid of the tasks of motherhood. Bathing Emma was scary to me, and I was confused about what size diaper to put on her and how often to change her. I didn't want to hold her because I feared I'd drop her. But I soon learned what the therapist meant by bonding with the baby through breast-feeding. Our special connection gave me a good feeling.

Now that Emma is 7 months old, I've learned that so much about motherhood can't be taught, but I'm glad I did so much work to get myself set up to be a mother. It's been challenging for me to care for a baby that needs so much love and attention from me. Many times I feel I need mothering because I didn't have much love or attention growing up. But I've been dealing with it by talking with my therapist. I've found that the more I show love and attention to my baby, the more I feel loved. I worry that if I slip up, Children's Services will come knocking at my door. But I also feel more confident that Emma won't end up growing up like me, habitually feeling starved for attention. I am slowly becoming the kind of mother I longed for.

Rosita Pagan describes how writing for *Rise* affected her:[6]

Writing for *Rise* has given me an opportunity to let go of those angry feelings I felt over the years, and having my stories published gave me a great feeling. I felt proud of myself. I accomplished something positive by writing for *Rise*, something I didn't even know I was capable of—writing for a magazine that can make a difference in people's lives.

Answering the questions was the most difficult part for me. My first few stories, especially, were about painful experiences in my life and my children's lives. Having to put it on paper made me relive it again, at least in my mind. My advice to the new writers for *Rise* is be honest with yourself and give honest answers. It will help you overcome those feelings that you have bottled inside. Remember, parents are probably out there facing the same experiences that you once faced and overcame, and are probably afraid of telling anyone. By writing for *Rise* you could be giving those parents the strength to carry on just like you did.

Latoya Baskerville is a parent who participated in a parent/foster parent workshop that became the basis for a guide book for parents and foster parents to work together:[7]

In fall 2008, *Rise* held a writing workshop for parents and foster parents to write about their experiences with each other. The workshop was a wonderful experience for me. I met other parents whose children were in the child welfare system. One parent actually reunited with her children during our workshop! I also met foster and adoptive parents who were sweet as can be.

We would write and talk for hours. Mainly talk, because we all enjoyed writing, so we would come in with our writing ready to show the editor, Nora. Keep in mind, Nora loved our writing, not our talking. So we would sneak and talk when she wasn't looking and then laugh like schoolchildren. It was a fun-filled adventure.

Our conflicts and differences of opinion were not obvious in the beginning but became evident the more we met with each other. Once we had already established trust and respect, it was safe to disagree with one another. Sometimes our differences of opinion took up our sessions, but we all felt safe and we always came back. We even invited each other to events outside the workshop.

We hope and pray that our writing will enlighten other parents and foster parents and encourage them to work together for the most important people, children in foster care. We also hope child welfare professionals will use our writing for education and training. The stories can help us rethink our beliefs and consider new ways to connect.

***

Rise is still a fragile organization whose budget is only $100,000 a year. McCarthy has adopted her second child from Ethiopia and continues to work part-time as she has since *Rise* began. But the staff has expanded to include journalist and social worker Rachel Blustain and writer Piazadora Footman, and has a strong and helpful governing board composed of leaders in the field who are professionals or parent writers. For the moment, *Rise* is a beacon in New York's child welfare system whose light reaches across the country.

BRIDGE BUILDERS

Highbridge is a South Bronx community literally in the western shadow of Yankee Stadium. It is in one of the poorest congressional district in the United States.[8] In 2002 it had the second-highest rate of placement of children in foster care of any neighborhood in New York City. It was here that a coalition of foundations chose to create a new model of child welfare services called Bridge Builders.[ii] The program was designed to reduce the incidence of abuse and neglect and the rate of unnecessary placement of children into foster care. The plan was that Bridge Builders eventually would be run as a collaboration between residents of the Highbridge community, some of whom had had children in foster care, and social welfare professionals.

Bridge Builders trained parents from the community to reach out to their neighbors and then provide or refer them to services. Poor Latino and black mothers, and a few fathers, who grew up in the South Bronx, some of whom had experienced the pain of the child welfare system, went door-to-door in housing projects, spoke at daycare centers and hospitals, and visited the neighborhood's three elementary schools to offer help to struggling families.

Families received assistance at the Bridge Builders' storefront on 164th Street and Ogden Avenue, near the geographic center of Highbridge. The storefront, unlike most other child welfare programs, was staffed by parents from the community who had experienced the child welfare system. They had changed their lives by doing things like successfully completing a drug treatment program or leaving an abusive partner. They had also received CWOP's 6-month training course in parent advocacy. These local residents were hired by Bridge Builders as family support workers to engage and provide services to struggling families before the families were overwhelmed by their burdens. They visited families' homes when trouble arose and led support groups for parents with children in foster care. A social worker supervised the

---

ii. Aryeh Naier, president of the Open Society Institute (OSI), wanted his foundation to create a significant project in child welfare partly because he had spent time in a residential institution in the United Kingdom when he was a displaced child after World War II. He asked Gara LaMarche, who was at the time head of U.S. Programs for OSI, to develop a project. Gara contacted me (we had met as Revson Fellows). I brought in two other long-time child welfare reformers, John Courtney and Berny Horowitz. We spent about a year designing a new service model and selected Highbridge after considering half a dozen other neighborhoods in the city. We asked Eric Brettschneider from Agenda for Children Tomorrow to bring residents and social service providers in the Highbridge community together to develop a unified proposal that would become the Bridge Builders service model. OSI required that its grant be matched by other foundations. Initially five foundations—the Child Welfare Fund, the FAR Fund, Ira W. DeCamp/JPMorgan, and New York Community Trust—pooled funds to launch Bridge Builders. Over time 15 foundations and ACS joined the donors' collaborative, providing a total of $1 million a year for Bridge Builders for about 5 years. John Courtney and I co-directed Bridge Builders for 8 years before people from Highbridge and the Bronx took over the administration of the program.

family support workers' activities, but most of the assistance and referrals were given by the eight parent advocates (called family support workers) who grew up in the neighborhood. They helped hundreds of people from the community who came to the storefront each month to fax a letter, for help filing a food stamps application, to get their child into an after-school program, for help dealing with child protective services, to get their child out of foster care, or to be trained about their rights in the child welfare system.

When the program was operating at full steam in mid-2007 eight community agencies were funded by Bridge Builders, which coordinated their services for families in Highbridge. One of these agencies, Bronx Defenders, represented parents in Family Court when their children were going to be put in foster care. For 2 years, a special part of the Bronx Family Court exclusively handled the child placement cases from Highbridge and Community District 4 in which Highbridge is located.[iii] Another agency, Legal Services of New York, represented or advised families about welfare benefits, housing problems, or when a child was in foster care. Among the remaining agencies Alianza Dominicana worked with young children and adolescents in its after school programs, Citizens Advice Bureau (now called Bronx Works) out-stationed a part-time social worker and a community parent in each of Highbridge's three elementary schools to work with families whose children were having trouble at home, Highbridge Community Life Center provided mental health services and job training, and Woodycrest Center on Human Development offered parenting classes.

The goals of the foundations that launched Bridge Builders were, first, to create a collaborative that would reduce abuse, neglect, and unnecessary removal of children from their families. Second, the foundations wanted to create a collaborative that would be administered by the community it served. And third, the foundations eventually wanted to obtain government money to run Bridge Builders, because the foundations were unable to do so in perpetuity.

Bridge Builders met the first goals but received only partial government support for its work. Inadequate funding, along with the difficulties of community members administering a complex organization, means that at present Bridge Builders faces an uncertain future.

Regarding the first goal—reducing abuse, neglect, and foster care placement—Bridge Builders was evaluated every year from 2004 to 2009 by

iii. New York City is divided into 59 community districts. The Bronx has 12 districts; Community District #4 is in the southwest Bronx.

the Chapin Hall Center for Children at the University of Chicago. The evaluation of 2008 was encouraging:

> The data suggest that in the fourth year of the Project, Highbridge begins to stand out from the comparison sites in several ways. Highbridge experienced an unadjusted decline in the number and rate of maltreatment reports and in the indication of those reports that was ahead of what was seen in the other sites. When averaging across the pre-project years and across the Project years, Highbridge also saw the higher rates of children exiting care to family among all the sites.[9]

The evaluation of 2009 was even more encouraging:

> In particular, over the past 3 years, the relative [child maltreatment] rate in Highbridge has been below the average of the comparison sites. In addition, as in the case of maltreatment reports, the average within year relative rates for the past 3 years show that placement is now less common in Highbridge...[10]

According to Dr. Fred Wulczyn, the lead evaluator, "Highbridge is at the vortex of where New York City and elsewhere are trying to take child welfare."[11]

The second goal was to have members of the Highbridge community administer the collaborative. This goal was based on the belief that if the people served by a program help design it and work in it, the program would more likely meet the needs of the people it served than if outsiders ran the program. Certainly people with particular skills—lawyers, social workers, counselors, to cite a few examples—would work in the program to provide expertise, but the intention was for people from the community to have a strong say in shaping the content and direction of the program and to work directly with families.

At the beginning, the foundations that launched Bridge Builders and the staff they paid to design and supervise the program, primarily Courtney and me, had the dominant role in shaping the organization. Courtney focused on program design and management; I zeroed in on fundraising and the transition to community administration. During the start-up years, a steering committee composed of community service providers and residents was created to oversee Bridge Builders. The foundations, Courtney, and I still had the primary say on funding decisions, but the steering committee modified and ratified our recommendations.

After about 5 years, when Bridge Builders had become a well-functioning service program with an effective administration, its leadership created a

4-year transition plan under which community members, service providers, and technical experts would gradually assume the administration of Bridge Builders. As of 2011, Bridge Builders was governed by an 11-member interim board of directors composed of Highbridge residents, service providers in Community District 4, and individuals with skills or access to resources that could be helpful to Bridge Builders. The executive director of the program, Joe Jenkins, is an indefatigable social worker who is both a black man and a Bronx resident. He is trusted by the parents from the neighborhood as well as the service providers in the collaborative.

Community-based governance, however, is not easy. Board and committee meetings are at times tedious, with community members talking at length about unclear ideas or seemingly extraneous information that are, nonetheless, important to them. Decisions are slow in coming because of the need to reach consensus among community members, service providers, and social welfare policy wonks. But a strong collaborative has been created in which members of the Highbridge community feel listened to and involved in running an organization that serves them, their families, and their neighbors. The foundations that originally approved the annual budget and grants to each service provider in the collaborative now operate as an advisory board and do not vote on the annual budget or grants to partner agencies.

The third goal of Bridge Builders was to have government provide the lion's share of money for the organization. Foundations would provide supplemental funding rather than the core support they provided to launch the organization. It has been a long, slow, and, as of 2012, incomplete journey toward government financing of Bridge Builders. As a result, the collaborative's budget was reduced from $1 million per annum, which it maintained for about 5 years through fiscal year 2008, to $420,000 for the fiscal year beginning July 2011. In 2012 its budget is likely to again be reduced by half.

ACS Funding of Bridge Builders

The story of ACS's coolness toward Bridge Builders under Commissioner Scoppetta, its in-kind support during Commissioner Bell's tenure, its direct funding under Commissioner Mattingly, and finally the decreasing attention of government, also under Mattingly, because of the fiscal crisis and ACS's shifting priorities at the end of the first decade of the twenty-first century, is illustrative of the difficulties inherent in parent- and community-led organizations collaborating with the city.

Bridge Builders was taking shape in 2001 toward the end of Commissioner Scoppetta's tenure. During Scoppetta's last weeks in office, John Courtney, Berny Horowitz, and I met with him to encourage ACS's involvement in Bridge Builders. During much of his time as commissioner we had battled with him and ACS. Courtney had been chairman of the board of CWOP, which Scoppetta had declared off limits to ACS. I had participated in the Thanksgiving Day demonstration at his house and had underwritten, through the Child Welfare Fund, the *Marisol v. Giuliani* lawsuit against the city's child welfare system. But toward the end of his tenure at ACS, largely through the influence of the Special Child Welfare Advisory Panel, set up as the centerpiece of the *Marisol* settlement to assist with reforming the city's child welfare system, Scoppetta became more receptive to Bridge Builders' approach and more willing to talk to us.

For our part, we began Bridge Builders without involving ACS, which we had seen as too aggressive in removing children from their homes. In time, we realized that without ACS's support and funding, Bridge Builders would not survive. We asked for a meeting with Scoppetta to discuss Bridge Builders, which he agreed to. The December 2001 meeting with him was encouraging. At one point, when his wife called on his private phone, he said to her, "I'm meeting with my new friends." He made no commitment to support Bridge Builders, but the door was open for further discussion.

He left office soon after the meeting and became New York City's Fire Commissioner. He was replaced at ACS by Bell, whose focus on reducing the number of children who needed to be put in foster care was consistent with Bridge Builders' view. The first steps in the collaboration between ACS and Bridge Builders included visits by Madeline Duran, the deputy director of the ACS Bronx field office, to the storefront to see Bridge Builders in action and her attendance at the organization's steering committee meetings. Bridge Builders' staff members also met with staffers in the ASC Bronx field office to develop protocols about when and how Bridge Builders would refer families to ACS.

After this groundwork had been laid and as trust between ACS and Bridge Builders slowly developed, in April 2004 Bell agreed that ACS would become a member of the donors' collaborative that funded and oversaw Bridge Builders. Although ACS did not yet provide direct financial support, it provided other valuable assistance. Deputy Commissioner for Community and Intergovernmental Relations Anne Williams Isom became the ACS representative to the donors' collaborative. Her enthusiastic support of the Bridge Builders' model of parent involvement was valuable in educating Bell and other ACS personnel about the program's merits, its benefits for families, and the good will it was creating for ACS.

Whereas families in Highbridge had previously feared ACS and resented its presence in their lives, parents from the neighborhood now worked closely with ACS to preserve families and no longer badmouthed ACS for taking children needlessly. Soon parents who worked for Bridge Builders would sing the praises of ACS, especially its senior policy staff members, for helping families and respecting parents.

From 2004 to 2007 ACS's support for Bridge Builders was in-kind rather than the direct funding that Bridge Builders sought. ACS's contributions were nonetheless crucial. It conducted special biannual data analyses for the three census tracts in which Bridge Builders operated; this allowed the program to determine the blocks and buildings that had the highest rates of abuse and neglect reported and the highest rates of children placed in foster care. This information helped Bridge Builders target its resources on the streets with the greatest need. Staffers in the ACS Bronx Field Office also worked closely with Bridge Builders to develop special relationships that would reduce the need for removal of children from their homes. For example, before calling in a report of neglect to the state central registry, a Bridge Builders' staff person would unofficially notify the ACS Bronx Field Office that a family was having trouble, that someone would call in a report of neglect, but that we had a network of social service supports and people available to help so that the child would be safe at home and would not have to be removed.

The most important in-kind contribution was Francis Ayuso, the ACS neighborhood-based service coordinator who had been working as a community liaison for Deputy Commissioner Isom. Isom assigned Ayuso to work half-time as the field coordinator of Bridge Builders. He was a skilled community organizer from Belize who had a gift for working with grassroots people from poor neighborhoods. He brought disparate members of the Highbridge community together and kept ACS informed about the strides Bridge Builders was making to empower parents, preserve families, and collaborate with ACS.

After Bell left office in 2004, his successor, Mattingly, increased ACS's role at Bridge Builders. The first visit he made to a neighborhood meeting as commissioner was at Bridge Builders. Afterward he said, "I think Bridge Builders is a perfect example of how a commitment to neighborhood-based services can lead to better services and outcomes."[12] In 2007 ACS created the Community Partnership Initiative (CPI), modeled on Bridge Builders, which funded three community collaboratives, including Bridge Builders.[iv] These organizations were created in community districts with

iv. The following year the number of CPIs increased from 3 to 11.

the highest rates of child abuse and neglect in the city. These collaboratives were designed to allow communities to have a greater say in how child welfare services are provided and to link child welfare agencies with other services, such as child care and Head Start, to find foster homes in the neighborhood and to increase visiting between children in foster care and their parents.

The $150,000 ACS provided to Bridge Builders annually beginning in 2007 caused a complication. To receive the ACS money, Bridge Builders had to agree to carry out its CPI activities not just in the three census tracts in one corner of Community District 4 where Bridge Builders worked but in all 18 census tracts in the district. The geographic expansion with limited funding diluted Bridge Builders' impact in the small area that Chapin Hall was evaluating.

The commitment from ACS was small relative to Bridge Builders' $1 million a year in foundation support. In early 2008, ACS tentatively agreed that it would double its funding to Bridge Builders and to the 10 other community collaboratives. But within 6 months the financial crisis struck, reducing ACS's discretionary funds and eliminating the proposed expansion of financial support to Bridge Builders. At the same time, the foundation funding to Bridge Builders had decreased in anticipation of increased government allocations, while Bridge Builders was increasingly serving families from all across Community District 4. By 2010 Bridge Builders' funding had decreased to just about half its original $1 million from foundations.[v] The programs it provided, the partners it funded, and the number of families it served all decreased proportionately.

As of the beginning of 2011, Bridge Builders continued to operate as a collaboration among the community, foundations, and providers, but it supported only one service program, CWOP, rather than the eight service providers it had funded. CWOP was being paid to provide a parent advocate and social work supervisor to staff the storefront. Bronx Defenders, which had been funded by Bridge Builders to represent parents in Family Court when their children are about to be removed from the home, is now underwritten by the Mayor's Office of the Criminal Justice Coordinator to represent half of all parents who appear at such proceedings in Bronx Family Court. Bronx Defenders has been able to use these resources to represent all parents from Highbridge in Family Court when a child is about to be removed.

---

v. In fiscal year 2010 Bridge Builders received only $350,000 from foundations, $150,000 from ACS, and $60,000 from the New York State Office of Children and Family Services as a subcontractor on a kinship foster care project overseen by Children's Village, a large foster care agency.

Other programs that were part of Bridge Builders now do less. For example, Bronx Works no longer outstations a social worker in any of the three elementary schools in Highbridge. The separate Bronx Court Part for Highbridge families ended when the Administrative Judge Richardson transferred to Manhattan.

Nevertheless, Bridge Builders has led policy makers and program staff members throughout the city to respect the ability of people from low-income communities to collaborate with professionals in running social service programs. According to Dale Joseph, assistant commissioner of ACS for community partnership and advocacy: "The Bridge Builders/ Highbridge Community Partnership has been at the center of many innovative community led strategies.... We are encouraged by this success."[13]

But Bridge Builders is vulnerable because of inadequate financial support. Its budget continued to decrease significantly and in 2012 it planned to create a management agreement with Children's Village whereby the large foster care agency would provide management and fundraising support in an attempt to preserve Bridge Builders and its community approach to services. Many outstanding service programs that began as demonstration projects have folded because they were not able to secure long-term government funding. After 10 years of operation, with very positive annual evaluations, Bridge Builders has proven its effectiveness but may not survive because of lack of money.

***

VOICES OF WOMEN ORGANIZING PROJECT

Susan Lob is a small woman in her 50s who speaks in a calm, slow voice that is well-suited to mediating the volatile, problematic lives of domestic violence survivors. In 2000 she created the Voices of Women Organizing Project, known as VOW. It became the only organization in New York City and among the first in the nation to provide survivors of domestic violence with mutual support and a pathway to collective action to reform the legal and service systems on which they rely. Though not a victim of domestic violence, Lob began working with domestic violence survivors through her efforts in the women's movement, tenant organizing, and welfare rights campaigns. She describes the anger that led her to create VOW:

> In 2000 I was part of a citywide domestic violence coalition and wanted to organize a demonstration against ACS because of its policy of removing children of domestic violence survivors. It was the years of the Giuliani administration,

and people were afraid to come to the demonstration. I was so pissed off I got a planning grant from the Child Welfare Fund and created VOW.[14]

In its early years, VOW had a membership of 50 to 60 grassroots women who had been battered; many of whom had their children taken from them and placed in foster care. A majority of the women were black—African-American or Caribbean—from poor and lower working-class backgrounds. The group also included some white or middle-class women and a few from the upper class.

VOW's mission is "to support and give voice to survivors of domestic violence so that they can organize to influence, change and improve the many systems battered women and their children rely on for safety, assistance and justice."[15]

VOW's most active and vibrant period lasted until about 2008. At that time, and continuing today, VOW trained women to be leaders and organizers and held monthly support groups to help its members heal from the trauma of domestic violence. Once trained through VOW's six-session course called SOUL (School for Organizing, Unity, and Leadership), these women worked in and led campaigns to reform elements of the child welfare system, Family Court, and housing programs that had so much influence on the lives of domestic violence survivors.

One successful child welfare campaign changed the way reports of child abuse and neglect are recorded. For decades child protective service cases were routinely filed in the name of the mother rather than in the name of the perpetrator. When a child was abused and the mother battered, reporting the case in the mothers' name turned the victim into the perpetrator. Members of VOW pressed the City Council Welfare Committee to hold hearings on the problem and testified. Afterward, ACS sent a bulletin to its staff telling them to implement a new reporting policy, listing the case in the perpetrator's name, not the mother's name.[16] Though policy changed, practice down the line was slow to catch up. Five years later there were still situations in which the mother was a victim of domestic violence, but the abuse report was filed in her name, not in the name of the perpetrator.[17]

VOW also focused on Family Court where battered women's custody disputes are handled and foster care and other child welfare decisions are made.[vi] The survivors of domestic violence complained that Family Court

---

vi. In 2006, more than 210,000 filings and depositions were heard by only 47 judges in New York City Family Court. The cases involved child support (55%), custody/visitation (26.5%), family offenses, i.e., domestic violence (7.5%), child protective proceedings (6.5%), and other issues (4.5%).

further abused them after they had been abused by their partners. As one VOW member put it, "Each time I appeared in court, the system reinforced his dominance over me by preserving his 'parental' rights without regard to my safety. I felt totally undermined by the court."[18]

To address shortcomings of Family Court, VOW organized the Battered Mothers' Justice Campaign and met in 2004 with Judge Joseph M. Lauria, then the chief administrator of the Family Court. According to Lob, after the meeting with the judge:

> Little changed. So we organized a coalition of 11 groups and 100 people, including several elected officials, to demonstrate with us outside of Manhattan Family Court. Demonstrations make the system want to negotiate.[19]

The demonstration took place on May 6, 2005, with Manhattan Borough President C. Virginia Fields presenting VOW's demands to reform the Family Court system. Two city council members, Margareta Lopez and Charles Barron, also spoke, pressing Family Court to protect battered women.

After the demonstration, VOW conducted a research project, *Justice Denied: How Family Courts in NYC Endanger Battered Women and Children,* in connection with the Human Rights Project of the Urban Justice Center. The project's data gatherers, who themselves were survivors of domestic violence and members of VOW, interviewed 75 women who had been victims of domestic violence about their experiences in New York City Family Court. The report documented numerous problems such as overburdened judges delaying the judicial process, court procedures in violation of due process (e.g., frequent ex-parte communication between the father's lawyer and the judge, or the mother's witnesses not being allowed to testify), domestic violence not being taken seriously by the judge, and the mother's lawyer not understanding issues of domestic violence. The report concluded:

> Each of these problems alone is of concern. In combination, they create a system described by the women we interviewed as an "Alice in Wonderland" world where justice is turned on its head, and decisions are not based on logic or fairness. The Family Court should be open to scrutiny, and yet decisions that destroy families routinely happen behind closed doors.[20]

The goal of the report and of the Battered Mothers' Justice Campaign in general was to "build a case for a large-scale investigation into Family Court's failure to protect battered mothers and children and to call for more transparency and oversight."[21] The New York *Daily News* reported that "...the charges made by the report have to be taken very seriously."[22] According to Lob, "We got a lot of attention from the report, including from Judge Lauria, who met with us [again]. He sent the report to all Family Court judges, but they are trying not to take responsibility for the problems. We keep pushing."[23]

The following year, 2009, Lauria was replaced by Edwina Richardson-Mendelson as administrative judge for New York City Family Court. Richardson-Mendelson, who had been counsel at Sanctuary for Families, a shelter for survivors of domestic violence, was more sympathetic to the concerns of domestic violence survivors.

VOW's work with the survivors of domestic violence has not been easy. As Lob said in 2008:

> It's really hard work organizing parents. A lot of attention needs to be paid to how you build trust among people, how you build unity. By definition everybody in the organization is somebody who has been betrayed by the people closest to them. So trust issues are difficult. People get their feelings hurt easily. Learning how to disagree respectfully needs to happen since people had the shit beat out of them when they disagreed. To do that across class and race is really challenging. This is the stuff that makes me go home crying at night. Organizing parents is the only strategy that can make a difference, but it takes a toll.[24]

Early the following year Lob resigned as executive director of VOW. She felt proud of what she had accomplished but was burned out from the difficulty of the work, the slow pace of change, and the endless struggle of raising funds to keep VOW afloat. She went to Columbia University's School of Social Work to teach community organizing. Her replacement, Raquel Singh, who began as executive director of VOW in May 2009, the same month that Richardson-Mendelson was appointed, is a fundraiser with no experience as an organizer. In fact, at the interview for the job she said she didn't know the term community organizing.[25] She was selected because of her ability to strengthen the finances, administration, and strategic planning of VOW.

Under Singh's leadership VOW's goals remained the same, though it did shift its emphasis from agitating outside the child welfare system and other systems that affect survivors of domestic violence to working within the systems, by providing self-help to survivors and increasing public awareness of their plight. According to Singh, "My goal is to build positive relationships and to make change that way."[26] By 2011 VOW had expanded its membership to 120 (including survivors, witnesses of domestic violence, and friends of survivors). Its board of directors has five members; three are survivors of domestic violence.

Under Singh's leadership, VOW's campaign to reform Family Court shifted from demonstrations and research-based attacks to increasing judges' awareness of domestic violence. VOW had hoped to train judges on matters involving domestic violence, but Richardson-Mendelson chose to use others to do the training without VOW's participation. VOW is also trying to improve the court's sensitivity to issues of domestic violence in custody cases and orders of protection. As part of that effort VOW wanted posters hung in Family Court listing the rights of survivors, but the court declined to have the posters hung. VOW was also developing a Court Watch Program, under which volunteers would sit in on Family Court proceedings to document whether court proceedings are fair. That campaign has been in the works for more than a year with court watchers to begin in the fall of 2012.[27]

VOW also has undertaken a campaign to reform ACS—to reduce the number of false and malicious reports against mothers that are made and investigated, one of the many problems with the abuse and neglect reporting system. Although state law requires that the state record the name of the person who reports a case of abuse or neglect to the State Central Registry, the state's Office of Children and Family Services (OCFS), which administers the Registry, permits anonymous reporting and does not track either who the reporter is or how often he or she has called in a report to the Central Registry.[vii] The law also prevents ACS from differentiating between reports that might be serious and those that are likely to be inconsequential, spurious, or malicious. If a landlord wants to dislodge a troublesome tenant, he can repeatedly and anonymously report that the woman is abusing her child. If an angry former boyfriend has anonymously and falsely reported a dozen times that his former girlfriend has neglected her child, ACS is required by law to investigate his next anonymous report. One example among thousands that occur each year is that of Ms. Z, who has been investigated by the city's child protective services over 50 times because of false reports filed by her former batterer.[28] One researcher estimates that between

vii. Martin Guggenheim, professor of law at New York University School of Law, and his students found that New York State law stipulates that the name of the person reporting a child protection allegation "shall" be recorded, thus prohibiting anonymous reporting. The person mentioned in the report, however, does not have a right to know who made the report. [Professor Martin Guggenheim, NYU School of Law, personal communication, January 6, 2010.]

5% and 10% of unfounded reports throughout the nation are made maliciously.[29] The current arrangement wastes public resources investigating spurious or inconsequential matters and results in countless violations of families' privacy, causing endless and overwhelming disruptions in their lives.

In 2009 VOW formed a coalition of domestic violence and child welfare groups to discourage false and/or malicious reporting. One goal was for ACS to create a method for tracking and reporting incidents of malicious reports, for example, by identifying situations in which more than 10 reports from the same reporter are found not to be confirmed abuse or neglect. VOW, however, has shifted its focus away from policy change to behavioral change. VOW organized a speak-out in early 2012 for ACS staff, with presentations by child survivors of malicious reports—children who have lived in a family in which their mother was falsely reported for abuse or neglect and was investigated by child protective services. The speak-out led to a series of trainings led by VOW to ACS staff on domestic violence and the effects of malicious reporting.[30]

VOW at its height enabled survivors of domestic violence to shine a light on the way battered women have been mistreated by the courts and by the child welfare system, contributing other important voices to the movement of parents and their allies to reform the child welfare system. VOW has made the difficult transition from the founding executive director to another and less combative successor. As VOW moved away from agitation and demonstrations toward an inside strategy of collaboration and education, it makes its voice heard through training and education. Its impact for the moment is diminished, though its new strategy is just being implemented by its new leadership. As Lob described VOW's work, "We are little specs swatting at a big system. It's an important role, but we can't be the only ones out there."[31]

***

PEOPLE UNITED FOR CHILDREN

Sharonne Salaam is a tall, stunning black woman who always keeps her head covered. She was born in Alabama and moved to Central Harlem as part of the great black migration north. She received a bachelor's degree from Empire State College and then an associate in applied science degree from the Fashion Institute of Technology.[32] Life was fairly routine during the 14 years she worked in the fashion industry and raised three children. "I was a regular person trying to make ends meet."

On April 19, 1989 her life was transformed. Her 15-year-old son Yusef was arrested along with three black and one Latino friends for the assault and rape in Central Park of a 28-year-old white female investment banker who became known as the Central Park Jogger. The boys charged in the attack were all convicted and spent a combined total of 44 years in prison. Yusef was imprisoned for nearly 7 years. He and the other boys were freed after Manhattan District Attorney Robert Morgenthau in 2002 recommended vacating their convictions after Matias Reyes, convicted for another rape, confessed to the attack on the Central Park Jogger, and DNA evidence confirmed his guilt.[33]

Throughout Yusef's ordeal, Sharonne maintained his innocence and fought for his release and exoneration. She became an activist working on his behalf and that of other youth incarcerated in New York State. In 1992 she began the process of incorporating an organization called People United for Children that began with the goal of helping youth incarcerated in New York's juvenile justice system. PUC in its early phase was composed of a group of volunteers who prepared and brought home-cooked meals to the imprisoned youth, brought in speakers and created educational programs for them, and helped prepare them for life after prison. According to Sharonne:

> When we started, so few people visited kids in juvenile facilities, we could bring visitors any time we wanted. We brought other parents to visit their children. So many people were coming, the facilities set up specific hours and days for people to visit. The change was a good thing.[34]

PUC also worked on a broader level to reform the practices is juvenile justice facilities, where, for example, children at the time could be kept in isolation 23 hours a day. "We worked to change that policy, decreasing the time kids could be kept in isolation to 7 hours maximum, not the whole day," says Salaam.[35]

Salaam soon realized, however, that problems for children in the juvenile justice system begin farther upstream in the child welfare system, which she saw as a main feeder for the juvenile justice system.[viii] She says that PUC "made the decision to take the preventive approach by stopping

viii. Nearly half the boys and two-thirds of the girls released from juvenile correctional facilities in the early 1990s were previously involved with child protection, preventive services, or foster care, according to a study by the New York State Office of Children and Family Services. Practitioners estimate these numbers are similar today. ["A Need for Correction: Reforming New York's Juvenile Justice System," *Child Welfare Watch* 18 (Fall 2009): 2.]

the cycle of children first entering the foster care system...."[36] In the mid-1990s PUC shifted its focus to reforming child welfare. By 1996 PUC had become, as Salaam later accurately wrote, "the Harlem community's best-informed advocates for foster care children."[37]

At its height in the late 1990s and early 2000s, PUC was active in many different aspects of child welfare reform: helping individual families, providing parenting classes, organizing demonstrations, holding speak-outs (in which people from a community talk about their problems with the child welfare system), lobbying legislators, meeting with New York Foundling Hospital (while the courageous though short-termed Michael Garber was executive director) to encourage foster care agencies to hire more parents with child-welfare experience, sitting on the advisory board of the *Child Welfare Watch*, and bringing a class action law suit against ACS for removing black children from their homes without adequate investigations. At the time, it was the most militant, outspoken grassroots organization pressing for dramatic changes in child welfare, and it succeeded in pushing the center of debate to the left.

PUC held weekly support group meetings, led by professionals and volunteers, to assist families negotiating the child welfare system and to teach them how to avoid having their children taken from them. PUC also partnered with Harlem Hospital to provide stress management to families. Salaam and volunteers went to court appearances with parents to provide support and guidance, and they went to families' homes as witnesses and allies when ACS scheduled a visit to investigate a family.

They organized speak-outs in the black community that were attended by hundreds of people who complained about abuse by ACS and child welfare agencies. In 2004 alone, PUC held seven large forums—including one at the Emanuel AME Church in Central Harlem. The meeting had the feel of civil rights gatherings in the segregated South in the 1960s, with people standing one at a time in the pews to testify to the treatment they had received at the hands of the child welfare system. They were surrounded by a hundred other seated black mothers and fathers, using hand-held fans to cool themselves, many prepared to tell a painful story about what was deemed a racist system that abused them and their families. The audience responded with words of acknowledgment and rising anger, putting ACS on notice that it was being watched by angry parents who were beginning to meet and work together.

PUC organized a Christmas Day demonstration at St. Patrick's Cathedral, protesting the deaths of several children in Catholic foster care agencies. On Thanksgiving Day it organized a picket and candlelight vigil outside the apartment building on Central Park West where Commissioner

Scoppetta lived, and another on Mother's Day protesting what were seen by them as illegal removals of children by ACS. And they regularly demonstrated outside ACS's offices at 150 Williams Street. Although the demonstrations were often small, generally numbering fewer than 50 people, the demonstrations contributed to an environment in which ACS and, to a lesser extent, the voluntary agencies became aware that parents were organizing, angry, and should be listened to.

PUC also administered the Family Unity Awards. For 6 years around Christmas time it organized a ceremony at the National Black Theater in Harlem that each year provided a plaque and $1,000 to about 15 parents who had overcome arduous difficulties to be reunited with their children. The awards ceremony, underwritten by the Child Welfare Fund, was intended to humanize parents whose children had been in foster care and to celebrate their achievements. Each year the ceremony was attended by hundreds of people from Harlem and the larger child welfare community, including a guest appearance by U.S. Representative Charles Rangel of Harlem in 2007.

Four of the award winners from 2001 and 2004 give a sense of the parents whose fortitude was recognized:[38]

- Fatmata Fornah emigrated from Sierra Leone in 1997 to escape that country's civil war. Shortly after becoming pregnant, her husband left her. Confused and alone in a strange land, she took out her anger on her children who were removed and placed in foster care. After much suffering and personal change, she was reunited with her three daughters.
- Rhonda Taylor-Becton overcame a history of addiction, crime, and imprisonment to regain custody of her three children. She had been clean and sober since November 4, 1994.
- Audra Black overcame drug addiction that began at age 15, a term in prison, homelessness, and the loss of the grandmother who raised her. After her children were removed from her custody, she changed her life with the help of Hour Children, a half-way house for mothers leaving prison. Black wrote, "While there are many things I regret about my past life, the thing that hurts most is that my grandmother couldn't see how far I've come."
- Yadira Caicedo's first born son was wrongfully put in foster care by ACS following an accidental injury. The child welfare agency responsible for her case would not return her son because her residence was in a basement apartment that the agency determined was unsuitable for children. Her second son was also removed because she and her husband were still living in the same apartment. In October 2003 Caicedo

and her husband regained custody of their two sons immediately after moving into the Dorothy Day Apartments in West Harlem, a supportive living facility, which provided a good apartment and an array of social services.

In 1999, while Rudolph Giuliani was mayor, PUC, in collaboration with the Center for Law and Social Justice, brought a class action lawsuit against New York City alleging that ACS removed black children from their families "without a proper investigation as to whether their children will be in danger if they remain in the custody of their parents." ACS's practices, the suit charged, violated the 4th Amendment of the U.S. Constitution, which prohibits unreasonable searches and seizures. Fifteen black parents who alleged that their children were removed illegally were named plaintiffs.[39]

The lawsuit was filed at the height of ACS's policy of removing children from their families if there was any doubt about the child's safety. By the time the court approved a settlement of the case in 2005 ACS had made many of the changes sought by PUC. The settlement had reinforcing but not ground breaking impact on the changes ACS was making in the child welfare system. The most important element was that ACS would expand its family team conferences (at which decisions are made about the future of a child in foster care) and preplacement child safety conferences (at which a decision is made whether or not to remove a child who may be in imminent danger from his or her family). The settlement reinforced what ACS had already begun—using child safety conferences and family team conferences to make decisions about the removal of a child from his or her home and continued placement in foster care. These conferences are now a routine part of the ACS decision-making process, though their impact has not been fully assessed.

Other provisions of the settlement affirmed ACS's use of its Office of Advocacy to ensure that class members in the future could file complaints and receive prompt responses, and obtain information about their rights. The plaintiffs each received between $10,000 and $15,000 from the city and PUC received $10,000 to provide educational programs, quite modest amounts given the magnitude of the violations that the lawsuit alleged.[40] Salaam is not sure of the lawsuit's impact: "Did we win that ACS would no longer remove children without investigating? I don't know. Since they write the [child protective] reports, they can write anything they want. There have been cases since where people came to us with kids removed without an investigation."[41]

The settlement agreement became contentious, though the conflict was not between the city and the plaintiffs, but among some of the plaintiffs and other members of the class who objected to the settlement. Several of the named plaintiffs, other unnamed members of the class, and Roland Bini, executive director of Parents In Action (PIA), claimed that there was not adequate notice about the settlement, that the terms of the settlement did not solve enough of the problems of the child welfare system, that the illegal actions by ACS against individual plaintiffs were neither solved nor did they receive adequate financial compensation, and that the primary beneficiary of the settlement was the lawyer for the plaintiffs. Bini circulated a letter on the internet that charged that the settlement was a "Betrayal to the Reparations Movement, Betrayal to Black Families; Betrayal to the Anti-Slavery Movement. All for the Love of Money."[42] Conchita Jones, one of the named plaintiffs, withdrew from the class. Salaam from PUC contends that Bini was upset because the law suit did not include Latinos[ix] and feels his actions sabotaged the lawsuit and diminished its impact and the financial settlement.[43] The settlement was approved despite Bini's objections.[44]

The conflict among the plaintiffs and the attack by PIA against PUC and its lawsuit, while not unique among the advocates who were working to reform the child welfare system, was unusual. During the 15 years that parents and advocates had been working to reform the city's child welfare system, almost all attacks and criticisms by parents and their advocates were directed against ACS and the voluntary agencies. Relative harmony within the parent advocacy community, despite significant differences in strategies, tactics, and even goals, contributed to the effectiveness of the parents' movement.

For several years PUC had an impact on child welfare debate through its militancy, Salaam's broad and ceaseless activity, and her connections to black city councilmen and state legislators. She says:

> We put out an awareness that people weren't satisfied with the way things were going. We worked for certain changes and things got better for everyone. And more people got involved in change and [defining] what change should be. Before that, people were staying under the radar.[45]

She also recognizes that her militancy made other organizations demand more from ACS and made the positions of moderate groups more acceptable to ACS. The extremes define the center, and PUC was on the far end of the spectrum. Salaam says, "We were able to push CWOP, and they were

---

ix. Two Latinos were originally part of the lawsuit but dropped out before the settlement was reached.

able to seek out more. People United for Children was a group that people could point to as the antagonistic entity."[46]

But PUC was never able or interested in building a strong organization, even with technical assistance from Community Resource Exchange (CRE), a group that assists struggling nonprofits to strengthen their administration. At its height PUC was primarily staffed by Salaam and one or two members of her family. Its annual budget, which never exceeded $150,000, came primarily from foundations and small contributions from individuals. PUC also received some in-kind gifts from people it helped. It never obtained significant government funding. After 2006 its funding almost completely disappeared. With a weak organization and with scant funding from foundations, PUC was unable to survive when Salaam became sick with cancer. It closed its office in 2009.

Salaam continues to fight, despite her illness. At present, she had considered organizing a march to the New York State capital, Albany, during the week before Easter 2012 to promote a law that would provide swift reparations to her son and to men and women imprisoned for crimes they did not commit, but the march did not happen. She is seeking $50 million in restitution for her son and the other boys who wrongly spent a total of 44 years in prison in the Central Park jogger case, though, she says, "We should have asked for $500 million."

Salaam also continues to work in child welfare but from a much diminished platform, with PUC no longer playing the significant role it once did. She works out of the Harlem office of New York State Assemblyman Keith Wright, where she holds meetings on the weekends for 10 or so parents who are having problems with the child welfare system. She periodically holds larger meetings but hasn't organized a demonstration in several years. "We are still an exciting voice," she says. "ACS is now more willing to hear a voice from their partners—the parents—but they do not always take that voice seriously."

***

Four other groups were part of the movement of parents reforming the child welfare system in New York City. Three of them folded: Birth Fathers Support Network, the Child Welfare Action Center, and Concerned Citizens for Family Preservation. The fourth, Parents In Action, dramatically changed its strategy.

Birth Fathers Support Network was founded in the early 2000s by three fathers who had been in prison and/or had lost their children to the foster care system. They wanted to reconnect with their children and help other fathers do the same. For a brief moment they energized the child welfare community, including commissioner Bell, who spoke eloquently on their behalf at the opening of their office in the south Bronx in 2003. The organization folded within 3 years of its founding because the administrative and financial requirements to run an organization were beyond the experience of the founders.

A second group that foundered after a few years was the Child Welfare Action Center, located at the Center for Law and Social Justice at Medgar Evers College in Brooklyn. The Action Center was set up by the Child Welfare Fund to coordinate activist child welfare organizations that the Fund supported across the city—parent groups, youth groups, grassroots groups, and well-established organizations. The Action Center's agenda was similarly broad. As the lead representative of the Child Welfare Fund, I was overly directive and in too much of a hurry to let the organization evolve in ways that would be useful to the advocacy community. Because the organization lacked a clear, organically developed direction, the director left and the project to coordinate advocacy efforts collapsed. The absence of an organization that coordinates grassroots parent advocacy has significantly limited the influence of parents.

Concerned Citizens for Family Preservation (CCFP) was the third group that folded. It was created in early 2003 by Folasade Campbell, a black social activist who had served for 6 years on the executive committee of the Staten Island Branch of the NAACP. She wanted a perch from which she could be more supportive of families and more critical of the child welfare practices. Although she was not a parent whose child had been in foster care, she was able to create a membership organization of professionals, activists, and child welfare-affected families. CCFP opened its office in Staten Island, the borough that includes the St. George/Stapleton community district, which in 2010 had 361 children placed in foster care, the highest number of such placements from any community district in the city in that year.[47]

CCFP described itself as "the go-to place on Staten Island for low-income people needing strong advocacy in the child welfare system."[48] It provided individual advocacy to families at child welfare family team conferences and in Family Court, since institutional legal representation for parents has not reached Staten Island.

CCFP was also an activist organization. In 2005, when the mayor's panel on the judiciary did not recommend reappointing Judge Ralph Porzio, who was sympathetic to poor families of color, to the Family Court on Staten Island, CCFP rallied on the steps of Borough Hall. He did not win reelection to the bench. CCFP also brought families to a rally at City Hall in Manhattan supporting the use of preventive services and testified at city council and state assembly hearings on the rights of children and families. These actions did help restore some of the preventive services cuts.

Short on funds and staff and too dependent on Campbell's energy and time, CCFP was not sustainable. In July 2010 she closed CCFP's office. Like Salaam, she continues to fight for child welfare reform but with a smaller voice and little or no organization behind her.

A fourth parent-led activist organization, Parents In Action (PIA), continues to operate, though it has dramatically changed from the time in 2000 it called child welfare a system of "slavery" to its current approach of collaborating with ACS. Bini, the founder of PIA, is an immigrant from Ecuador. In 2000, according to him, he was charged by ACS with medical and educational neglect, because, ACS alleged, he failed to have his 7-year-old son's eyes tested and have him tested for special education classes. He believed his son's problem was lack of English language competency (since Bini, and his former wife from whom he was separated, spoke Spanish to their son), not mental deficiency. He believes he was charged with neglect because he protested against the school's inadequate Spanish-language program and against the lack of input permitted black, Latino, and Bengali parents in his son's school. Regardless of where the truth lies, ACS dropped the charges against him, though his son remained in foster care for 5 months.

How Bini and his son were treated by ACS fueled Bini's anger and led to his creating PIA. In its early years, the organization had almost no budget, and the few individuals connected to it were volunteers. Bini supported himself and the organization with income from his day job designing websites. PIA initially was mostly the swirl of activity around Bini—advocating for individual parents who believed they were mistreated by ACS or by foster care agencies, teaching parenting and advocacy classes, both in Spanish and English, and speaking against ACS at meetings convened by other organizations. At these forums he publicized the injustices committed against individual parents by ACS or by specific foster care agencies. He also organized many small but loud and inflammatory demonstrations against the child welfare and family court systems. As one PIA flyer said:

> Family Court is an institutionalized system of injustice set in place to give an aura of legality to the white collared racketeering criminal enterprise of family destruction and child slave trade.[x] There is no jury or due process in Family Court. Parents only win 2 cases out of 1000 in a 1028 hearing.[49]

x. Malcolm X also referred to the child welfare system as slavery. In his autobiography he describes how the state put his mother in a mental hospital and placed him

PIA organized dozens of street demonstrations against the child welfare system—at Family Court in Queens, at Family Court in Manhattan, at the headquarters of ACS, at the headquarters of Catholic Charities in Manhattan, and at St Vincent's and other foster care agencies. The largest demonstration was at Incarnation Children's Center in Washington Heights in Manhattan, which was attended by several hundred people drawn to the protest because Incarnation had tested HIV medication on children in foster care without parental consent.

PIA organized a demonstration at Mayor Michael Bloomberg's house that would forever change PIA's activities and strategy. Bini had been advocating on behalf of Vanessa James, a mother whose 5-year-old daughter had been placed in foster care, because the mother allegedly had Munchausen's Syndrome by Proxy, a condition in which a parent feigns a child's illness to get attention. "Ms. James is a difficult person, but not a bad mother," said Bini. To protest the child's removal from her mother's custody, he organized a demonstration at Bloomberg's house at 79th Street and Fifth Avenue. Previously PIA demonstrations had attracted little attention. But for this one Bini sent emails inviting members of two militant black organizations that were being monitored by the police to attend the protest. ACS was informed by a police intelligence unit of Bini's connection with these groups. ACS then passed this information to the ACS-funded Community Partnership Initiative in Queens, where Bini was an officer. ACS forced him out of his position.

His dismissal from the Community Partnership, his concern that he would be ostracized by ACS, his awareness that ACS had improved, and perhaps his concern for his own well-being, heightened by the police intelligence investigation, led to an abrupt turnaround in his reform strategy. "For practical purposes we shifted our strategy to work with ACS," Bini says. "We couldn't help people if we didn't."[50] PIA now collaborates extensively with ACS. ACS refers clients to PIA's parenting skills and anger management classes. PIA is also trying to get on the Family Court roster, so judges can refer clients to the organization. They no longer organize demonstrations and they no longer refer to child welfare as slavery. According to Bini, "ACS has changed starting with Bell. It still needs improvement, but it has changed for the good. We need to be the friendly opposition."

in foster care. "We were 'state children,' court wards: (The Judge) had the full say over us. A white man in charge of a black man's children! Nothing but legal, modern slavery—however kindly intentioned...I truly believe that if ever a state social agency destroyed a family, it destroyed ours. We wanted and tried to stay together. Our home didn't have to be destroyed. But the welfare, the courts, and their doctor, gave us the one-two-three punch." [Alex Haley and Malcolm X, *The Autobiography of Malcolm X* (New York: Ballantine Books, 1964): 21.]

All of these groups were part of a broad, vibrant movement of parents and their allies that worked from the mid-1990s to 2011–2012 to reform New York City's child welfare system. Along with CWOP and its allied organizations, these groups helped change the attitude of the child welfare community toward parents who lose their children to foster care, humanized some programs and policies, and pushed the leadership of the child welfare system to remove fewer children and provide more resources to meet the needs and protect the rights of poor parents. These changes and the pressure from these groups contributed to the reduction in the number of children in foster care as discussed in Chapter 7. As ACS and the child welfare system improved, the groups increased their collaboration with ACS and diminished or stopped their agitation, lawsuits, and protests outside the system. The groups that remain, *Rise*, Bridge Builders, Voices of Women, and Parents In Action, collaborate in one way or another with a much improved, much more responsive, ACS. The groups that chose to remain on the outside, that had difficulty raising money, and that did not build a strong organization folded.

All of these groups, both those that folded and those that remain, had a powerful impact that helped compel the child welfare system to be more responsive to the needs of families and to the rights of parents. Now that the two most militant organizations either have closed (People United for Children) or are collaborating with ACS (Parents In Action), as are the other parent-led organizations, there is less external pressure on the child welfare system to change.

One key lesson from the experience of these organizations is that although individuals bring about change, they can take things only so far. Without an organization with structure, staff, funding, and a clearly defined mission, the activities are likely to fizzle. The leaders who generated whirlwinds of activity, but did not simultaneously create strong organizations, burned themselves out, their nominal organizations folded, or they dramatically changed their mission.

CHAPTER 6

Parent Participation across the Country

"New York is on a different planet. It's what others aspire to," says Lisa Paine-Wells, the leader of the Annie. E. Casey Foundation's national Parent Partner initiative.[1] She was comparing the level of involvement and activism of parents who have become embroiled in New York City's child welfare system to the actions of similar parents in other cities across the country. Although parent activism in New York is far ahead of that in other cities, child welfare-affected parents have been working in organizations elsewhere to persuade government and child welfare agencies to let parents have a say in child welfare programs and policy decisions. Parents who have lost custody of their children and then regained it have also been hired by child welfare agencies in more than 20 states to help other parents regain custody of their children. The hiring of such parents by child welfare agencies and the organized, grassroots activity of parents in the child welfare system are unprecedented, though the power of these groups to influence policy is still limited and the number of parents who have a full-throated voice in the child welfare system is still a small percentage of the approximately 230,000 families that have children in foster care.[2] But there is no doubt that parents who believe that they have been mistreated or helped by the child welfare system are beginning to have a collective, albeit mostly local, voice in the child welfare debate.

One exception to the local focus is the work of groups of parents and their allies, both inside and outside government, over the past several years to produce *From Rights to Reality (FRTR)*, which has been called "a plan for parent advocacy in family-centered child welfare reform." In essence it is a national bill of rights for parents entangled in the child welfare system.[i] *From Rights to Reality* consolidates many of the best practices that have helped families have a stronger voice in their own cases and a greater likelihood of raising their children at home safely. It identifies 15 rights for parents, though most parents affected by the child welfare system do not yet have these basic rights. *From Rights to Reality* is designed to unite parents and parent advocacy around a common set of goals.[3]

FROM RIGHTS TO REALITY

15 Rights of Parents Affected by the Child Welfare System

1. I HAVE THE RIGHT TO not lose my child because I'm poor.
2. I HAVE THE RIGHT TO services that will support me in raising my child at home.
3. I HAVE THE RIGHT TO speak for myself and be heard at every step of the child protective services process.
4. I HAVE THE RIGHT TO be informed of my rights.
5. I HAVE THE RIGHT TO a meaningful and fair hearing before my parental rights are limited in any way.
6. I HAVE THE RIGHT TO quality legal representation.
7. I HAVE THE RIGHT TO support from someone who has been in my shoes.
8. I HAVE THE RIGHT TO have my child quickly placed with someone I trust.
9. I HAVE THE RIGHT TO frequent, meaningful contact with my child.
10. I HAVE THE RIGHT TO make decisions about my child's life in care.

i. The initiative to create *From Rights to Reality* was guided by *Rise* magazine in New York City, the Center for the Study of Social Policy in Washington, D.C., the National Coalition for Parent Advocacy in Child Protective Services in Claremont, California, and Parents Anonymous, also in Claremont, California. Fifteen parent/professional advocacy and service organizations in child welfare participated in drafting the rights and contributed stories by mothers and fathers. Several of these organizations are described in this chapter.

11. I HAVE THE RIGHT TO privacy.
12. I HAVE THE RIGHT TO fair treatment regardless of my race, culture, gender, or religion.
13. I HAVE THE RIGHT TO services that will support me in reunifying me with my child.
14. I HAVE THE RIGHT TO offer my child a lifelong relationship.
15. I HAVE THE RIGHT TO meaningful participation in developing the child welfare policies and practices that affect my family and community.

***

Although no national campaign has emerged to push for all these rights to become standard practice in children welfare,[ii] significant efforts have been made across the country to promote several of them. Three have received particular attention: the right to have meaningful participation in developing policies and practices that affect my family and community (15), the right to quality legal representation (6), and the right to support from someone who has been in my shoes (7). This chapter focuses on activity regarding these three rights.

I HAVE THE RIGHT TO MEANINGFUL PARTICIPATION IN DEVELOPING THE CHILD WELFARE POLICIES AND PRACTICES THAT AFFECT MY FAMILY AND COMMUNITY (15)

The federal government encourages parent participation in child welfare policy development but that involvement has mostly been in family support and family preservation programs, rather than in protective services or out-of-home placement. One national evaluation conducted for the Department of Health and Human Services found that many efforts by states to involve parents, where it did occur, primarily provided "one-time consumer involvement." Although the involvement "provided some short-term input, [it] did not support the development of a cadre of consumers who actively participated alongside professionals in problem-solving activities."[4]

Grassroots groups across the country, however, are promoting a sustained and deeper influence of parent in all aspects of child welfare policy. Several dozen of these groups with parents who have had child welfare experience are working to increase parents' influence in shaping child

ii. The document has been distributed to the 14,000 subscribers of *Rise* magazine and its 2,000 internet users and has been further distributed by several groups and individuals around the country. [Nora McCarthy (editor, *Rise*), interview with the author, March 28, 2011.]

welfare programs and policies. In most of the groups, parents are in leadership positions, generally working in close partnership with professionals—social workers, lawyers, and/or community organizers.

These groups range in size, strength, and location. Most are quite new, having been formed within the past 5 to 10 years. They receive limited funding, have small staffs, and have had little or no formal training in organizing or child welfare. The strongest of the groups are based within larger antipoverty and welfare rights organizations.[iii] These large organizations came to realize that a substantial portion of their membership had overwhelming child welfare issues that had to be addressed. The organizations include Welfare Warriors in Milwaukee (Mothers and Grandmothers of the Disappeared Children is the name of the in-house child welfare advocacy group), Poor People's Economic and Human Rights Campaign in Louisville (Women in Transition), and Every Mother is a Working Mother in Philadelphia (DHS-Give Us Back Our Children).

DHS-GIVE US BACK OUR CHILDREN, PHILADELPHIA

DHS-Give Us Back Our Children is the strongest of these grassroots advocacy groups outside New York City in which parents and professionals are

---

iii. Other smaller groups are free-standing child welfare advocacy organizations that are not part of larger antipoverty organizations. For example, the Family Advocacy Movement (www.Familyadvocacymovement.com) of Omaha, Nebraska was created by parents and grandparents in response to Nebraska's well-intentioned but problematic "Safe Haven" law, which allows parents to voluntarily relinquish a child to state custody. Parents created the organization to reform child welfare so that they would not have to abandon their adolescent children to receive mental health services.

Dozens of other parent-led groups are not incorporated, and at times they are not even groups but individuals who feel abused by the child welfare system. For example, the website Kidjacked (http://kidjacked.com/about.asp) was created by Annette Hall who grew up in foster care and now wants to help parents whose children have been removed from their custody. The Arizona Family Rights Advocacy Institute (http://groups.yahoo.com/group/azfra/) works on behalf of parents who have been falsely accused of abusing or neglecting a child. It was set up by Robin Scoins after her newborn son was taken from her when she falsely tested positive for crystal meth because of sloppy testing procedures. It took 9 months for her to get her son out of foster care. [Sarah Fenske, "Public Enemy Number One: She Went After CPS But Now the State May Be Coming After Her," *Phoenix News*, March 22, 2007, http://www.phoenixnewtimes.com/2007-03-22/news/public-enemy-number-one/.] John Ford, whose adopted daughter with special needs was removed from his custody, created the North Dakota Coalition for Child Protection Services and Foster Care Reform. He joined forces with Sheri McMahon, a parent whose son with disabilities was placed into foster care twice. Together they are trying to create a child welfare ombudsman's office for the state. [Teri Finneman, "Child Services Proposal Rejected." Posted on September 19, 2010, Northdakota.areavoices.com/2010/09/19/child-services-proposal-rejected/.]

working together to reform child welfare policies and programs. Although it is so new that it has not yet been incorporated and is operating with a tiny budget and volunteer staff, it has begun to have an influence on the high rate of removal of children by the Department of Human Services (DHS) in Philadelphia.

Its history begins with Tilli Ayala, a Latina and Native American mother who was in her late 30s when she began demonstrating against DHS.[5] In the summer of 2004 Philadelphia's DHS removed Ayala's children, ages 3 years and 6 months, from her custody. The charge was that her husband (now her former husband) had walked along a beach saying he had a baby for sale. He maintained it was a prank; DHS placed the two children in foster care.

To get her children back, Ayala did all that DHS required: She went to parenting classes, found a new apartment, and got a job as a home health care worker. Nevertheless, her children remained in foster care. In May 2005, exasperated and angry, Ayala began a lone protest every Thursday afternoon on the corner of 15th and Arch streets in Philadelphia, the site of DHS headquarters.

After almost 2 years of standing alone or with a few other mothers who came to the DHS office to deal with their cases, her demonstration on March 8, 2007 coincided with a large Women's Day demonstration in Love Park across the street from the DHS office. Pat Albright was at the demonstration. A former welfare recipient, Albright is an activist with Every Mother is a Working Mother (EMWM), a grassroots antipoverty organization with a chapter in Philadelphia. Albright invited Ayala to join their demonstration, and in the ensuing weeks and months members of EMWM marched with Ayala during her weekly demonstrations outside the DHS office. These women included Barbara Clayton, a white grandmother, frustrated after years of unsuccessfully trying to gain custody of her grandson from DHS; Nina Boyd, a black mother living in a white neighborhood who had her children removed, unfairly she believed; and Mary Kalyna, a social worker who was fired from a local child welfare agency because, she says, she identified too often with her clients rather than with the agency.

It took months to gather a core group of women large enough to create an organization, but by November 2007 what would eventually be called DHS-Give Us Back Our Children came into being as a project of EMWM. Ayala left the group after about a year and a half, frustrated at her inability to reunite with her children. Her daughter was placed with the white father's mother in the suburbs; her baby son was placed with the father's sister. DHS-Give Us Back Our Children continues to operate with a core group of eight to 10 women, about half of whom have had the experience of having their children placed in foster care.

DHS-Give Us Back Our Children is a project of EMWM, a welfare rights organization founded in 1996 with roots in the 1960s and 1970s. It has chapters in Philadelphia, Los Angeles, and San Francisco that fight for welfare reform and the rights of poor women.[6] Eventually, EMWM recognized that many of the welfare recipients they were working with had children in foster care, often removed unnecessarily or illegally by DHS.[iv] To address their problems, EMWM helped launch DHS-Give Us Back Our Children, a self-help, support, and action group of mothers, grandmothers, and other family members, former social workers, foster parents, and other supporters. The group works "against the unjust removal of children from their families by the Philadelphia Department of Human Services."[7] According to Phoebe Jones, who has worked with EMWM for years and helped create DHS-Give Us Back Our Children, "We see our job as getting the professionals—lawyers, case workers, housing people—to do what they are paid to do."[8]

DHS-Give Us Back Our Children staffers hold weekly support group meetings for about 20 mothers who are trying to get their children back from DHS. They act as parent advocates, accompanying mothers to court hearings and meetings with case workers, though none of the women has had formal training as parent advocates or organizers. Without a salary from the organization or formal training to support them, many of the mothers leave the group when their children are returned or in frustration when their children aren't returned.

DHS-Give Us Back Our Children continues to picket against DHS on the first Thursday of every month, pressing for changes in the department's policies and programs. In collaboration with EMWM and other groups, DHS-Give Us Back Our Children members participated in a demonstration on March 12, 2011 calling for a wide range of changes: end budget cuts, discrimination, war, poverty, and other violence. One of the stops on the March demonstration was at the DHS office at 15th and Arch demanding help for families rather than removal of their children.

One of DHS-Give Us Back Our Children's recent projects was producing a short film[v] that profiles three women who had their children removed

---

iv. EMWM in Philadelphia and the women from DHS-Give Us Back Our Children helped form a similar group of mothers in Los Angeles called DCFS [Department of Children and Family Services]-Give Us Back Our Children. The members of the Los Angeles group are also unpaid volunteers and work in ways similar to DHS-Give Us Back Our Children in Philadelphia, trying to help individual mothers reunite with their children and advocate to lower the extremely high rate at which children are removed from their homes in Los Angeles.

v. The film is titled *DHS-Give Us Back Our Children: Mothers and Others Come Together to Reclaim Children from the Foster Care Industry.*

from their custody unfairly and struggled to be reunited with them. One mother, Lawanda Connelly, holds two masters degrees. In the film she says, "If it could happen to me, it could happen to anyone else." The movie has been shown on local public television and to groups of parents and their supporters in a dozen cities to nurture parent activism and to create bridges between those groups and DHS-Give Us Back Our Children. At a showing in East Harlem in May 2011 to 30 parents and their allies, many of the parents who struggled with the same issues were crying, remembering their similar experiences. Tamek Sellars, who worked in the Bronx as a parent advocate at Children's Aid Society, said, "It dredges up a lot of hurtful feelings. I'm still in court."

The movie was dedicated to Robin Frazer, a mother with whom DHS-Give Us Back Our Children began working in 2009. Frazer had been living in a mental health facility that did not allow children to live there with their mothers. While she was still in the hospital, right after she gave birth, DHS removed her child because of concerns about the child's safety as the mental health facility had not arranged for an alternative placement where the mother and child could live safely. The child was placed with someone whom Frazer disliked and with whom she did not want the baby placed. Although DHS-Give Us Back Our Children served as her advocate, it did not have a lawyer on staff; its efforts to have Frazer regain custody of her child were unsuccessful. In June 2010 Frazer committed suicide.

DHS-Give Us Back Our Children has had some impact on child welfare policy in Philadelphia. It gained the right for advocates to sit in on family court hearings as allies of mothers whose children had been or might be removed from the home.[vi] Its criticism of DHS in several stories in the *Philadelphia Daily News* by Dana DiFilippo about children removed unfairly by DHS and mothers' fights to be reunited with their children was deemed unhelpful by DHS Commissioner Anne Marie Ambrose, who said at the time, "I've been called a 'baby killer' and a 'baby snatcher' [by DHS-Give Us Back Our Children]. It hasn't been a productive relationship."[9]

Nevertheless, DHS-Give Us Back Our Children and the articles in the *Philadelphia Daily News* have begun to have an impact, or at least the child welfare system in Philadelphia County has begun to remove fewer children

---

vi. A memo from the City of Philadelphia Law Department directed "staff attorneys not to object to the presence of representatives from Every Mother is a Working Mother at court hearings...." [Barbara Ash, chief deputy city solicitor, child welfare unit, City of Philadelphia Law Department, Memorandum to CW Attorneys, CW Legal, subject: Every Mother is a Working Mother Network, 12/14/10.]

from families. In the year ending March 2009, for every 1,000 children living in poverty, Chicago removed six children from their homes, Los Angeles removed 14, and Philadelphia removed 40. In the year ending in March 2010, the child removal rate in Philadelphia dropped by 10% faster than the national decrease in that year of 6.5%.[10]

***

PARENTS ANONYMOUS

Another organization, Parents Anonymous, is beginning to involve parents in reforming child welfare policy, though its focus to date has been on providing self-help, mentoring and training of parents. Parents Anonymous was founded in 1969 by a parent and a social worker to reduce child abuse and neglect by providing peer support for parents who are having difficulty raising their children and have come into contact with the child welfare system; it does not focus on organizing parents. It is a large organization, reporting that it has 267 local affiliates that provide weekly family support groups, parent training, and parent leadership programs through a collaboration of professionals and parents with child welfare experience.[11]

Parents Anonymous' origins and focus are similar to other self-help "Anonymous" groups, such as Alcoholics Anonymous or Narcotics Anonymous, which focus on individuals' acknowledging their problems rather than focusing on their rights. As a result, Parents Anonymous' primary impact has been on helping individual families, reported to be millions by now, rather than changing child welfare policies or programs.[vii]

vii. Some individual chapters of Parents Anonymous have been more active in trying to shape child welfare programs to be more responsive to the needs and rights of families. In New Jersey, for example, the Parents Anonymous chapter joined forces in about 2005 with the Statewide Parent Advocacy Network (SPAN) to press the State Department of Children and Families to incorporate parents who had been involved in the child welfare system to serve on the state's human service advisory board and to have parents hired by the system. For a brief time the state child welfare agency was responsive to their pressure and for a time included child welfare-affected parents on a statewide, cross-systems advisory council to provide feedback on a newly created Department of Children and Families. But with a new governor in 2010 and a new commissioner, shifts in policy priorities, budget cuts, reduced pressure from the resolution of a lawsuit, and the absence of organized parents pushing for change, the state shifted its focus to hire parents from the mental health system. As Kathy Roe, executive director of Parents Anonymous New Jersey, says, "The mental health system has the 'good parents' with the 'bad kids.' We serve the 'bad parents' with the 'good kids.'" [Kathy Roe (executive director, Parents Anonymous New Jersey), email communication with the author, March 30, 2011.]

A recent evaluation found it to be "a promising program for the reduction of child abuse and neglect."[12]

Recently, however, Parents Anonymous has tried to enable parents embroiled in the child welfare system to have a national role on policy. In 2010 it was the driving force in creating the National Coalition of Parent Advocacy in Child Protective Services (www.parentadvocacy.org), consisting of more than 40 organizations in 20 states and Washington, D.C. Its mission is "To mobilize parents/caregivers and advocacy organizations to create positive public policy and program changes that prevent removal of children from their families by child protective services, strengthen and ensure the rights of families whose children have been removed, and return children to their families."[13] One of its first activities was to create a bill of rights for parents in the child welfare system. Many of these rights are similar to those in *From Rights to Reality*, although Right #15, the right to "meaningful participation in developing the child welfare policies and practices that affect my family and community," is absent, perhaps reflecting the National Coalition's focus on support groups for parents rather than on their participation in policy and practice.

I HAVE THE RIGHT TO QUALITY LEGAL REPRESENTATION (6)

In at least 12 states, parents do not have an absolute statutory right to counsel after the initiation of child protection proceedings against them. In at least six states, parents do not have an absolute statutory right to counsel in termination of parental rights hearings.[14,viii] Even in states in which a strong statutory right exists, parents' rights are not protected. In some states parents are represented by lawyers who do not specialize in child welfare law and may not be knowledgeable about how to engage and assertively represent their clients. Lawyers for parents are also paid very poorly in many jurisdictions, with no money available to pay for discovery or to pay lawyers to meet with their clients outside of court or to go beyond a cursory in-court defense. Lawyers often work alone, even though working in teams with social workers and/or parent advocates may be more successful.[15]

Lawyers nationally have had some success in reforming the quality of legal representation for child welfare-involved parents. In an increasing

---

viii. The Supreme Court of the United States held that the Due Process Clause of the 14th Amendment does not automatically confer the right to counsel to indigent parents facing the termination of the their parental rights. [*Lassiter v. Department of Social Services*, 452 U.S. 18 (1981) Id at 31–32.]

number of states, lawyers are required to receive training in child welfare law to practice in family court.[ix] Back-up support to assist lawyers or the families they are representing is becoming available in some jurisdictions. New publicly funded models of legal representation are being tried; they provide institutional legal representation for parents rather than representation by a lawyer working alone. In some of these new models, lawyers work in teams with social workers, with paraprofessionals, and, in some cases, with parent advocates who have had child welfare experience.[16]

Two of these national developments are central to improving legal representation for parents and enabling parents' participation in child welfare proceedings. The first is the beginnings of a national organization of lawyers who represent parents in child welfare. The second is the presence of parents with child welfare experience on legal teams representing parents in Family Court.

A national organization of lawyers representing parents in child welfare proceedings: Housed in the Center for Children and the Law in the American Bar Association (ABA) is the National Project to Improve Representation for Parents Involved in the Child Welfare System. This project, which began in 2006, has been championed by Martin Guggenheim, a professor at New York University Law School. In 1990 he created the first law clinic in the country whose primary focus is training lawyers to represent parents in family court.[x] Seventeen years later he successfully pushed New York City government to underwrite high-quality legal representation for parents in family court. Through the ABA's parent representation project he is working with lawyers throughout the country to improve legal representation for parents in child welfare cases nationally.

The parent representation project provides training and technical assistance for attorneys, judges, and legislators to improve legal representation of

ix. In many jurisdictions courts that handle child welfare cases are called dependency courts. The term family court is used in this chapter to include all courts in which child welfare cases are heard.

x. Today only three law schools in the United States have legal clinics that focus on parent representation: The University of Michigan Law School Child Advocacy Law Clinic provides in-court training and classroom instruction to law students interested in child advocacy; the New York University School of Law Family Defense Clinic provides students with an in-depth view of child welfare policy and practice; and the University of the District of Columbia's David A. Clarke School of Law, through its HIV/AIDS law clinic, provides students with the opportunity to represent parents and guardians in child welfare proceedings in Washington. [American Bar Association, Center on Children and the Law, *Legal Representation for Parents in Child Welfare Proceedings: A Performance Based Analysis of Michigan Practice* (Washington, DC: ABA, 2009) available at http://abanet.org/child/parentrepresentation/michigan_parent_representation_report.pdf.]

parents in child welfare proceedings. In August 2006 Mimi Laver, who was on the staff of the ABA's Center for Children and the Law, successfully pressed the ABA House of Delegates to approve Standards of Practice for Attorneys Representing Parents in Child Abuse and Neglect Cases, making the standards official ABA policy.[17] She is now the director of the national parent representation project, which is underwritten by Casey Family Programs.

One of the project's national activities is hosting a listserv for parents' attorneys (Child-ParentsAttorneys@gmail.AmericanBar.org). Three hundred lawyers and a few social workers, parent advocates, and parents across the country receive guidance in representing individual parents and on class action litigation from this site. Lawyers advise each other on legal strategy, precedents, or the names of lawyers who could represent a parent. The national parent representation project and its listserv work closely with Richard Wexler, executive director of the National Coalition for Child Protection Reform (www.NCCPR.info), which he founded in 1991. A journalist by training, a fighter by temperament, Richard is a one man band for the rights of parents confronting the child welfare system. On a shoestring budget, he monitors child welfare activities across the country, provides documentation and press releases to local groups fighting to reduce child removals, speaks on panels everywhere, blogs on national and local child welfare issues, maintains a website with resources for parents, lawyers, and advocates, and organized a national conference in 2008 for parent advocates and child welfare-involved parents. He has been one of the most effective forces in the country for increasing support for the rights and needs of parents entangled in the child welfare system.

Another project of the ABA's national center is sponsoring an annual Reunification Day to celebrate parents who have reunited with their children. These events are organized in collaboration with the National Council of Juvenile and Family Court Judges, the National Association of Council for Children, and Casey Family Programs. The first was held in 2010 with 20 jurisdictions across the country hosting events. In 2011 Reunification Day became Reunification Days, with events organized between Mother's Day and Father's Day to celebrate parents and to change the national perception of parents with children who had been in foster care.

A future goal of the national parent representation project is to create a national membership organization for attorneys who represent parents in the child welfare system. Building toward that goal, in 2009 the Project organized the first national conference of lawyers representing parents in child welfare proceedings and held a second national conference in 2011 with close to 300 in attendance. Although these forums spread the word about the importance of adequate legal representation for parents and increased the number of participants on the project's listserv, the economic recession and the lack of foundation funding have made it unlikely that a new membership organization will be created anytime soon.[18]

Child welfare-involved parents working on legal teams representing parents in family court: In a handful of states, law firms have recently begun hiring parents who have been embroiled in the child welfare system to be part of legal teams representing parents currently facing proceedings in family court. This approach reflects the developing awareness that trained parents with previous child welfare experience can gain the active involvement of parents, identify their needs, and make sure their voice is heard in the legal process. In Santa Clara County, California, the Dependency Advocacy Center represents parents in the local family court. The team uses parent mentors—mothers and fathers who have been through the child welfare system themselves, have reunited with their children, and have been sober for at least 5 years. In New Jersey, the Office of Parental Representation, a unit of the Office of the Public Defender, represents parents in both pretermination and termination hearings. The lawyers work with support staff and parent advocates to identify services for parents and assist them in obtaining these services and to provide traditional investigative services. The Vermont Parent Representation Center, founded in 2010, represents parents in child welfare cases and lobbies for parents at the state level where policy decisions are made. The center uses an attorney, a social worker, and a parent advocate as its legal team.[19]

In Michigan, the Detroit Center for Family Advocacy, created in 2009, provides legal advocacy and social work services to low-income families to prevent unnecessary child removals and to reduce the time children spend in foster care. It uses a team consisting of a lawyer, social worker, and parent advocate. The center accepts cases only from the Osborn neighborhood in Detroit, which has one of the highest rates of removal in the state. The story below, by Nancy Colon, describes her experience with inadequate legal representation and then her work as a parent on a legal team at the Detroit Center for Family Advocacy.

NANCY COLON[20]

I Needed My Lawyer to Be My Advocate

> From the first day that the child welfare system came into my life, I felt confused, afraid to ask for help and alone, with no one to guide or support me. It took me a long time to understand my service plan and access services.

Once I found a job and a house and was getting therapy and taking parenting classes, I thought my kids would come home. At every court date, I expected my children to be released to me. Finally I asked my attorney why they were still in foster care and he explained that I had to complete my treatment plan before the court would consider reunification. My attorney was friendly and nice, and I thought he was a good lawyer because he took the time to answer some of my calls and meet with me before each hearing. But now I see that he did not help me understand my situation. I never knew what to expect from the next court hearing or why we kept returning to court. He also did not challenge the court or the child welfare agency in any way.

At times I wanted to speak up in court. My children told me that they were being abused in foster care, and I wanted the agency to move them to a new foster home. But I didn't dare to ask too many questions. I was intimidated by the referee and my lawyer seemed intimidated, too. He stayed quiet in court. My attorney could have been much more aggressive in pushing the court to return my children to me. Or, if I'd had an attorney at my first team decision-making meeting, I could have gotten preventive services instead of having my children removed.

Now I am a Parent Advocate at the Detroit Center for Family Advocacy. Our mission is to keep kids out of foster care and reduce the number of children in care by providing legal assistance, support, and resources to families. I am proud to sit with the parents and provide support. I share my story and encourage parents to get help and to advocate for themselves.

I HAVE THE RIGHT TO SUPPORT FROM SOMEONE WHO HAS BEEN IN MY SHOES (7)

Before 1994 there were almost no parents employed in the child welfare system anywhere in the country. Today several hundred parent advocates—parents who have had children placed in foster care, changed their lives, reunited with their children, and been trained as advocates—are working in child welfare agencies throughout the country to engage families, to assist them, and to link them with a range of services.

Some research has evaluated the use of parent advocates as mentors or partners of parents whose children are in foster care.[21] The studies have generally shown that these parent engagement programs using parent mentors "are growing in number nationally but they largely remain untested... Nonetheless, preliminary results are promising and anecdotal feedback from parents and social workers is positive."[22] Some of these programs truly enable parents to better negotiate the child welfare system, to fight for the best interests of their families, and to help bring their voices to case decision making. In other situations, though, agencies have used peer support or parent mentors to bend parents to the wishes of the agency, which may not always be in the best interest of the children or their families.

The Annie E. Casey Foundation (AECF) had been the main organization promoting the use nationally of parents with child welfare experience to engage and then provide ongoing support to parents encountering the same experience. AECF is the largest and most influential foundation in the country focusing on reforming child welfare systems. It was established in 1948 by Jim Casey, one of the founders of United Parcel Service (UPS). The foundation primarily works through state and local governments, providing grants and technical assistance to fashion more innovative and cost-effective responses to the needs of children and families.[xi]

AECF's focus was not primarily to involve parents with child welfare experience in parent organizing, to increase the power of parents, or to have parents influence child welfare policy; its goal was to have parents hired (or, more often, to work part-time with stipends) in child welfare agencies to engage parents and provide ongoing guidance and emotional support to those who are struggling to be reunited with their children. This work had been done through AECF's Parents as Partners program, part of a larger initiative called Family to Family. By the time the Family to Family ended in 2009, dozens of urban areas in more than 20 states had participated. Family to Family focused on reforming foster care by making it less disruptive to people's lives, more individualized, and more culturally sensitive and community based.[23] It was primarily in this last area—partnerships with communities—that AECF promoted parents with child welfare experience to work in foster care agencies.

xi. Casey Family Programs (CFP), founded in 1966, was also established by Jim Casey. It aims to provide foster care, improve foster care, and ultimately reduce the need for foster care in the United States. It is the largest operating foundation in the United States that focuses exclusively on foster care and reforming the child welfare system. Its primary goal is to reduce the number of children in foster care by 50% by the year 2020.[http://www.casey.org/AboutUs/.]

CFP has also promoted the engagement of parents and their participation in shaping child welfare programs and policies. Its approach is similar to the strategy of AECF—working with state, county, and city governments through a comprehensive reform strategy, often including parent engagement and participation. CFP has supported parent engagement initiatives in many of the states in which AECF is involved, as well as in other states.

In 2001, as a national movement was developing for parents with child welfare experience to have a role in child welfare decisions and practice, AECF convened a national forum in Los Angeles on its Family to Family program. It invited a small, informal theater group of parents who had been entangled in the child welfare system to act out the parents' experiences and aspirations concerning the child welfare system. The theater group was created by a New York City foster care agency, St. Christopher's, one of the first agencies in the country to hire a parent who had had a child placed into foster care. St. Christopher's began hiring such parents in 1994.[xii]

Sandra Jimenez, an ebullient, articulate, and fast talking former child welfare parent, was in the group that performed for AECF.[xiii] She had been a court stenographer in New York City, started using drugs, and lost one child to foster care and others to relatives. She became sober, participated in the Child Welfare Organizing Project's (CWOP) 6-month training for parents, and became an effective spokeswoman for parents' rights in child welfare.

About a year after the performance, Jimenez became a consultant to AECF. In that role, she modified the CWOP training curriculum to create a 3-day parent training program called Building a Better Future for the foundation. The curriculum she developed focused primarily on parent engagement rather than on organizing parents or on policy reform. It is used to train parents with child welfare experience to be mentors to other parents. As the AECF was spreading its Family to Family Program across the country, in about 2002 it began to introduce parents with child welfare

xii. St. Christopher's at the time was headed by a charismatic, iconoclastic Latino named Luis Medina, who, among other reforms, hired parents with child welfare experience. He was seen as a visionary leader and excellent administrator, receiving the Child Welfare League of America's Outstanding Management Award in 1998, and expanded the number of children in the agency's care. For reasons that no one can fully explain, he stopped paying attention to the agency's affairs and eventually the Administration for Children's Services held him responsible for encouraging or turning a blind eye to the falsification of agency case records. The city terminated its foster care contracts with St. Christopher's in 2005 and Medina left the agency. ["St. Christopher's, Inc. Receives Outstanding Management Award from Child Welfare League of America," *Progress* (Winter 1998–99): 1; Leslie Kaufman, "Foster Children at Risk and an Opportunity Lost," *New York Times,* November 5, 2007.]

xiii. St. Christopher's received grants from the Child Welfare Fund beginning in 1994 to give parents a stronger voice and a greater role in program and policy development and accountability at the agency. The grant was used to create the Family Council (which assessed the agency's progress regarding client participation) and to train parent advocates. Sandra Jimenez was one of the parent advocates trained by and working for St. Christopher's. [Child Welfare Fund, Summary of Grants, 1993–1994.]

experience into its Family to Family programs as a way to engage parents currently embroiled in child welfare disputes. The first site where parents underwent training—under the guidance of Jimenez and her training partner, Randy Jenkins, a social worker—was in Louisville, Kentucky. Soon AECF expanded to Detroit, Michigan, Raleigh, North Carolina, Contra Costa County and Los Angeles, California, and, eventually, to Cedar Rapids and Des Moines, Iowa. AECF provided start-up funds for the state child welfare agency to implement a Parents as Partners Program, which included some combination of training, technical assistance, support for state oversight and administration, and funds for stipends or salaries for trained parents. Voluntary child welfare agencies that contracted with the government agency hired the parents, most often as part-time workers receiving a stipend and no benefits.

The parents who worked part-time had small caseloads of five to 10 families; those who worked full-time had larger caseloads. All of the parent mentors engaged in a wide range of activities, most often helping parents negotiate the child welfare system. They visited families in their homes to give emotional support and helped mothers accomplish what they needed to do to reunite with their children. They accompanied mothers to health, welfare, or legal appointments. They went to family court with mothers, though they were generally not permitted to speak in the court proceeding on the mother's behalf.

In 2009, at the end of AECF's involvement in Parents as Partners, roughly 200 parents with child welfare experience were working in child welfare agencies in eight states that had received money from AECF.[xiv] The parents primarily worked in contracted child welfare agencies on part-time stipends, though a few worked as full-time salaried staff with benefits. Almost none was employed by a public child welfare agency.

Evaluations conducted at several of the most robust AECF-supported Parents as Partners sites found that the use of parents with child welfare experience strengthened case practice, enhanced how parents felt about their child welfare experience, and improved rates of reunification of children and their families. One study looked at the outcomes for

xiv. The states were California (Los Angeles, Alameda, Contra Costa County), Iowa (Cedar Rapids, Des Moines, Iowa City), Kentucky (Louisville, Northern Bluegrass Region), Maine (Portland), Michigan (Detroit), Missouri (St. Louis), North Carolina (Raleigh), and Ohio (Cleveland). These figures are based on a small, informal survey in February and March 2011, conducted by Lisa Paine Wells, consultant to AECF. The survey gathered information from Casey-supported sites in which parents with child welfare experience worked in a Parents as Partners Program. Additional parents with child welfare experience are working in other states, supported in part by Casey Family Programs.

children whose parents were served by Parent Partners in Contra Costa County after their children were placed in foster care. The study compared their outcomes with those for children whose families were not served by Parent Partners. Approximately 60% of children with a Parent Partner reunified with their parents within 12 months of removal, compared to 26% of children whose parents were not served. The study also found that "parents [served by Parent Partners] had an exceptionally high degree of satisfaction with the services received." For the parent mentor, the experience "was personally redemptive as well."[24]

Another evaluation, of the AECF-supported Parent Advocate Program in Jefferson County, Kentucky, looked at 374 families served between September 2005 and April 2008. Although the families that had the help of a parent advocate had higher risk ratings for family problems than families not served by a parent advocate, 70.3% of children exiting out-of-home care and served by parent advocates were reunified with their parents, compared to 56.7% of families without a parent advocate.[25]

When AECF ended support for its Parents as Partners programs in 2009, there have been mixed results in sustaining these programs, despite the very positive evaluations. As of 2011, several states had continued their programs using a combination of state and federal funds, local foundation support, or money from United Way. Michigan, for example, had 20 parents each working as many as 30 hours a week both during and after the period of support from the AECF and CFP. Iowa was able to expand its program after the departure of the AECF. As described in detail below, 63 parents with child welfare experience work in 49 of the state's 99 counties.

On the other hand, several states have not provided financial support to sustain their programs. In Raleigh, which had had six parent partners, the program ended. In the Louisville area, the number of parents working in the child welfare system decreased from 20 at the program's height to 11 in 2011. Those who remained receive stipends only for part-time work.

PARENT PARTNERS, IOWA

Iowa is the state in which the Parents as Partners program has been most successful in terms of garnering government funding, replication beyond the few AECF-funded sites, and the likely long-term sustainability of the program. Parents as Partners is now part of the Department of Human Services (DHS) Community Partnership for Protecting Children, a series of programs and approaches to improve child welfare practice by blending the work and expertise of professionals and community residents, including parents who have had children in the foster care system.[26]

The Community Partnership is coordinated by an activist turned government administrator, Lisa Lint, who spent her early career running an organization of women in Montana who had been victims of domestic violence and then volunteered to help other women struggling with similar problems. For the past 11 years she has worked for the Iowa DHS. She is both a strong administrator and a champion of the program, working to maintain the continued support from the DHS leadership while ensuring the program's values and integrity on the ground. Her leadership has been an essential ingredient in the program's success.

One of the projects she oversees as part of the Community Partnership is the Parent Partners program that promotes and funds the employment of parents with child welfare experience in child welfare agencies. Each parent partner has a caseload of individual families who are trying to reunite with their children. They attend team decision meetings (which are similar to the aforementioned family team conferences in New York City), go to court or other appointments with their client parents, and provide emotional support to the families. That their work is not an isolated intervention but part of other reforms—increased use of preventive services, more placements in kinship families, lower caseloads among case workers, and quality assurance reviews—is another reason for the program's success. The following profile of Denise Moore describes a mother with child welfare experience who became a Parent Partner in Iowa.

DENISE MOORE

Profile by Andrew White[27]

Denise Moore began using drugs when she was a teenager. By age 26, she was a mother of two and addicted to methamphetamine. Twelve years later, pregnant with her sixth child and dealing drugs, police recorded her on a wire selling meth to an undercover cop. Moore ended up on intensive probation—and the state sent her children to live with her mother and brother. "I was missing from their lives long before that," she says today.

But Moore continued to get high. "I couldn't stop using," she says. She wanted her kids back, so she'd go to Alcoholics Anonymous meetings, but she was still getting high. "I kept thinking I could beat the system." One day her caseworker from Iowa's child welfare agency, the Department of Human Services (DHS), sat her down in front of her kids and told them she had relapsed yet again. "I saw my son's face fall," Moore recalls. "He was crushed. I didn't believe in AA. But I saw this face, and I stopped using."

She's been clean ever since. "My life would not have changed without that caseworker," she says, pushing her long hair away from her face to reveal her habitual, genuine smile.

Today, 4 years later, Moore shakes her head in disbelief at the turn her life has taken. Her 19-year-old son is in college on a football scholarship, and she is raising her other five children, ages 4 to 17, while working full-time with DHS and its Polk County office, in Des Moines. She helps other parents put the pieces of their lives back together so they can get their kids back from foster care—or avoid losing them in the first place. "No one is more credible to these families than someone who has done meth," explains DHS child protective social worker Tracy White. Moore and a half dozen other women with first-hand experience of the child welfare system lead training sessions with child protective caseworkers, helping the workers to understand exactly why people like them—former addicts, survivors of domestic violence, women who have found their way back to being nurturing parents—can be very effective at encouraging other parents to work with the agency, to do what's right for themselves and their kids.

They know what it takes to get the agency out of their lives. Another part of Moore's job is to coordinate the Polk County Community Partnership for Protecting Children (CPPC), one of dozens of partnerships started across the state in recent years that aim to break down the walls that have long divided child welfare agencies from the larger community. Through the partnership, Moore sits at the policymaking table with high-level child welfare officials, juvenile court judges, nonprofit executive directors, and frontline caseworkers and their supervisors. She organizes community leaders, activists, and other parents to take part in the governing council that helps guide improvements in the county's child protection and foster care system.

In a DHS district office that manages 5,000 investigations each year, has responsibility for 1,000 foster children, and oversees another 1,100 children living with relatives, community people such as Denise Moore have an influential voice. For Moore, this is a radical and almost inconceivable change in her life. "One and a half years ago I couldn't get a job at the Dollar Store or Perkins Restaurant because of my felony," she says. "It's an honor to do what we do," she adds, as she travels from one mid-day meeting to the next with one of her fellow parent advocates. "Who would have ever thought that people like us would do what we do?"

***

The Parent Partner Program began in Iowa in 2007 with support from AECF. It took a full year to convince the leadership of Iowa's DHS to invite Casey-funded trainers to come to the state to present the idea of Parent Partners and to train parents to work with families. But once the leadership of DHS saw the approach first-hand, they embraced it and have been supporters ever since. Parent Partners in Iowa has grown from a small program of 17 parents in four sites to 13 sites covering 49 of the 99 counties of Iowa. By March 2011, 63 Parent Partners were working with 262 families who had children in foster care.[28] They work part-time, receiving $10 an hour without benefits.

The parent partners, along with the site coordinator and a local DHS representative, are trained in the standard 3-day workshop developed by AECF. The training is conducted by a professional social worker and a parent who has had child welfare experience. It is designed to give the trainees a greater understanding of the child welfare process and to provide them with the skills to assist parents to move more successfully through the child welfare system. "The training is more of a facilitated discussion than a formal training," says Sandy Lint, who participated in it.[29] Jimenez, who developed the training, calls it "Self-Advocacy 101."[30]

The Parent Partner program grew rapidly, and though its leadership would like to set up programs in all counties in Iowa by 2013, the program is not expanding and its future funding is not certain. Currently the funding for Parent Partners comes primarily from state government, with local programs weaving in money from federal, nonprofit and private grants. Nevertheless, the program is still not part of the institutionalized child welfare funding. For that to happen, state DHS would have to require the large, powerful, statewide nonprofit providers who contract with the state to provide child welfare services to include Parent Partners in their programming. Instead, agencies will be "required to respond how they will participate in statewide conversations on Parent Partners," says Lint. That is a long way away from the state requiring agencies to hire parents with child welfare experience. According to Lint, "Cultural change takes a long time. I've seen quite a few initiatives come and go. And we always reach this point, but we don't have the resources to do it right and on a big scale."[31]

***

Unprecedented activity by child welfare-involved parents and their allies has slowly spread across the country, inspired by the example of CWOP and the reforms and reformers in New York City. These activities have been funded primarily by the Annie E. Casey Foundation and Casey Family Programs. A few city and state governments have also provided money, but most local governments, as well as the federal government, have been slow to support these initiatives.

In most states the parents' bill of rights contained in *From Rights to Reality* is still more a goal than a reality. Generally parents do not have a meaningful voice in shaping child welfare policy, though parent and professional partnerships do exist in isolated locations to influence child welfare policy. For the most part, these groups are small and operate in hostile environments, limiting their impact.

Similarly most parents still do not have adequate legal representation in family court and even fewer have a parent advocate working on their legal team. Nevertheless, lawyers and advocates across the country, spearheaded by the national parent representation project at the ABA and by the National Coalition on Child Protection Reform, are working on behalf of parents, at times in direct collaboration with them, to expand their rights and improve their legal representation in family court.

Much of the parent activity across the country focuses on getting parents firmly engaged in their own cases. Andrew White, director of the Center for New York City Affairs and a professor of urban affairs at the New School University, in 2008 reviewed the Family to Family programs in California, Iowa, and Washington, D.C., which include the Parent Partners program that uses parent mentors to prompt child welfare clients to become engaged in their cases. He concluded that "These initiatives have all reached a size, a level of visibility and a degree of philosophical investment by powerful public sector supporters that they appear unlikely to be washed away by any radical shift in government priorities."[32]

After Casey's catalytic involvement in Parent Partners ended in 2009, several of the programs in Casey's 20 target states have been sustained and two or three jurisdictions have increased the number of Parent Partners. But several of the programs have decreased the number of Parent Partners and one state ended its program because of lack of funds.

The recent involvement across the country of child welfare-affected parents and their allies—foundations, lawyers, advocates, and leaders in government and service agencies—is hopeful. It is far from certain, however, that parents' involvement nationally will become a permanent or prominent feature of the child welfare system. It seems likely, though, that without continued parent activism and pressure from parents and their allies, the practices of having parents work in child welfare agencies, of parents having broad legal rights in and out of family court, and of parents participating in child welfare policy debates will remain on the margins of case practice.

What is happening across the country is primarily engaging parents to participate more fully in the status quo with all of its limitations. Parent participation is not primarily focused on creating and using the power of parents as a collective force for change. The example of CWOP and the parents' movement in New York has taken root in only a very few cities. The impact of parent participation in child welfare across the country is still limited.

CHAPTER 7

What Improved, What Hasn't, and What's Beginning to Slip

In 1995 New York City had one of the worst child welfare systems in the United States. It had staggered from crisis to reform and back to crisis for at least the previous half century. That year roughly 50,000 families, most of them poor and black or Latino, were investigated by child protective services for neglecting or abusing their children. Among the third who were found to have maltreated their children—most often because of problems involving poverty, unskilled parenting, substance abuse, or poor housing—about half received no assistance nor did the city remove the children from their homes.[1] Often the families' difficulties festered until the situation exploded. Then the city's response was to place the children into foster care at an alarming rate. In the early 1990s, the number of foster children reached almost 50,000, more than any other time in the city's history. Less traumatic and less expensive interventions could have protected many of these children and kept them with their families.

Since the mid-1990s parents who have been embroiled in the child welfare system and their allies have worked with leaders in the city's Administration for Children's Services (ACS) to reform New York City's child welfare system. Their efforts brought about unprecedented improvements that are more profound, provide more benefits to children and families, and appear to be longer lasting than any reforms in the recent past. Toward the end of the first decade of the twenty-first century, the child welfare rollercoaster reached a high point, though recent budget cuts and shifts in focus by both ACS and advocacy groups have caused the system to slip backward.

This chapter describes the changes that have taken place in child welfare in New York City in the years between 1996—when Mayor Rudolph Giuliani and the City Council created ACS after the death of Elisa Izquierdo and the filing of *Marisol v. Giuliani*—and 2011, when ACS Commissioner John Mattingly left office. During those 15 years, ACS and the voluntary agencies, the courts, and the state and the federal governments put into place thousands of changes in policies, funding, programs, administration, staffing, legal representation, monitoring, training, and the relationship between the public and the private sectors. It would be tedious to recount all of these reforms and the twists and turns along the way.[i] Instead, this chapter focuses on the changes that had the greatest effects on children and families, and even then I have had to be selective, choosing what I think are the most important issues. The chapter reviews what has improved, what has not, and what has begun to regress. In many of the areas, the changes are not exclusively positive or negative, but more nuanced. I'll try to briefly describe those differences.

WHAT HAS IMPROVED

The three most important changes in New York City's child welfare system between 1996 and 2011 were a reduction in the number of children in foster care, improved legal representation for parents, and the participation

---

i. For those who are interested in an inside baseball review of changes in the child welfare system, several reports will help, though they cover only part of what has changed in New York City's system since 1996. The first source is the 21 issues of the *Child Welfare Watch* produced between 1997 and 2012. They provide an analysis of the broadest range of issues in child welfare in New York City during the period 1996–2011. A second source is Children's Rights, Inc., *At the Crossroads: Better Infrastructure, Too Few Results* (July 2007). It reviews changes from about 2000 to 2006 in significant areas of child protection, foster care, preventive services, and the family court. Another report, by Children's Rights, *The Long Road Home: A Study of Children Stranded in New York City Foster Care* (November 2009), reviews the case records of 153 children who had a permanency goal of return to parents or adoption and were in foster care for more than 2 years as of September 30, 2008. Both reports are filled with scores of indicators on the progress and lack of progress in child welfare. A fourth source is Citizens' Committee for Children, *The Wisest Investment: New York City's Preventive Service System* (April 2010), which is a review of changes in preventive services between 1995 and 2010.

of child welfare-affected parents in child welfare programs, in shaping policies, and in their own cases.

REDUCTION IN THE NUMBER OF CHILDREN IN FOSTER CARE[ii]

The number of children in foster care decreased from its highest point in the city's history, 49,365 in fiscal year 1992,[2] to its lowest point of 13,781 in May 2012.[3] The number of youngsters in care remained below 17,000 for 6 years starting in fiscal year 2006. This extraordinary reduction of almost 75% is the result of fewer children being removed from their families as well as of children being returned home more quickly. Whereas 12,000 children were removed from their homes in fiscal year 1998, 6,313 were removed in fiscal 2011.[4]

Several factors have contributed to the dramatic decrease in the number of children in foster care. First, child welfare has two competing goals. One is to protect children; the other is to strengthen families, so parents can better care for their children. Although these two imperatives compete, protecting children had long been the dominant approach both in New York City and around the United States. Beginning in the last years of the twentieth century, there was a shift in New York City's child welfare system toward supporting families before the extreme measure of removing a child from the home is taken. In 1996 ACS's mission statement said that "Any ambiguity regarding the safety of the child will be resolved in favor of removing the child from harm's way."[5] As of 2011, the statement read: "Children's Services' mission is to ensure the safety and well-being of New York City children."[6] To carry out this new approach, families receive assistance from preventive service agencies with whom ACS has contracts. These agencies provide case management, parent training, anger management, and general psychological counseling, as well as referrals to community-based service providers for respite care,[iii] day care, homemaking aid, alcohol or substance abuse treatment, medical and health services, housing assistance, and job training.[7]

ii. Consistent ACS data sets are often not available that cover both the first decade of the twenty-first century and the period before 2000. This chapter therefore frequently relies on "Watching the Numbers" from the *Child Welfare Watch*, which uses ACS and New York State's Office of Child and Family Services data to report New York City child welfare trends from fiscal year 1992 to fiscal year 2011.

iii. Respite care is the provision of a person to provide short-term, temporary relief to those who are caring for a child who might otherwise require placement in foster care.

In 1996, 28,872 children were in families receiving preventive services; by 2002, 33,537 children were members of such families.[8] For much of the ensuing decade the number remained similarly high (33,022 in 2008), but beginning in 2009 there was a significant decrease in the number of children receiving preventive services. The total fell to 27,532 in fiscal year 2010 and to 23,294 in fiscal year 2011.[9] This decrease, with its potential for undermining the reforms that have strengthened families and reduced the number of children in care, is discussed below.

In the past when parents were investigated and found to have neglected or abused a child, more often than not the only response from the city was to remove the child from the home, rather than assist the family in overcoming its troubles. Here, too, a change in the city's approach is evident. In January 2006, almost 45% of indicated cases of abuse and neglect were closed without services. In January 2009, only 14% of such cases were closed without services, though many of the families were referred to community-based services with no follow-up by ACS reported to determine if the services were provided.[10]

The shift in ACS's policy toward an emphasis on helping families rather than removing children, and the provision of social services for families in difficulty, enabled many more children to remain safely with their families. The approach, however, as implemented by ACS, has not been without problems. First, many more children and families need assistance than are currently helped by preventive service agencies. The increase in the number of children and families receiving preventive services has been far less than proportional to the decrease in the number of children in foster care. According to a survey of preventive service agencies conducted by the Citizens' Committee for Children, the preventive service system operated at approximately 100% of capacity between 2006 and 2010. Twenty-six of 31 preventive programs surveyed reported they had turned away families in the prior 6-month period because their programs were full.[11] And the problem is compounded by the fact that many of the most important services families need are consistently not available, including mental health services, housing assistance, and substance abuse treatment.[12]

During the period of reform, ACS for the most part successfully resisted the knee-jerk reaction of so many other jurisdictions: Remove children from their families and keep them in care as a reaction to political pressure after a high-profile death of a child. The city has made substantial progress in helping families, but by 2011 it had become clear that the gains might be insufficient or, worse, undermined without additional services to help vulnerable families.

IMPROVED LEGAL REPRESENTATION FOR PARENTS

In 1962 New York State created the Juvenile Rights Division of New York's Legal Aid Society to provide lawyers to represent children in Family Court. That office currently represents an average of 34,000 children annually in the five boroughs of New York City in child protection, termination of parental rights, Persons In Need of Supervision (PINS) petitions, and juvenile justice proceedings.[13] During the next 45 years neither the city nor the state created a comparable office for lawyers to represent parents in Family Court.[14] Instead parents whose children were about to be removed from their homes, who wanted their children returned to them, or who faced termination of their parental rights had only meager legal representation. As *The New York Times* wrote in a 1996 editorial:

> Parents who are about to lose their children because of abuse or neglect are often at a legal disadvantage. Welfare authorities have the legal muscle of the city behind them. The children are generally represented by an experienced Legal Aid lawyer with a support network of social workers. But the parents are generally stuck with harried court-appointed lawyers who are juggling many cases, and who often show up unprepared and late for hearings.[15]

Until 2007, all poor parents in Family Court proceedings were represented by these lawyers (called 18B panel attorneys) who were underpaid, worked without an office or assistance from paralegals or social workers, and whose clients were unable to speak with them between court appearances.[16] It was not surprising that in 1996 parents prevailed in only 1.6% of fact finding hearings, the Family Court equivalent of a trial.[17]

Legal representation for parents in New York City Family Court changed dramatically in 2007 when the New York City Office of the Criminal Justice Coordinator provided $9.4 million to pay three existing, well-regarded legal offices to represent about half of the parents who appear in child removal proceedings in Family Court in the Bronx (Bronx Defenders), Brooklyn (Brooklyn Family Defense Project of Legal Services NYC), and Manhattan (Center for Family Representation). In 2011 the Center for Family Representation received the contract to represent parents in Queens. The other half of the parents in those boroughs, and all poor parents on Staten Island, continue to be represented by the 18B panel attorneys.

The story of how this historic change came about illustrates how government sometimes operates against its own best interests and against the best interests of the people it serves. The idea of separate legal services for parents had been championed for years by New York University law professor Martin Guggenheim. He is a passionate advocate for parents' rights, even above children's rights, and in 1990 he created the first law school program in the United States that trains lawyers to represent parents in family court. His legal expertise and his persuasive, logical, understated speech led all three child welfare commissioners from 1996 to 2011 to include Guggenheim on their advisory boards, despite his dedication to representing parents rather than the children.[iv]

In 1992 Guggenheim, with the support of the administrative judge of New York City's Family Court, Kathryn McDonald, convened a meeting with the deputy mayor for criminal justice services, Fritz Alexander II, and the head of the Office of Court Administration, Matt Crossen. "I made a persuasive case that funding quality legal representation for parents would save the city considerable money because the foster care population would get smaller," Guggenheim says. He then learned what he refers to as "the lesson of broken government." He was meeting with Alexander because his office oversaw the city's criminal justice coordinator (CJC) and pays for legal services for parents. But Alexander had no responsibility for foster care. "He turned to me and told me that, although I may well be right about how his spending more money on lawyers might save the city on foster care, ... I was asking him to spend more of his budget on lawyers and whatever savings it might achieve would not be part of his budget," says Guggenheim.

He was confronted with another of poverty's Catch 22s. "I had the support of the chief administrative judge and the Office of Court Administration. But the person who had to agree for this to happen only wanted to know how the plan would help him. Recognizing that it wouldn't, he turned me down."

Why then did John Feinblatt, the criminal justice coordinator under Mayor Michael Bloomberg, agree to fund institutional representation for parents in Family Court in 2007? Guggenheim speculates:

> I think the main catalyst for this change was the *Nicholson* lawsuit. More precisely, after Judge Weinstein [who was the judge for the lawsuit] ruled that the city had to pay 18B lawyers $90 per hour for court-assigned representation of parents accused of neglect when they were themselves victims of domestic violence, the long movement to raise the rates of assigned counsel finally resulted in legislative action. Once the legislature raised the rates to $75 per hour for Family Court lawyers (up from $40 per hour for in-court and $25 per hour for

iv. Commission Richter appointed Guggenheim to his advisory board in 2011.

out-of-court), the CJC finally had an incentive to try to limit costs. Since he knew his budget was about to soar, he started paying serious attention to an alternative to the 18B arrangement. In short, the goal for the change may simply have been to save money within the same budget.[18]

Guggenheim argues that even though the city provides funding to cover not quite half of all families against whom a petition to remove their child has been filed, adequate legal representation for parents in Family Court is the most important change to improve the legal rights of parents since the founding of Family Court. "It is not much of an exaggeration to say that there was no lawyering going on for the past 40 years to support families in Family Court," Guggenheim said in 2010.[19] At present, according to former Family Court Judge Bryanne Hamill, these new public interest law firms provide "some of the best lawyering I've seen in any court."[20]

One of the important changes in legal representation is that two of the three law firms provide parents with a multidisciplinary legal team consisting of a lawyer, a social worker, and a parent advocate who previously had a child in foster care. The team provides holistic support for families, recognizing that families need guidance and social services as well as legal representation to prevent placement of a child in foster care or make reunification of the family possible.

The results have been impressive. The Center for Family Representation reported that in 2011, it "kept 73% of our clients' children out of foster care entirely. For those who entered and left care their median stay was just 2.2 months, significantly shorter than the New York State median of 19.9 months and the New York City median of 6.4 months."[21]

The legal glass for parents, however, is less than half full. Approximately half of poor families are still represented in Family Court by overworked 18B panel attorneys. Staten Island, the borough that in 2011 had the community district with the highest number of children in the city placed in foster care (St. George/Stapleton), still does not have a city-funded public interest law firm to represent parents in Family Court.[22]

A second problem is that public funding does not cover legal representation before a family appears in Family Court. When families investigated by child protective services have problems that may contribute to neglect or abuse—such as housing, utilities, welfare, health, and/or marital issues—these public interest law firms are not paid to provide the legal assistance needed to address them. As a result, these difficulties often go unaddressed until the family appears in Family Court, at which point ACS seeks to remove a child.

Finally, Family Court judges are still notoriously overloaded with cases causing long delays in families reuniting with their children. Although the caseload burden was documented as early as 1991, the number of Family Court judges has not increased since then. This was true even after the number of cases coming before the judges increased as a result of the 2005 New York State Permanency Law, which mandated two, instead of the previous one, permanency hearings per year for children in foster care. In May 2009 the 26 judges in the child protection specialty had an average caseload of 774 children. Such enormous caseloads contribute to long delays in the hearing of cases. In 2008 the mean length of time from a child's entry into care (remand) and the determination that the child should be placed in care (disposition) was 14 months, a very long time in a child's life to be away from his or her parents.[23]

THE PARTICIPATION OF CHILD WELFARE-AFFECTED PARENTS

Before 1996 parents involved with the child welfare system had little say about what happened to their children and almost no say about the child welfare programs and policies. Parents who neglected or abused their children were demonized by the media, the general public, the protective services personnel who investigated their families, and the social workers who handled their cases. Child welfare professionals and the public often saw these parents as the cause of their own problems. They focused on parents' choice to neglect or mistreat children, rather than acknowledging the limited choices they had and the enormous pressures they confronted. As the executive vice-president of one of New York City's child welfare agencies told me in 2011 not for attribution, "Demonizing parents makes it easier for workers to do their jobs." And even if some workers in child welfare did not demonize parents, they did not empathize with them, either.

For decades, in fact for centuries, parents whose children have been through the child welfare system have struggled, mostly alone, to reunite with their children, by changing their behavior and/or fighting the injustices committed against them and their families. What changed in New York City after 1996 was that some of the parents began to find each other through organizations such as the Child Welfare Organizing Project (CWOP), *Rise* magazine, Voices of Women Organizing Project, and People United for Children that were set up specifically to help them and to champion their cause. Several hundred parents were trained to be spokespersons and leaders, and they learned to understand, to accept, and then to describe for others the traumas they confronted, the strengths they had, the mistakes they made, and the changes they were making, both personal and political.

Once these trained parents began to recognize their strengths, which helped them survive overwhelmingly difficult circumstances, and to acknowledge that they had the courage not only to change their lives but to help others do the same, they began to speak publicly about the ills of the child welfare system that at times made their troubled lives more difficult. They became a presence that could not be disregarded.

Parents alone, however, would not have had the strength to bring about the vast changes that were needed in the child welfare system. They allied with professionals who had similar goals—advocates who joined or helped form their organizations, lawyers who represented them in family court, foundation officers who underwrote their work, and social workers in child welfare agencies who listened to their concerns. Perhaps their most important allies were ACS commissioners William Bell and John Mattingly, who championed their cause and implemented reforms that would better meet their needs and protect their rights.

The genuineness of their stories, the generosity of their spirit, the personal changes they made in spite of their pain and punishment, and the help they were providing to others surprised those who met them, read their stories, or heard them speak. Child welfare professionals began to empathize with them as experienced people, rather than see them as the one-dimensional demons portrayed in the press. As decades of research show, contact reduces prejudice.[24] That is what happened in child welfare. The changes in attitudes, however, were greatest among the child welfare leaders who had contact with parent advocates; change was slower in the attitudes and practice of line staff members, unless they had regular contact with parent advocates. Jane Golden, head of foster care at the Children's Aid Society (CAS) and a champion of parent advocates, described the shift in CAS since she arrived at the agency in 1999:

> The culture here at first was a very old fashioned way of looking at families. There was a lot of suspicion and distrust of birth families. Workers said, "Why do we need them at case conferences?" The culture started to shift under Mattingly and Family Team Conferences, which required parents to be at the table because parent participation was part of the ACS Scorecard [the system ACS uses to evaluate foster care agencies]. Birth parents are more involved now.[25]

Since 1995, with the pressure from well-organized activist parents and their allies, parent participation in child welfare decisions has begun to change, though it is still a long way from being part of the core of child welfare practice. Parents are participating more regularly in their own case decisions. They and their allies are participating in policy decisions that shape child welfare programs and, perhaps most significantly, they are beginning to play a role in service delivery programs, to which we now turn.

Parent advocates participating in service programs: Child welfare-affected parents are working in child welfare service programs for the first time in New York City (or in the United States, for that matter).[v] Although they have contact with only a small percentage of child welfare families, their number and the families they reach have been increasing. These parent advocates have taken the steps necessary to be reunited with their children and have been trained to be advocates for families who are struggling with the child welfare system. Parent advocates work in foster care and preventive services agencies, where they coach families who are embroiled in the child welfare system, helping them negotiate the hurdles of reunification. They also work in public interest law firms as part of the legal teams that represent parents in family court. They work, too, in the new Community Partnership Initiative, the attempt by ACS to involve communities in child welfare service delivery and decisions. And they work inside ACS, both in its Office of Advocacy, where they train ACS staff members and help parents who have problems with the agencies handling their cases, and in ACS's START program for parents who have used drugs and have been investigated by child protection services in the Bronx. Rather than describe the work of parent advocates in each of these areas, I will focus on their role in foster care agencies, which is where most parent advocates work.

Parent advocates are parents who have been entangled in the child welfare system, have changed their lives, have been reunited with their children, and have been trained as advocates either by CWOP or by the foster care or preventive service agencies in which they work. Many are working in the same foster care agencies in which their children were placed. In handling their case loads, they urge parents to become actively involved in the process of reunifying with their children, conduct home visits, supervise visits between parents and their children in foster care,

v. Child welfare-affected parents, who also had been drug involved, began work-ing in preventive service programs in the late 1980s and early 1990s, particularly in the Family Rehabilitation Program for substance-abusing clients. They specialized in outreach, engaging clients, and assisting with securing entitlements and preventing evictions. Child welfare-affected parents did not begin working in foster care agen-cies until the mid-1990s.

and accompany parents to court and to social service and health appointments. They also attend family team conferences or other agency meetings to ensure that the parent's voice is being heard and that the parent is well-informed. Parent advocates facilitate communication between the clients and the agency staff. They work to ensure that the needs of the family are being adequately addressed.

According to Chapin Hall at the University of Chicago, which evaluated the use of parent advocates in New York City foster care agencies:

> Case planners, case aides, and supervisory staff may advocate for clients in similar ways. What makes the parent advocate role distinct is their status as persons wholly committed to support the parent in any way necessary ("I am here to help you in whatever way you need"), and who can relate to the experience of being a client at the agency. All staff groups interviewed claimed that the parent advocates were able to gain the trust of parents in ways not possible for other staff. It is the authenticity of their experience ("I've walked in your shoes") that promotes their ability to engage clients and gain their trust.[26]

As one parent advocate cited in the Chapin Hall study said, "I am there to find the solutions. Sometimes [the case planners] just can't see what I see because of my unique position. Or they just don't have the time and don't think that way."[27]

At first, agency leaders did not believe parents who had neglected or abused their children could work in a foster care agency, let alone work directly with parents and children, but New York State law permits it as long as the agency believes the parent advocate is not a danger to the family.[28] The first child welfare-affected parent began working in a foster care agency, St. Christopher's, in 1994. The number of parent advocates and the number of agencies that employed them slowly increased over the next decade.

The Chapin Hall evaluation said that "By and large, parent advocates are seen to enhance the effectiveness of what the agency already does to help the parent: their role is thought to enhance what clients and staff do to move the case forward."[29]

I expressed a similar conclusion in my opening remarks at the parent advocate forum described in the preface of this book: "Every executive director, supervisor or caseworker I have spoken with who employs parent advocates or has worked with them emphasizes that parent advocates have improved case practice."

Because of the advocates' effectiveness, by 2011 there were at least 50 parent advocates working in 22 foster care or preventive service agencies.

Another 50 parent advocates worked in public interest law firms, advocacy organizations, or other parts of the child welfare system, such as substance abuse or mental health programs.

Parent advocates working in foster care agencies did present complications. Some social workers had difficulty accepting parents as professional peers. According to the Chapin Hall evaluation:

> Overall the directors and supervisors believe that line staff had become open
> to and accepting of the parent advocates. For example, four of the five directors interviewed referred to "initial resistance" to the parent advocates that
> seems to have been "overcome" or "resolved." They claim that staff appreciate
> the ways in which the parent advocates help support their work and engage
> the parent in case planning and decision-making. Still, supervisors and parent
> advocates alike claimed that a small minority of case planners are "territorial"
> and avoid working with the parent advocates.[30]

Despite this progress, there is still a long way to go before parent advocates are a central part of child welfare practice. Advocates are working with only a very small percentage of families that could benefit from their involvement. Jane Golden of CAS says that "Of the 650 families in our agency, about 85% could benefit from a parent advocate. The other parents are completely absent."[31] At present, there were more parent advocates who had been trained and were NOT working as parent advocates and wanted to be than there were parent advocates who were working in foster care agencies. One reason for this was that there was no designated funding stream for parent advocates, so agencies had to cobble together ways to pay for them. There is a risk that parent advocates will be another "boutique" program that remains on the margins of case practice or even disappears as so many other exemplary models have for lack of funding. Nevertheless, by almost all accounts, parent advocates have been a welcome addition to foster care case practice, both for the agencies and for the parents whose children are in care.

Parent participation in child welfare policy: Child welfare decisions are discussed and made in thousands of meetings and less formal contacts involving commissioners and their deputies, in public hearings held by city, state, and federal legislators, in court proceedings or forums at which judges participate, in research reports and policy papers by academics and policy wonks, and in hallway discussions and meals over pizza or Chinese food in now smokeless rooms. Parents of children in foster care are still on the periphery of many of these meetings, but they and their organizations, primarily CWOP and its allies, meet regularly with representatives of ACS, and its New York State counterpart, city councilmen, and state legislators, and testify at hearings when ACS's budget and programs are discussed. They are part of the environment that influences child welfare policy.

The main venues in which parents make their policy preferences known outside of government are the advisory board of the *Child Welfare Watch*, in the pages of *Rise* magazine, as members of the Parent Advocate Network, and through ACS's Parent Advisory Work Group. Parents have been on the *Child Welfare Watch* advisory board since its founding in 1997; in 2011 five of its board's 27 members are parents. The *Watch's* influence in child welfare policy was discussed in Chapter 3. Since its founding in 2005, *Rise* has published articles detailing the experience and recommendations of child welfare-affected parents. Its influence was also described in Chapter 5.

The newest voice in the child welfare policy debate is the Parent Advocate Network (PAN), whose members are 120 child welfare parent advocates in New York City; about 20 regularly attend the monthly meetings of the network. Its goals are to support the parent advocates emotionally and professionally, to provide them with training, and to serve as a collective voice for parent advocates in their agencies and in the child welfare system. The network was designed in 2009 and had its first meetings in 2010, so it is still very new and has yet to have a significant impact. In addition, although the network is housed at CWOP, it was created by the Parent Advocate Initiative, the membership of which included not only advocates and foundations but also ACS, New York State's Office of Children and Family Services (OCFS), and the Council of Family and Child Caring Agencies (COFCCA) representing foster care and preventive service agencies. As a result, its policy focus will likely reflect the compromise of collaboration among government bodies, child welfare agencies, and advocates. Promoting the expanded use of parent advocates throughout the child welfare system is a likely focus of PAN since all of the above parties agree that parent advocates enhance child welfare practice.

In ACS, the official forum through which parents participate in child welfare policy discussions is the ACS commissioner's Parent Advisory Work Group (PAWG). It was set up by Bell and formalized by Mattingly to gather the opinions of parents and to get their reactions to programs and policies being considered by ACS. (PAWG is described in Chapter 3.) As Mattingly summarized the group's role:

> Parents have a lot to say on the periphery but they haven't gotten into the heart of things. They know what it's really like, that's why you bring them in. They are not systems change people; they are parents. You can't expect them to design something for us.[32]

Nevertheless, parents have pushed themselves into the child welfare policy arena and gained a voice in the child welfare debate. Their voice, however, still has limited influence; their ability to be heard remains largely dependent on the good will of individuals in governmental bureaucracies, legislative chambers, and child welfare agencies. More often than not, it is their allies, both outside and inside ACS, who have the most influence in bringing the perspective of parents to child welfare policy discussions. For example, a coalition of 60 advocates, including three parent advocates, as well as foster care and preventive service agency directors, academics, journalists, lawyers, and foundation officers, signed a letter in 2006 strongly urging the mayor to retain Mattingly as ACS commissioner in spite of Nixzmary Brown's death and four other high-profile deaths of children known to ACS. When Mattingly was asked why he was retained as commissioner after the press, councilmen, and members of the state assembly called for his resignation, he referred to the letter:

> When people got together, the advocates, the parents, the agencies, people who don't agree with each other, and said, "Let's give this time," that was a critical step. Parents don't carry political weight but providers and advocates together, that was a big, unusual thing.[33]

The voices of child welfare-affected parents have been heard in the child welfare system. Their experience and opinions have influenced policy makers as well as their allies. Whether their voice will gain strength—or even continue to be heard—is discussed in the final chapter.

Parents participating in their own case decisions: Although parents in New York State have for decades had a right, at least on the books, to participate in decisions about what will happen to their children when they enter the child welfare system, in practice parents had often been denied that right.[34] State regulations entitled parents with children in foster care to participate in Service Plan Reviews, which were meetings in which key decisions were made by caseworkers outlining what a parent had to do to be reunited with his or her child.[35] Parents in New York City with children in foster care were rarely present when these Service Plan Reviews took place.[36,vi]

---

vi. Parents rarely attended service plan reviews because their presence was often considered a formality, rather than an important part of the decision-making process. As a result, meetings were scheduled at times that were convenient for the case worker, not for the parent, or the parent did not receive timely notification about the meeting, or the parent did not feel comfortable attending the meeting without

Beginning in 2002 with the arrival at ACS of Bell, and championed by Mattingly when he became commissioner, is a new approach intended to be more inclusive. In the past caseworkers made all decisions regarding the foster child with little or no input from the family. Today decisions about what happens to a child and his or her family are supposed to be made collectively, with meaningful participation by parents, their relatives, and their friends, in what are called family team conferences.[vii]

Family team conferences are held at regular intervals around key decision points to both encourage consensus-based decision making and to promote steady progress toward agreed upon goals for the family. The conferences take place when ACS is considering removing a child from his or her home (called a child safety conference), after a child has been in care for 72 hours, 30 days, and 90 days, when a move to another foster home is being considered, or when a decision to return a child to his or her family is being considered (called family team conferences or family permanency conferences). These meetings are attended by the parent, family members, the case planner from the foster care agency, the case planner's supervisor, a facilitator from ACS (sometimes), and a community member who might be an ally of the parent or knowledgeable about resources in the community in which the family lives.[viii]

an ally or a lawyer. [Jill Chaifetz, *The New York City Foster Care System in Crisis: The Continued Failure to Plan for Children* (New York: The Door, February 1998).]

vii. Family team conferences are part of a larger ACS initiative called Improved Outcomes for Children (IOC), which created sweeping changes in the way ACS works with voluntary child caring agencies that provide services to families. There are several components of IOC, but the one that most directly affects families is using family team conferences to make case decisions. There are four features of IOC: (1) The elimination of the role of the public agency as case manager and the consignment to the voluntary agency of expanded authority to make case management and other service decisions on behalf of clients; (2) the implementation of an enhanced practice model that relies on family team conferences that include service providers, families, community stakeholders, and at times ACS staff; (3) a rigorous system of quality assurance monitoring; and (4) the funding of agencies upfront rather than retroactively and assignment of greater flexibility over the use of fiscal resources to them. [Fred Wulczyn, Sara Feldman, and Nadra Qadeer, *Improved Outcomes for Children, Implementation Study, Interim Progress Report (Draft)* (Chicago: Chapin Hall Center for Children/University of Chicago, March 2008): 3.]

viii. This group decision making, involving the entire family and the community, originated among the Maori people in New Zealand. It was then brought to the United States and championed by the Annie E. Casey Foundation when Mattingly directed the foundation's work in child welfare before becoming ACS commissioner. [Judge Leonard Edwards (ret.) and Dean Inger Sagatun-Edwards, "The Transition to Group Decision Making in Child Protection Cases: Obtaining Better Results for Children and Families," *Juvenile and Family Court Journal* 58(1) (Winter 2007): 4, 5.]

In the middle of his tenure, Mattingly was asked what he thought his major accomplishments would be. He said:

> What we've done up to now is set some directions that can be changed, so I don't want to say they are accomplishments. We are on the way to some things that I think are quite possibly remarkable. Things like the child safety conferences and the family permanency conferences I think are the kind of a systemic change that flows from a new practice.[37]

The family team conference approach was pilot-tested in 2007 with nine foster care agencies, affecting about a third of the children in care or coming into care, and then was implemented system wide beginning in July 2009 after Mattingly received permission from OCFS to do so. At present, most of the information about the impact of this new approach has been anecdotal. The reports were mixed, but in small pockets of the system, improvements were visible.

An evaluation by Chapin Hall was conducted less than a year after family team conferences were in place. Nevertheless the evaluators found that there was widespread acceptance of the process and that "the family team conference model offers a robust alternative to the way in which ACS carried out its oversight responsibilities..."[38]

One encouraging preliminary finding was that attendance by parents approached 50% of conferences held between November 15, 2007 and March 15, 2008.[39] That percentage was likely to increase as the logistics of holding family team conferences (e.g., getting all participants into the room at the same time) and the inherent barriers to change are overcome. Although parents attended only half of the conferences,[ix] that percentage was a dramatic improvement over the 20.6% of parents who attended similar service plan reviews 15 years earlier.[40]

When a well-trained parent advocate is present in a child safety conference there is often a genuine exploration of alternatives to putting a child in care. Parent advocates from the Child Welfare Organizing Project have participated in 700 preplacement conferences in East Harlem and

---

ix. Family team conferences are extremely difficult to arrange logistically. They can involve 10 or more people—parents, relatives, foster parents, case workers, social workers, a parent advocate, and other individuals from the community some of whom may work at any of several agencies and others of whom may have jobs outside the child welfare system that they are not free to leave. Child safety conferences, which occur before children are placed in foster care, have as many participants but have the additional complication that they take place within a few hours of the time they are called.

the South Bronx as allies of the parents. They report that frequently the conferences decide to have children remain with their families. Similar conclusions are reported by the Center for Family Representation, whose parent advocates also participate in child safety conferences.

On the other hand, when parent advocates are not present, as is often the case in family team conferences that deal with issues such as a child being reunited with his or her parents, both parents and parent advocates who have attended these meetings report that the proceedings are often a rubber stamp for decisions that were made before the meeting.[41] According to data prepared by ACS, there was no difference in the outcomes for children between agencies that used family team conferences and agencies that did not.[42] These data from ACS, however, were from 2009 when the new approach to decision making was less than 2 years old.

WHAT HASN'T IMPROVED

The basic design of New York's child welfare system is the same as it was 15 years ago. It is a residual, remedial system that provides help to children and families only after a child has been reported to be abused or neglected. It is not a preventive, universal system that helps all families, middle class or poor, in the normal course of their lives before their problems become overwhelming. Poor children of color, particularly black children, continue to be disproportionately represented at every stage in the child welfare process; the disproportionality increases the further into the child welfare pipeline the children go—from investigation through indication, placement, and the length of time children remain in care.[43]

Child welfare continued to be underfunded. Foster care agencies were paid less than the reimbursement standard set by OCFS to care for children adequately.[44] Fewer preventive service slots than needed were available to help struggling families. Other essential services, particularly in areas of mental health, housing, and substance abuse, were not adequately available. Budget cuts since 2008 had made a difficult situation worse.[45]

The mindset of many caseworkers who deal directly with families and ultimately make the decisions on individual cases had not changed, though more voices were now part of the decision-making process. Too often these frontline workers—those who engage families, conduct risk and safety assessments, develop and implement case plans, assess progress toward permanency, and ensure that families take appropriate steps to achieve it—blamed parents for their problems rather than empathized with them. A recent study by Children's Rights Inc. of children remaining in foster care longer than 2 years concluded that "The quality of case planning for many children was poor."[46]

Beneath these aspects of child welfare that remained unchanged, the situation was more complex. Although many of the indicators of child and family well-being that needed improvement 15 years ago still needed improvement in 2011, some things had changed. This section focuses on two areas of the child welfare system that have a substantial effect on children and are emblematic of the mixed results during the 15 years in question: the experience of children who are placed in foster care and child protective services.

The Experience of Children Placed in Foster Care

The median length of time that children remain in foster care before returning to their parents has fluctuated. In fiscal year 2000, children stayed in care an average of 6.4 months. That figure increased to a recent high of 11.5 months in fiscal 2007 and then fell to 5.3 months in fiscal 2010.[47] However, nearly 40% of the children in the city's custody at present had been there for more than 3 years.[48] The experience of the almost 15,000 children in foster care in 2011 in many ways was similar to what foster children encountered in the past, though there had been improvements in some areas. Betsy Krebs, executive director of Youth Advocacy Center, who works with children in foster care, says, "The foster care agencies are running businesses, and they don't have a vested interest in kids succeeding in the long-term."[49]

Three areas are the best indicators of the quality of the experience of children in care: where they are placed (i.e., with relatives or strangers, with their siblings, in which neighborhoods), the rate of abuse they suffer, and, perhaps most important, their lives after they leave foster care.

Where children are placed: It is generally agreed that children are better off living in foster care with a relative than living in the home of a stranger. In fiscal year 1993 44.1% of children in foster care were living with a relative. That year was the highpoint in the city's use of kinship foster care, one of the main ways ACS's precursor agency solved the bed shortage at the end of the 1980s. For more than the next 10 years the numbers of children in kinship care decreased, reaching a low of 24.3% in fiscal year 2006. By fiscal year 2010 the number of children in kinship care had increased to 35.0%, the highest percentage since 2000.[50]

Placing a child in care with his or her siblings, rather than separated, is also generally agreed to be beneficial. There has been no improvement in this area. Forty-eight percent of sibling groups were separated when they were placed into foster care in fiscal year 1996; 48.1% were separated in fiscal year 2010.[51]

Another issue significantly affecting the child's well-being is where the foster home is. It is generally agreed that children are better off if they are placed in a home in their neighborhood so they can maintain their friendships, continue to attend their school, and visit with their family more frequently. ACS's goal is "to keep children in their home community district [there are 59 community districts in New York City], allowing them to maintain ties to all that is familiar, thus reducing the trauma of being placed into foster care." In 2001 ACS's Renewed Plan of Action set a goal of 75% of children placed in their community district of origin.[52] This goal has eluded ACS.

In 1998, the first year for which consistent data are available, only 4.9% of children were placed in the community district in which they had been living. Community placements increased until fiscal year 2004, when 23.7% of the children lived on their home turf. Thereafter community placements dropped, falling to 10.5% in fiscal year 2010.[53,x]

The rate of abuse of children in foster care: Children are removed from their families and placed into foster care to protect them from harm. Nevertheless, there is a high and increasing incidence of confirmed abuse of children while they are in foster care placements. In fiscal year 2003 1.8% of children in family foster care (excluding children in group settings) were confirmed to have been abused or neglected while in care. In fiscal year 2009, 7.1% of such children were confirmed to have been abused or neglected in that year,[54] far higher than the rate of confirmed child abuse and neglect among the general population, though there is likely greater public scrutiny of youngsters in foster care than of children in their own homes.[55]

Outcomes for children when they leave foster care: How well children do when they leave foster care depends on whether the child is discharged to his or her family, to adoption, or ages out of foster care to live independently. We focus on the outcomes for children whose goal was return to their families, which in fiscal year 2010 was more than half (51.1%) of the children in care.[56,xi] The results are mixed.

---

x. Since then ACS has changed the definition it uses for in-community placement. Contiguous community districts are now considered to be an in-community district placement. This modification increased the percentage of children listed as having been placed within their "community of origin," though, in fact, it reflected little if any actual improvement.

xi. For those interested in the outcomes for children discharged to independent living, the *Child Welfare Watch* 19/20 (Winter 2010/2011) is a special double issue reviewing the situation of New York City adolescents discharged to independent living.

A recent study by Children's Rights Inc. looked at children with a goal of returning to their families who had been in foster care longer than 2 years but had not been reunited. The study documented deficiencies in their care that blocked reunification. More than half (51%) of the children had more than three different caseworkers handling their case in the previous 2 years. This brings to mind the words of Jeanette Vega (Chapter 2), who said that when her son Remi was in care, "caseworkers were coming and going like flies." Many children and parents did not receive the services they needed for reunification. Seventy-two percent of the families who were identified by their caseworkers as needing family therapy did not get that help. Thirty percent of the parents needing substance abuse treatment did not get it.[57]

One useful indicator for assessing the outcome for children who leave foster care is the recidivism rate: how frequently a child returns to foster care. Many factors contribute to recidivism—unsolved family problems, inadequate preparation of the family for the difficulties of reunification, or a deterioration in the family's or the child's situation. Often these problems can be addressed with additional services such as ongoing family counseling, support groups, or material assistance, such as a job, income support, or better housing. Without those supports, too often families continue to struggle with the problems that landed their children in foster care in the first place.

The rate of recidivism improved slightly between 1996 and 2011. In fiscal year 1996, 13% of children who were discharged returned to foster care within a year; in fiscal year 2010, 11.3% returned to care within 2 years.[58]

Child Protective Services

Child protective services (CPS)—the division of ACS that investigates reports of abuse and neglect and recommends whether a child should be removed from his or her family—has improved in many ways since the mid-1990s. These improvements are discussed below. Nevertheless, the basic structure and function of CPS remain unchanged. Its primary function is to investigate reports of abuse and neglect, rather than to assess the needs of a child and family for assistance and provide the required help. Under the leadership of commissioner Gladys Carrion, a long-time friend of poor families, OCFS tried to inch child protective services throughout the state toward assessing families' needs rather than exclusively investigating them. At the urging of OCFS, the New York State legislature passed a bill (Chapter 452 of the Laws of 2007) allowing local social service districts to try a new approach to child protective services called family assessment response. Counties could identify low-risk cases of neglect that would be assessed for services and provided help, rather than be investigated for abuse and neglect. "The reason for this alternative response," according to a report to the governor and legislature evaluating the program, "is that serious child safety issues are not found in the majority of families reported for suspected neglect. The family situations are more likely to reflect needs for support or advocacy rather than needs for investigative fact-finding and court ordered formal government intervention."[59]

Nineteen counties in New York opted to participate in this approach. ACS opposed the approach for New York City. The evaluation of the counties that participated was positive. The approach led to a decrease in the percentage of families for which a child removal petition was filed in family court, families who were given an assessment to identify their service needs were significantly less likely to have a child welfare case opened within 6 months of the focal report than were comparable families who received an investigation, and families were much more likely to report receiving help from their workers than similar families who received an investigation.[60] The evaluation recommended that the legislation for the family assessment response be made permanent.

Many families should be investigated for maltreatment, but the majority of CPS reports are for neglect, not for abuse. As the state's evaluation of the family assessment response concluded, "Child safety issues are not found in the majority of families reported for suspected neglect." ACS's approach—investigating all reports of abuse and neglect—wastes resources, takes attention away from high-risk cases needing investigation, and perpetuates the mislabeling of poverty as neglect.

Between 1996 and 2011 many of the most important CPS performance indicators have gone up and down. After a high-profile death of a child known to ACS reveals long-standing problems in the system, corrections are made that improve the situation temporarily, until the next high-profile death reveals other problems. At present, following two recent high-profile deaths of children mishandled by CPS and other agencies—those of Nixzmary Brown in 2006 and Marcella Pierce in 2010—many of the most important CPS indicators have improved as a result of ACS's hiring of more staffers, improving training and coordination, and strengthening supervision. Although the improvements have been impressive, the changes are unlikely to be sufficient to prevent future high-profile deaths of children known to ACS. In fact, the number of children who died or have been killed each year who were known to ACS (i.e., a child who has been either reported to child protective services, has been investigated by ACS, is in the custody of ACS, or has been returned home from foster care) has remained relatively constant: 43 fatalities in fiscal year 1996, 32 in 2001, 30 in 2006, and 39 in 2010.[61] In essence, the changes in CPS have not affected this most telling indicator of child safety.

The changes in protective services that ACS has implemented have made a significant difference in other areas. One of the accomplishments during his tenure as commissioner of which Mattingly is most proud was the implementation of ChildStat in 2006. Each week it brings together ACS senior management, including the commissioner, and CPS managers from local offices to examine data trends and individual cases. Through this process, local offices are both held accountable and receive supportive technical assistance from senior management on both systemic and individual case issues. According to some people both inside and outside of ACS who have sat in on these reviews, they are impressive and have improved the work of child protective services.[62] Others are less positive. Martin Guggenheim, professor at NYU School of Law, says, referring to ChildStat meetings, "They don't talk about what families need, or what was provided but what questions did the worker ask. Did you investigate correctly?"[63]

New York City reports data on hundreds of CPS indicators. Four are key to understanding the quality of CPS investigations and the help that families receive. These are caseload size, the proportion of children who are maltreated a second time within a year, turnover of child protective staff, and the percentage of families for whom a report of abuse or neglect has been confirmed and who have not received services. The changes in these indicators not only reflect the improvements that have been made in protective services but also the setbacks and the distance still to go.

Caseload size: Low caseloads are critical to ensure that CPS workers can perform timely and comprehensive investigations of allegations of abuse and neglect and assess the safety of each child. The Child Welfare League of America recommends a caseload of 12 active investigations per month per caseworker.[64]

The CPS caseloads have fluctuated widely since 1996. Generally they have been low when CPS was functioning well and high when it was functioning poorly. The average caseload in 1996, at the time of Elisa Izquierdo's death, was 23. The number fell to 12.8 in 1999, before rising again to 16.6 in 2006 at the time of Nixzmary Brown's death. In fiscal year 2011 the CPS caseload had fallen to 9.4, a sign that workers were more likely to have sufficient time to conduct adequate investigations.[65]

Children who experience repeat maltreatment within a year: According to ACS, "this outcome provides a measure of the child welfare system's success at keeping children who have been found to be victims of abuse and/or neglect safe."[66] The data below present the percentage of children confirmed to be victims of abuse or neglect who are investigated again within a year and are confirmed to be victims of a subsequent report of abuse or neglect. In 2000 the percentage was 9.3%. It rose to 14.8% in 2005 and to 17.0% in July 2011.[67] The trend was in the wrong direction. In the first decade of the twenty-first century, there was more than an 80% increase in the percentage of children found to be abused or neglected who were confirmed to have been abused or neglected again within a year.

Staff turnover: As described in Chapter 1, working as an investigator for child protective services is one of the most difficult jobs in the city. As a result, the turnover has remained high, though it improved in the years to 2009. Mattingly reported to the city council preliminary budget hearings in 2009 that because of ACS's success in maintaining manageable caseloads, recruitment campaigns, and improved frontline supervision, "our monthly attrition rate in Child Protective Services is at a historic low, below 2 percent."[68] That computes to an annualized attrition percentage of about 24%, a high rate, particularly in a recession economy. Many CPS workers have therefore been on the job for less than a year and possess limited experience in conducting investigations, limited skill in identifying families' needs, and limited knowledge of the resources available to assist families.

Families for whom a report of abuse or neglect has been confirmed and who have not received services: After a CPS worker determines that there is evidence of abuse or neglect, he or she decides what services, if any, are needed to address the abuse or neglect. The options are foster care, referral to preventive services agencies under contract with ACS, or referral to other community-based services, such as public assistance or a health clinic, not under contract to ACS, or no services. In the past a very high percentage of families in which abuse or neglect was confirmed received no services or even referrals for services. The percentage of families who have not received services or who have not been referred for services steadily decreased in the first decade of the twenty-first century. In the second quarter of 2006, 38.4% of families in confirmed reports of abuse or neglect received no services[69]; in the second quarter of 2011, only 14.2% of families did not receive services or referral for services.[70] Despite this apparent progress, roughly a third of the families referred for preventive services were not even connected within 30 days with the agencies that provide those services, let alone receive those services,[71] and ACS does not even record the percentage of families referred to other community services who actually receive those services. In 2011, for example, among 3,474 indicated reports in which both abuse and neglect were confirmed, 65.4% of the cases were completed with services, 12.2% were closed with no services, and 22.3% of the cases were referred to community-based services.[72] ACS, however, does not indicate whether the families that were referred to community-based services actually get to those agencies, if the agencies provide any service, or if the agency provided the help the family needed. ACS is strongly promoting evidence-based research as the standard to determine a program's efficacy. ACS would do well to use the same standard for itself in reporting whether families who are confirmed to have abused or neglected their children actually receive services.

WHAT HAS BEGUN TO SLIP

ACS's support for parents, families, and communities began to slip in 2005–2006 after several high-profile child deaths caused ACS to shift its focus to protective services, the area of child welfare that has often caused the undoing of family-focused reforms and the firing of commissioners, both in New York City and throughout the country. The economic crises and deep budget cuts that began in 2008 further diminished ACS's attention to and resources for families.

Preventive Services

Five highly publicized child fatalities in late 2005 and early 2006, including the death of Nixzmary Brown, in which ACS staff members as well as staffers in other agencies mishandled the case, led members of the city council and the state legislature to call on the mayor to fire Mattingly. Broad-based support for him from service providers and advocates enabled him to retain his position, but he had to shift ACS's focus and resources to protective services. At the same time that the child deaths revealed problems in protective services, the publicity surrounding the deaths caused a dramatic increase in reports of abuse and neglect, which rose from 50,251 in fiscal year 2005 to 64,190 in fiscal year 2007 and remained at roughly that level for the next 5 years, adding to ACS's already heavy workload.[73] ACS undertook several initiatives to improve children's safety, including increasing the number of protective service staff members who investigate abuse and neglect reports. ACS also increased the number of children receiving preventive services from 28,663 in June 2006 to 33,022 in June 2008.[74]

Another high-profile death in September 2010, this time of Marcella Pierce, a medically fragile child—in which ACS staff members as well as staffers in other agencies mishandled the case—pushed ACS to again address aspects of protective services. But by this time an economic crisis had engulfed the country; city and state funds for child welfare services were significantly reduced, including money for preventive service programs. The reductions resulted in a 30% decrease in the number of children served from 33,022 in June 2008 to 23,294 in June 2011.[75] As Jim Purcell, the CEO of the Council of Family and Child Caring Agencies that represents preventive service providers, said,

> We understand that the city is facing critical budget problems, but by closing access to preventive services for thousands of families whose children are at risk, the city is jeopardizing the safety—and the very lives—of many thousands of vulnerable children.[76]

In addition to the absolute reduction in the number of children served, ACS reduced the length of time, from 18 months to 12 months, that a family could be served in preventive service programs, as a way to increase the number of families served.[77] Parent and family advocates expressed concern that the reduced length of service would harm families.

Another change in the city's preventive service system reflected ACS's recent shift away from its focus on families. ACS has never systematically evaluated the performance of preventive service agencies. Instead, it gathers administrative and programmatic information about them, such as the number of families served, the length of time a family receives services, and the types of services provided by the 119 preventive service programs with which ACS has contracts. However, ACS does not evaluate the effectiveness of the services or what the parents who are served by the programs think of the assistance they receive. In 2006 ACS began a partnership with CWOP to design a way to interview parents about their experience as consumers of preventive services. Parents would be asked: Did you receive the help you needed? Did you feel respected by the staff? What could have improved the help you received?

The collaboration between ACS and CWOP to gather feedback from parents who used preventive services began with a grant from the Child Welfare Fund in 2006; in 2009, as had been agreed at the time of the grant, ACS began funding the project directly. According to CWOP parents and professional staff members, and to personnel from ACS's Office of Research and Evaluation who worked to develop a parent satisfaction survey, the project was productive and enthusiastically supported by both organizations. In the pilot phase, over 150 parents in 10 preventive service agencies were interviewed about their experiences with the preventive service agencies. The preliminary findings were surprising. The main problems were not the lack of concrete services or a mismatch between what was provided and what the family felt they needed. The main issues focused around respect. According to Mike Arsham, executive director of CWOP, "Parents were focused on relationship issues with staff in the programs. Will you respect me as the head of my household? Will you undermine me in the eyes of my kids? Will you be my ally or will you throw me under the bus? We therefore focused the interview instrument on these issues."[78]

As useful as the project might have been to improve casework, the preventive service agencies did not want to be evaluated in general, and they certainly did not want to be evaluated by the parents they were serving. They pressured ACS to abandon the project. "Agencies were screaming against the evaluation. 'No way are parents going to evaluate us. They are not reliable informants, and we don't trust ACS to do this fairly,'" Arsham says.[79] ACS was particularly vulnerable at the time to agencies' pressure since foster care and preventive service providers had already been attacking ACS—in fact one agency, Little Flower, filed a successful lawsuit against ACS—for its mishandling of the foster care and preventive service contracts that would define the city's relationship with child welfare agencies for the next 10 years.[xii]

xii. Every 10 years ACS issues a request for proposals (RFP) for all foster care and preventive services for which it contracts with voluntary agencies for the next 10 years. An RFP for $675 million was issued in the spring of 2008 but was cancelled in November of that year because of complaints from the agencies regarding ACS's excessive requirements in the contracts, insufficient funding to carry out the required tasks, and administrative problems in the application process. The RFP was reissued in May 2009. After the contracts totaling $630 million were awarded in April 2010, the agencies protested again, complaining about problems in the grading system to evaluate programs. Little Flower Children's Services, which had previously had a contract to care for 1,400 children in foster care, did not have its contract renewed and filed a lawsuit in the Supreme Court of the State of New York alleging that "its contracts would not be renewed, not because of Little Flower's performance, but as a result of a deeply flawed procurement process that ACS initiated." ACS acknowledged its mistakes in the grading process, and rescinded the contracts that were awarded in April 2010. The grading system was revised and contracts were reawarded in September 2010, with Little Flower receiving contracts to care for 700 children in foster care. [J. Glazer, "Remodeling Child Welfare by Answering This Request." *City Limits*, 692 (June 29, 2009); *Little Flower Children and Family Services v. City of New York*, New York City Administration for Children's Services, Supreme court of New York, complaint, June 14, 2010.]

In addition to the protests by the preventive service agencies, ACS's reduced focus on families was also a factor in the decision to terminate the parent feedback system. The staff members in the Office of Research and Evaluation who championed the parent feedback system and who wanted to evaluate preventive service agencies left ACS in 2010 as the enthusiasm for parent-oriented reforms in ACS was cooling. As ACS's priorities shifted, the replacement staff members in the Office of Research and Evaluation were given responsibilities other than hearing from parents. The city's budget cuts formally ended the parent feedback project in June 2010.

The Community Partnership Initiative

From the time that ACS was created in 1996 it has had a goal of moving child welfare services to a "neighborhood-based system" that would increasingly place child welfare services and decision making in the communities whose children and families ACS serves. Under Commissioner Nicholas Scoppetta ACS made a preliminary but significant move in that direction. ACS revised its contracts with all preventive and foster care providers, assigning agencies to serve specific boroughs or community districts, effective July 2000.[80] As a result, service provision became more rationalized—with specific agencies responsible for services in specific community districts, rather than serving children and families all over the city. But decisions continued to be made downtown at the headquarters of the major foster care providers, and services were often far from where the families lived.

In 2006 Mattingly developed an initiative with the potential to transform the way child welfare services are provided. It was called the Community Partnership Initiative (CPI), which would create collaboratives between communities, foster care agencies, and other social service providers. "The primary goal of the initiative was to promote 'a rethinking and reorientation' of child welfare work toward integrated, localized service models that can be tailored to the unique needs and resources of individual communities," according to the evaluation of CPI conducted by Chapin Hall.[81] The initiative was launched in three community districts—Bedford-Stuyvesant, Brooklyn; Highbridge, Bronx; and Jamaica, Queens—and was expanded the following year to eight other community districts with the highest rates of abuse, neglect, and foster care placement in the city.

In 2007–2008 ACS began funding 11 community partnerships—but with the modest sum of only $150,000 each. The expectation, however, as spelled out in the RFP issued by ACS in the spring of 2008, was that "... ACS intends to identify Community Coalitions to cover all of NYC..." There was also a requirement that "All ACS Family Foster Care and Preventive Services contractors...will be required to participate in local Community Coalitions."[82] Plus, there was a commitment by ACS that the money for each collaborative would at least double.[83] None of that happened. The RFP was rescinded in November 2008. When it was subsequently reissued in May 2009, the requirements for citywide expansion and foster care and preventive service agency participation were removed. The funding level was reduced from $6 million to $1.65 million, angering parents and their allies, who took little comfort from the fact that ACS did not eliminate the CPIs entirely at a time when other family-focused programs, such as the Office of Family Visiting and Parent Education, and the Office of Domestic Violence, were either eliminated or drastically cut.

The consequences of keeping CPI on the sidelines as an underfunded pilot project were significant. Individual community collaboratives suffered from the loss of anticipated funding (see the example of Bridge Builders Community Partnership described in Chapter 5). More significant, however, is that ACS's pulling back from the community partnerships reflected its abandonment of a restructured child welfare system that would have greater community participation and decision making and less autonomy for foster care and preventive service providers. Without an expanded partnership with communities, ACS's future reforms would at best remain where they are—or, worse, continue to slip—rather than move toward the significant improvements needed for parents, families, and communities that had been the advocates' hope and ACS's promise.

***

On February 23, 2010 the advisory board of the *Child Welfare Watch* met in a large, windowless conference room at the New School University on Fifth Avenue and 13th Street. These meetings had taken place twice a year for almost 15 years to discuss child welfare and to develop recommendations for the upcoming issue of the *Watch*. The group that day consisted of more than a dozen leaders working in the trenches of child welfare reform.[xiii] It

---

xiii. Attending the meeting were Andrew White, editor of the *Watch*; Mike Arsham, CWOP; John Courtney, Fund for Social Change; Kara Fincke, Bronx Defenders; Anita Gundanna, Fund for Social Change; Wayne Ho, Coalition of Asian Children and Families; Oma Holloway, the Door; Sandra Killett, parent advocate, Children's Village; Jeremy Kohomban, President and CEO of Children's Village; Larry Murray, former Assistant Commissioner, New York City Department of Juvenile Justice; and several staff members of the *Watch*. Andrew White, editor of the *Watch* and a faculty member of the Center for New York City Affairs, and I co-chaired the meeting.

represented a large part of the spectrum of people and organizations outside of ACS working to reform child welfare in New York City.

The meeting began with a discussion of what had changed in New York City's child welfare system. Although the meeting was not designed to reach consensus, everyone, even the sharpest critics of the city's child welfare system, acknowledged positive changes over the past decade or two. Those who spoke uniformly found the dramatic decrease in the number of children in foster care to be the most important change. On the other hand, the group felt that although the orientation and policies among many of the senior administrators of ACS and the child welfare agencies had changed, the values and practices on the ground—both in ACS and in the voluntary foster care agencies—had not changed, except in isolated pockets. For example, the quality of child protective services was inconsistent and varied by borough. Those who spoke also saw the system as beginning to slip, not back to where it was in 1995 but further away from where the reformers had hoped it would be but never reached.

A year and a half later, on July 26, 2011, Mattingly announced his resignation from ACS as of September. Although *The New York Times* article reporting his departure focused on problems in child protective services during Mattingly's watch, especially the death of Marcella Pierce in September 2010, the praise for him was widespread, including from Marcia Lowry who brought *Marisol v. Giuliani* in 1995 that set the reforms in motion. She said, "There are far too few child welfare commissioners anywhere in this country that share his courage, strength, integrity and tenacity."[84] Richard Wexler of the National Center on Child Protection Reform was more guarded in his assessment. "There are two John Mattinglys—the one who ran ACS before Nixzmary Brown died and the one who ran it after ... only the first one backed up the words with action."[85]

The changes that occurred in New York City's child welfare system between 1996 and 2011 began with Scoppetta, ripened with Bell, and reached their highest point under Mattingly. Tracy Field, director of the Annie E. Casey Foundation's strategy group that had worked closely with ACS on its reforms, in October 2011 stated, "I'd give New York City a B− [on the reforms it's made]. Perhaps at its high point it was a B+. I think there is more to do."[86]

Throughout those 15 years, parents and their allies successfully pushed to make many of those reforms a reality: reducing the number of children removed from their families, increasing services available to families, and securing legal representation for parents in family court. But the number of families receiving preventive services has decreased by 30% from 2008 to 2011, and decreased again in fiscal 2012.[87] The continued reduction in this assistance to families could have severe consequences. The Community Partnerships in which poor communities would have an increased say in child welfare decisions was sidelined and several offices within ACS that responded to families' needs such as the Office of Family Visiting and Parent Education, and the Office of Domestic Violence, were either eliminated or drastically cut. As the parents' movement waned, some of the reforms lost steam. This pattern is discussed in the next chapter.

CHAPTER 8
Conclusions

The child welfare system in New York since 1996 has improved more and remained improved for longer than during any previous period in at least the last half century. The parents' movement, working closely with their allies, was a decisive factor in bringing about and sustaining the changes. Several arguments support this conclusion.

WHY WERE THE CHANGES IN NEW YORK SO EXTENSIVE AND SO LONG LASTING?

Many factors in the past 20 years contributed to improvements in child welfare nationally that also contributed to improvements in New York City's system. Several pieces of federal legislation[i] shifted government policy toward reducing the number of children in foster care nationally from its highpoint of 567,000 children in 1999 to 400,000 children in 2012. This decrease of 29% is far less than the 64% decrease in New York

---

i. Promoting Safe and Stable Families Act (1993), Adoption and Safe Families Act (1997), and Fostering Connections to Success and Increasing Adoptions Act (2008).

City during the same time period.[1,ii] The crack cocaine epidemic that began in the mid-1980s fueled the increase in the number of children entering foster care nationally. The epidemic ended in the early 1990s reducing the number of children coming into care. The U.S. economy also improved nationally until 2008, putting less pressure on families, which also contributed to the decrease in children in care nationally. But New York City improved more, and has remained improved for longer than almost anywhere else in the country. Why?

Parents played a decisive role. The major factor that had not been present in previous reform efforts was the organized activism of parents who had children taken from them. Without their personal, forceful, sustained, and collective involvement, the changes would not have been as deep or lasted as long. Before parents began organizing in 1994, they had fought alone to be reunited with their children, but never in the history of the United States had parents embroiled in the child welfare system created a movement to fight to reform child welfare.[2] These parents, working in collaboration with their allies, created a dozen new activist organizations. The Child Welfare Organizing Project (CWOP) trained 150 parents to be activists and leaders. Child welfare-involved parents and their allies demonstrated against child welfare agencies, at family court and in front of ACS. They participated in victorious class action lawsuits. They met with commissioners and worked as trained parent advocates in foster care agencies, in law firms, and in the Administration for Children's Services (ACS). They spoke in schools of social work and law, wrote and published articles in *Rise* magazine and elsewhere about their experiences, and sat on the *Child Welfare Watch* advisory board presenting their recommendations for reform.

CWOP became by far the strongest and most influential of these parent/professional partnerships in New York and throughout the nation. The movement's effect on both individual case decisions as well as on ACS policy was unimaginable in 1996. As Commissioner Mattingly said to a cheering audience of child welfare professionals and parents at the March 16, 2011 Parent Advocates Forum, "Where would we be without CWOP?"[3]

Parents worked closely with their allies who included social workers, lawyers, foundations officers, academics, staff in ACS and child welfare agencies, and, most important, two visionary and skilled commissioners, William Bell and John Mattingly, who saw that strengthening families was

---

ii. The decrease in New York City is 72% from the maximum of almost 50,000 children in care in 1992 to fewer than 14,000 children in care today.

the best way to protect children. Neither parents by themselves nor their allies by themselves could have brought about these changes; together they created the depth and duration of the change. As Commissioner Bell said to parents at an event in 2004 organized by CWOP, "The New York City child welfare system has fundamentally changed over the last several years...because you have forced us to change, because you have said openly and loudly, 'Things cannot continue to go the way that they have been going.' And we've listened to that."[4]

An important element of the movement of parents and their allies was the creation of a critical mass of lawyers trained in family court law. In 1990 there were at most a half dozen lawyers trained to represent parents in New York City's family court; in 2011 there were about 100.[5] The creation of lawyers trained in family court law has meant that parents not only have lawyers to represent them in family court, but also that these lawyers are available to advocate or lobby on behalf of child welfare-affected parents in general. According to Martin Guggenheim, a professor at New York University School of Law:

> Child welfare is a field in which parents' perspective had never been at the table for law making and policy purposes. Now you can't have a meeting in a New York courthouse where you don't have a parents' lawyer. They are now institutional representatives of a movement.[6]

There have been other periods in the history of New York City's child welfare system when visionary and skilled commissioners implemented reforms, but they did so without a parents' movement pushing for the reforms. In those cases, reforms were effective but short-lived. In 1979, for example, child welfare Commissioner Gail Kong implemented a monitoring system that improved the performance of foster care agencies and decreased the number of children in foster care from 21,000 in 1979 to 16,230 in 1984. But pressure from the foster care agencies, without a countervailing force, slowly undermined the monitoring system, contributing to an increase in the number of children in care beginning in 1984, reaching 21,000 by 1988, and almost 50,000 in 1992. The recent round of reforms implemented with pressure from parents and their allies has lasted more than 15 years, with the number of children in care remaining below 17,000 for the past 7 years.[7] Parents and their allies became an effective countervailing force that continued to push for reform when the existing forces in child welfare might have let the reforms slide backward as happened repeatedly in the past.

The movement grew at a time when the influence of the voluntary agencies was diminishing. As the number of children in foster care dropped from 50,000 to fewer than 14,000 today, foster care became a buyer's market. As a result, the city could pick and choose which agencies would receive children and which agencies would be closed, decreasing the influence of foster care agencies. As the number of children in foster care declined so did the number of foster care agencies, dropping from 79 in 1979 to about 30 in 2011. The agencies that remain tend to be those that are better managed, are more effective in returning children safely to their families, and whose executive leadership tends to be sympathetic to ACS's policy direction of preserving and strengthening families as the first response to protecting children.[iii] These agencies are also supporters of parent advocates; the majority have hired them to work with families in their agencies.

As the size of the foster care market shrank, reducing the influence of the voluntary agencies, its leadership changed. John Cardinal O'Conner, the Catholic archbishop of New York, had been a powerful force in the child welfare system from the time of his arrival in New York City in 1984. He used his power to help eliminate or weaken several reforms that he felt undermined the independence of the faith-based agencies. After O'Conner's death in 2000, the agencies, left without a powerful spokesperson, relied instead on individual agencies, various religious federations, and the Council of Family and Child Caring Agencies to coordinate their activities. They were unable to match the stature and influence of O'Conner. The voluntary agencies retained considerable sway in child welfare, but their power during the first decade of the twenty-first century diminished, creating room for the voice of parents to be heard.

RECENT CHANGES IN THE PARENTS' MOVEMENT

Two significant changes occurred in the parent advocacy movement between roughly 2007 and 2010. These changes reduced the power and impact of the movement but also added weight to the hypothesis that the parents' movement was a decisive factor in bringing about reforms.

iii. However, they also tend to be larger agencies and more diversified into other systems. While the system remains small or contracts, their size is not a problem. If, or when, the number of children in care expands and foster care becomes a seller's market, the city will be dependent on a smaller number of providers. Today four agencies, Graham Windham, Good Shepherd Services, New York Foundling, and SCO "serve over half the children in the system." [Bill Baccaglini, executive director, New York Foundling, cited in "NYCT Gives Four Agencies $200,000 for Solution-Based Casework," *New York Nonprofit Press*, August 2012, http://nynp.biz/August2012. html.

The first change was a shift from outside agitation to inside collaboration. The second was a decrease in the number and strength of parent organizations pressing for child welfare reform. The simultaneity of these changes diminished the impact of the parents' movement.

CWOP shifted from having an exclusively outside strategy—agitating, criticizing, and demanding change—to collaborating with ACS and foster care agencies. Emblematic of this change, in 2007 it signed a memorandum of understanding with ACS that requires ACS, whenever it is contemplating the removal of an East Harlem child from his or her home, to call CWOP to send a parent advocate to the child safety conference. CWOP receives New York State funds to do this work.

As ACS and the child welfare system improved and CWOP became more mainstream, CWOP became more comfortable with ACS and less critical of it. In subsequent years, both Voices of Women and Parents In Action also switched to an inside strategy. The *Child Welfare Watch* became more mainstream and less critical of ACS, while continuing to produce well-regarded analyses of New York's child welfare system. As Andrew White, the editor of the *Watch,* said in 2011, "The *Watch* has become part of the DNA of the child welfare system."[8]

At first, parent advocates worked primarily outside the foster care system. Over time they too were increasingly incorporated into child welfare agencies. By 2011, 50 parent advocates were working in 22 foster care agencies. They were seen by the leadership of ACS and child welfare agencies as an effective and legitimate part of casework practice.

In the middle of the past decade, while ACS was increasingly listening to parents, supporting quality legal representation for them, and funding programs that increased the benefits they received, the shift to an inside strategy strengthened the parents' movement and its impact on child welfare. But as the decade wound down, and parent organizations moved toward an inside strategy, the outside pressure on ACS diminished. As Mike Arsham, the executive director of CWOP, said in 2011, "An inside strategy would not have been possible without outside agitation."[9]

REASONS FOR THE CHANGES IN THE PARENTS' MOVEMENT

By 2010, outside agitation against the child welfare system had all but disappeared for several reasons. The anonymous donor behind the Child Welfare Fund (CWF) shifted her funding focus to providing mental health services for children rather than reforming the child welfare system and I stepped down as executive director in 2009, ending my role as coach, coordinator, and funder of the movement promoting parents' influence in the child welfare system. Although I continued to urge parent involvement in child welfare—primarily through the Parent Advocate Initiative and Bridge Builders—my departure from CWF diminished the coordination and funds available to organizations working on behalf of parents.[iv]

Several parent-led organizations encountered difficulties that were exacerbated by the reduced funding from CWF. People United for Children (PUC), which always struggled to raise money, closed its doors in 2009. Voices of Women Organizing Project (VOW), shaken by the loss of its founding director, shifted to an inside strategy. Concerned Citizens for Family Preservation, relying on parent volunteers for much of its advocacy work on Staten Island, closed its doors in 2010. Parents In Action (PIA) moved from demonstrating in the streets, denouncing ACS at public forums, and calling foster care a modern form of slavery. PIA now collaborates with ACS in helping individual families reunite with their children.

The original shift from outside agitation to inside collaboration occurred when the movement of parents, CWOP, and their allies was growing in strength and ACS had resources to be responsive to the movement's concerns. Its incorporation into the system's mainstream reflected the strength of the movement rather than its cooptation. But by the end of the first decade of the twenty-first century, with little outside agitation or pressure pushing ACS to reform, the parents' movement stalled.

The shift of parents and their advocates to an inside strategy and the loss of outside pressure occurred at the same time as two dramatic changes in ACS. First, several high-profile deaths of children known to ACS—most notably those of Nixzmary Brown in 2006 and Marcella Pierce in 2010—caused ACS to shift its focus to fixing protective services. Mayor Bloomberg stood by Commissioner Mattingly, but shifted resources from helping families to fixing protective services. Second, the crisis in the economy starting in 2008 significantly reduced the money available to ACS, further diminishing the resources for families.[10,v]

iv. I do not want to overstate my role in promoting child welfare reforms from my position at the Child Welfare Fund, but as Martin Guggenheim, a leading child welfare reformer, wrote to me: "I regard you as the single most important advocate in NYC over the past 20 years because you helped nurture every group and individual committed to progressive child welfare reform and many of these people and organizations could not have flourished without you." [Martin Guggenheim, professor, New York University School of Law, email communication, May 23, 2011.]

v. The impact of the financial crisis on New York City's child welfare system was exacerbated by a significant decrease in federal funds to New York City for foster care. The city found "several cases" in which documentation for federal Title IV-E funding had not been adequate. Rather than face an unfavorable federal audit, the

The loss of parent pressure from the outside and the reduced resources and diminished attention to parents on the inside reinforced each other, contributing to an erosion in the parts of the child welfare system that had benefited parents and families.

In essence, at the same time that the parents' movement diminished in strength, parent-focused reforms diminished. Simultaneity of course does not imply causation, but the sidelining of parent-focused reforms at the same time that the parents' movement stalled does show the interconnection of the two and is consistent with the view that parents played a significant role in bringing about the reforms.

LESSONS LEARNED

Many lessons emerged while working to reform child welfare over the past two decades. Four lessons stand out as most instructive as parents and their allies continue reforming child welfare in New York City, and others across the country begin to create similar movements elsewhere.

First, social movements thrive when participants feel that they are part of something larger than themselves. They come to recognize that their personal problems are shaped in large part by forces beyond their individual control. They can see that those forces can be influenced by the mutual aid, compassion, and collective action from their movement, "collective efficacy" as described by Harvard sociologist Felton Earls.[11] In the process, people develop a sense of their own self-worth and a sense of a shared identity that can energize and sustain them. CWOP and a few other organizations in the parents' movement trained parents and provided them with paid jobs that enabled them to help others going through what they went through. These activities created a shared identity and a sense of "collective efficacy" that sustained the members of the movement.

Second, power is the key to success. Whether you choose an inside strategy—collaborating with the establishment—or an outside strategy—agitating from the streets or bringing a lawsuit in the courts—a movement needs to create power. People of good will who run a system, a bureaucracy, an agency, or a program generally will make changes only to the extent that those changes meet their interests. When their interests and

city gave up $140 million in federal foster care funding. Federal funding fell from 40% to 24% of the total foster care budget. [Kathleen Mahar, "How Has Shift Away from Foster Care Affected Funding, Spending, Caseloads?" (New York: New York City Independent Budget Office, October 2011): 5.]

the interests of their clients collide, as so often happens in child welfare, a countervailing force is needed to bring about reform.

Power comes from different sources—money, information, people, and connections. The area in which we should have put more emphasis was in creating connections with other movements of people fighting for parallel changes in other systems. The disabilities movement, for example, gained strength not only by linking disabilities—the blind, the deaf, the physically disabled, and the developmentally disabled—but by connecting with activists in other areas—veterans and workers who had people with disabilities among their ranks.[12] Although the parents' movement in New York City briefly tried to join forces with developmental disabilities activists, and CWOP has had contact with child welfare and antipoverty activists in other cities, the process of linking to other movements did not have the attention it deserved.

Third, individuals bring about change, but they can take things only so far. Without an organization with structure, staff, funding, and a clearly defined mission, the activities are likely to fizzle. The child welfare leaders who generated whirlwinds of activity, but did not simultaneously create strong organizations, burned out, and their organizations folded. Funding and technical assistance may help, but not always. How to enable a visionary and inspiring leader who lacks the skills and experience to create and sustain an organization is one of the unsolved puzzles of this work.

And finally, the parents' movement was one way to create a sustained countervailing force to bring about long-lasting change; it may not be the only way. Class action lawsuits that lead to broad court-ordered consent decrees have significantly improved child welfare systems. Illinois, for example, is one of the few jurisdictions that has significantly reduced the number of children in foster care over a sustained period of time—from 52,000 in 1997 to about 17,000 in recent years—and has made other significant improvements in its child welfare system. These include promoting family preservation, increasing parent/child visiting, and moving children to permanent placements more quickly.[13] In 2003 Illinois operated under eight state and federal court consent decrees that forced the state to make these improvements.[14] A full analysis of the situation in Illinois and other states operating under broad court-ordered consent decrees is needed, but class action lawsuits and court-ordered consent decrees can be a countervailing force to change child welfare.

Elected officials who represent the interests of poor families might also be a force for change. But they will need grassroots pressure on them from parents, the poor, and the general public to remain focused on child welfare and to remain in office, which brings us back to the need for a movement of parents and their allies.

The parents' movement in New York, like all social movements, has a life cycle. It developed in the early 1990s and grew for the next 15 years, contributing to significant changes in the child welfare system. Although its force has waned in the past 5 years, the values it promoted have become mainstream within child welfare practice. Fewer than 14,000 children are in foster care where once there were almost 50,000. Publicly funded law firms now represent almost half of all parents in family court when their children are in danger of being removed. Most foster care agencies in New York City have hired parent advocates to help parents reunite with their children. More struggling families than in the past receive preventive services to ameliorate their problems.

But these reforms are vulnerable and provide only partial solutions. More than half of the families with children who are about to be removed do not have quality legal representation in family court. Most foster care agencies have hired only one or two parent advocates, though thousands of families could benefit from their involvement. Preventive services for families have been cut and much of what families most need is largely unavailable—jobs, improved housing, drug treatment, and mental health services.

The child welfare system is dramatically different today than it was 20 years ago. But pressure from parents and their allies is still needed to keep the system moving forward or at least to keep the child welfare rollercoaster from sliding back downhill. The annex to this book describes a vision for future reform and a strategy to get there.

Epilogue

Commissioner Mattingly attended the Child Welfare Organizing Project's (CWOPs) fourteenth graduating class of Parent Leaders on Monday July 25, 2011. It was the commissioner's final public appearance before announcing the following day that he would resign after serving for 7 years as child welfare commissioner, the longest serving child welfare commissioner in the city's history.[1] The following day Mayor Bloomberg announced that Ronald Richter would be the new commissioner of the Administration for Children's Services (ACS) beginning in September.[2]

Unlike the three previous child welfare commissioners, Richter had not worked in a voluntary child welfare agency before becoming commissioner. He had represented children in family court for 10 years becoming deputy attorney-in-charge for Legal Aid's juvenile rights division. In 2005 Mattingly appointed him to serve as deputy commissioner of ACS for Family Court Legal Services, representing ACS in all matters before the city's five family courts. While at ACS his effective leadership and attention to the rights of both children and parents enabled him to please the broad spectrum of competing interests in child welfare. At one end of the spectrum he recruited police officers to work with child protection investigators; at the other end he enabled Bridge Builders to secure a special part in family court to handle all child welfare cases coming from the Highbridge community. After 2 years he left ACS to work in the mayor's office as the family services coordinator. After another 2 years, in 2009, Mayor Bloomberg appointed him to serve as a family court judge in Queens.

Richter's appointment as ACS commissioner was hailed by all segments of the child welfare community. Jim Purcell, the head of the Council of Family and Child Caring Agencies, which represents all foster care agencies, said that "Mayor Bloomberg has made a terrific choice."[3] Mike Arsham from CWOP wrote that "We applaud his appointment."[4]

Four months into Commissioner Richter's term in office he issued the ACS 2011–2013 Strategic Plan, anticipating that he would likely serve until only December 2013, the end of Bloomberg's third term. Although the plan was well received by service providers, it raised concerns among the parent advocacy community. Fifty-one leaders in child welfare, including 15 parents, signed a letter to the commissioner raising their concerns. "The plan seems more geared to strengthening child protective services than to strengthening families. A comprehensive plan would address both."[5]

Richter agreed to meet with a delegation of the advocates. The meeting in April was more encouraging than the advocates anticipated. ACS would continue as planned to strengthen protective services and bring juvenile offenders who had been placed upstate, back to facilities in New York City—important and appropriate priorities. At the meeting Richter reported that ACS would consider one of the advocates' main recommendations—having parent advocates attend every child safety conference held throughout the city. These conferences determine if a child should be removed from his or her family. The parent advocate serves as an ally of the parent in the conference, helping the parent understand his or her rights and options. A 2012 evaluation by the National Resource Center for Permanency and Family Connections of parent advocates participating in child safety conferences in East Harlem showed fewer children were placed into foster care when a CWOP-trained parent advocate attended the session.[6,i] The evaluation may have added to Richter's already high regard for the use of parent advocates, though he did not feel the evaluation rose to the level of evidence-based research.

Richter agreed to address other concerns of the advocates. The advocates' letter stated that the Strategic Plan had "no mention of the racial bias that pervades child welfare." Richter reported that ACS will implement an "undoing racism" training for senior management and other ACS staff, a small but important step to addressing a long-standing problem in child welfare. Although ACS would not increase the funding for general preventive services that has decreased over recent years, it will provide additional support for families with teenagers. Teenagers are the subjects of a third of the reports of child abuse and neglect.[7]

---

i. Several of ACS's senior management prefer that parent advocates attend some child safety conferences while other members of a family's community—civic or church leaders—attend other child safety conferences. At present, a final decision has not been made regarding which approach would be used. Regardless of the outcome, it seems likely that trained parent advocates will participate in more child safety conferences.

Other priority issues raised by the advocates were not embraced by ACS—having more parent advocates hired by foster care agencies, expanding the legal representation of parents in family court, or increasing the funding for the Community Partnership Initiatives.[ii] Nevertheless, Commissioner Richter agreed to future meetings to continue the discussions.

Change occurs slowly, especially in large systems such as child welfare. But the reforms set in motion 20 years ago by the parents' movement and championed by their allies continue under Commissioner Richter. As he so aptly said in a recent interview, "It's always hard to draw political attention to issues that affect children and families as opposed to business interests where powerful lobbyists have sway."[8] That is where parents and their allies have come in to shift the balance of power. The child welfare system may inch forward under Commissioner Richter, but the progress is likely to be more significant and come about more quickly if parents and their allies remain as a strong, countervailing force.

ii. ACS hired Chapin Hall to evaluate the Community Partnerships. The evaluation has not yet been completed.

ANNEX I
A Vision and a Strategy

A VISION

Child welfare in New York and throughout the United States is a residual service in which a family receives help only after the child has been abused or neglected. The residual perspective is based on the belief that the troubles of families derive from shortcomings in the parents—moral, psychological, physiological, or some other personal failing.[1] Foster care within the United States has emerged as the major tool in this model to deal with parental and family shortcomings. The alternative approach is a universal, preventive model in which financial supports and social services are available as a right to all families experiencing difficulties not just to the very poor, at all points in their life cycle before their problems become overwhelming. In the universal, preventive model, removal of the child and placement into foster care are used as a last resort, as is the case in most European countries.[2] The universal, preventive model is based on the belief that individuals are responsible for their actions, but that social and economic conditions beyond their control often shape their choices.

Many of the elements of that system, including the rights of parents in it, were recently codified in *From Rights to Reality*, by parent advocacy organizations, government agencies, and foundations.[3] It calls for a child welfare system that is based on the rights of parents and children in which quality legal representation is available to parents in all legal proceedings. It is a system that helps families with the wide range of services and supports they need before their problems become overwhelming, rather than only after they have fallen off a cliff, as is the situation now. These services include not only case management, parenting classes, anger management, and counseling currently available through preventive services programs, but jobs, better housing, better health care, child care, emergency assistance, properly functioning schools, health and mental health services, and drug treatment programs, which are often not available.

When families are charged with abusing or neglecting their children, child protective services should at least create a dual-track system as have all or part of 18 other states, including 19 counties in New York State.[4] By that approach, low-risk situations, such as educational neglect, in which child physical safety is not an issue, are assessed to find out what help the family needs, rather than investigated for punishment. In many European countries social service agencies are the first responders when families are having trouble rather than child protection investigators. This is a methodology that could be tried in the United States as well. Under this system, the state would intervene to remove the child only if the social service agency is unable to provide adequate help to ensure the child's safety.

When families are found to have neglected or abused children and help to the family would ensure the child's safety, those resources should be provided so children can remain at home. If they cannot remain home safely, they should be placed in foster care. Whenever possible, children in foster care should be placed with a relative or if that is not possible, in a nonrelative foster home in the community in which they were living so that they can continue to attend their school, maintain their friendships, and be in regular contact with their families, a primary factor determining how quickly children return home. Out-of-home placement should be brief, and when children leave foster care, they and their families again need a range of supports to ease the transition back to home and to prevent the original problems from resurfacing.

The question is how can these changes be brought about in economically troubled times during which many government leaders advocate scaling back government? What is the strategy to create a child welfare system that continues to improve or at least does not come crashing down as has happened so often in the past?

A STRATEGY

If government does not increase or further reduces its responsibility to the poor, the country will face more crises from increased child neglect and abuse and more children in foster care. There will be more homelessness, more sickness, and more crime, involving children in foster care as well as children who leave foster care. A 2010 study led by Mark Courtney at the University of Washington followed adolescents who left foster care in mid-west states until they were 23 or 24 years of age. Sixteen percent of the males were incarcerated at the time of the study; 45% of the women had been incarcerated at some time. Twenty-four percent of the young adults had been homeless, half more than once. Fifty-two percent were unemployed and 75% of the women were or had been pregnant. Nearly 25% had neither a high school diploma nor a GED.[5]

We either pay upfront to protect children or we pay at the back end for foster care after a child is abused or neglected. If 50,000 children were in New York City's foster care today as in 1992, at an average cost of $49,000 a year per child in 2010, the cost would be $2.45 billion a year, rather than $789 million a year for the 16,000 children in care in 2010.[6] The $1.7 billion in savings should be used up front for preventive services at an average cost of $10,000 per family or $4,000 per child.[i,7]

How then can a child welfare system based on rights, prevention, and support for families be created? How can we create the force or, as some say, the political will to make the needed change? How does child welfare get to the head of the line with police and fire departments when it comes to receiving government money? More important, how can a movement be forged pressing for government policies that champion social responsibility including universally available social supports?

Although the ideas presented here are specific to New York City, they apply to other localities as well. First, child welfare advocates, parents, and their allies can expand their work and influence inside the child welfare system. Collaborating with the Administration for Children's Services (ACS) and working as parent advocates within foster care and preventive service agencies have been major victories; the alliance of parents and professionals in child welfare has been unprecedented. Their expanded pressure is needed to preserve the reforms in place and to keep the system moving forward. Social workers who have been on the sidelines of these reforms could explore whether hiring a parent advocate could improve casework with families. Agency administrators might hire parent advocates and create forums in their agencies in which families can express their concerns and recommendations. Boards of directors might invite parents to join with them in making decisions about their agencies; currently no foster care agency in New York City, and probably none in the nation, has a parent with child welfare experience on its board of directors.

i. Assuming an average of 2.5 children per family served in preventive service programs.

Alliances might also be made with organizations of foster care youth who are organizing within the child welfare system. Currently the most effective of these groups is California Youth Connection (CYC). A national spin-off, the National Foster Youth Action Network, was set up by CYC's founder, Janet Knipe, to expand foster youth organizing across the country. The Action Network's goal is for national policy makers and state child welfare systems to involve current and former foster youth as equal partners in the development of child welfare policy and legislation.

The Child Welfare Organizing Project (CWOP) and other advocates can continue their discussions with ACS to increase the number of communities in which trained parent advocates are paid to attend child safety conferences. The law firms that are paid by government to represent half of the parents who are about to have their children removed by family court can press for the other half to be represented by them or by other public interest law firms. Staten Island—the borough with St. George/Stapleton (the community with the highest rate of children placed in foster care in the city)—should not be the one borough without institutional legal representation for its parents. The independent evaluation that these law firms propose conducting is an important step in that direction.

Working inside the system does not mean giving up your right to forcefully criticize what is harmful in child welfare. The foster care agencies have the Council of Family and Child Caring Agencies (COFCCA) lobbying ACS and the state. And when the agencies feel they have been treated unfairly, they sue the city as Little Flower Children and Family Services recently did when it believed its foster care contract should have been renewed and wasn't. Parent advocacy organizations can do the same.

CWOP, other parent advocacy organizations, and their allies need to also have an outside strategy. If they don't, parents working inside the system will be too weak to sustain the changes that have been made, let alone move the system forward. The child welfare rollercoaster will slide downhill, perhaps not to its nadir in 1995, but more children will be placed into foster care, more families will be destroyed, and more stories of children whose lives have been shattered by ACS and child welfare agencies will fill the media. To regain its strength and influence, CWOP and other parent organizations need to expand their alliance with professionals in child welfare and create alliances in other social service areas and with broader social movements as well.

One way to link with these other organizations is to view child welfare through a civil rights prism. Ninety-six percent of the children in foster care in New York City are black, Latino, Asian, or other minorities[8]; when half of their parents appear in family court they do so without adequate legal representation. That child welfare leaders label these problems as "disproportionality" rather than racism, indicates why a broader perspective and broader alliances are needed to reform the system.

Many child welfare organizations can be part of this alliance: CWOP; VOW; the former leaders of PUC and Concerned Citizens; Richard Wexler at NCCPR; the 100 lawyers and their organizations who represent parents in family court; Citizens' Committee for Children; foundations such as Casey Family Programs, which has a national goal for 2020 of reducing foster care by half; the New York Foundation, which promotes community organizing; and other funders who support parents and their allies—to name a few. The Social Service Employees Union might be part of such a coalition in areas in which their interests overlap with child welfare clients. A coordinating body would strengthen their impact.

Child welfare reformers can gather more force by making alliances beyond child welfare with advocacy organizations in other social service areas in which child welfare is an important concern. Juvenile justice, child care, homelessness, mental health, and substance abuse have important overlaps with child welfare parents and children. When many of these constituencies joined forces with elected officials in April 2011, with 800 people demonstrating at City Hall protesting budget cuts in child care and early education, the city council restored much of the funding.[9] A subsequent demonstration had an even bigger impact. "In a city where financial institutions are too big to fail," as the article in the *New York Nonprofit Press* reported, "yesterday's May12th Coalition rally in which more than 20,000 people marched on Wall Street was finally too big to ignore." The event brought together diverse groups with a common interest in expanding social services—labor unions, grass roots advocacy organizations, Catholic Charities, and human service providers. Subsequently cuts in preventive services and other social service programs were restored.[10]

Alliances can also be forged with parent organizations in other fields such as developmental disabilities, mental health, and public education. Parents in each of those fields have become powerful change agents.[ii]

ii. Risks are associated with their success. Parents of children with developmental disabilities, for example, contributed to closing the Willowbrook Developmental Center, where abuse of the residents was rampant, on Staten Island in the 1980s. Since then, parents of children with developmental disabilities created organizations that became service providers on contract with the state to provide group homes for the developmentally disabled, and dramatically reduced their public criticisms of and pressure on the state agency that serves the developmentally disabled.

Alliances could be formed outside of social services with antipoverty organizations that have broader agendas. These alliances can be with activist groups whose constituents are also embroiled in the child welfare system. These include organizations that are working for jobs and health care for the poor, to end the exploitation of women, to help people in prison, and for the rights of immigrants. Some of these groups such as Every Mother is a Working Mother, Welfare Warriors, and the Poor People's Economic and Human Rights Campaign have already taken note that their constituents have been entangled in the child welfare system and have begun to organize and press for reforms on child welfare issues. It would strengthen the power of all groups if child welfare reform was embraced by these and other antipoverty organizations and if child welfare groups focused on the broader reforms promoted by those organizations.

One of the most important alliances that child welfare-affected parents and their allies could make is with the general public. With the help of journalists and parent activists the public can become aware of who the parents in the child welfare system are and how the system fails them. As Steven Cohen, the staff director of the Special Child Welfare Advisory Panel, concluded, "Most of the families involved with the child welfare system are committed to their kids and are torn up by not being able to raise their kids safely and by confronting systems that hurt rather than help them."[11] Members of the public who read horror stories in the media about parents who have viciously abused their children can be made to realize that these stories represent a miniscule portion of the parents whose children are removed from their custody. The stories of why the children of Tracey Carter, Wanda Chambers, Sandra Killett, Shawrline Nicholson, Jeanette Vega, and Youshell Williams were placed in foster care are far more common.

We who care about our own children and other people's children should push government to help families as the best way to help their children. This can be accomplished by contacting elected officials to ask that preventive service programs be expanded; standing with parents and their allies outside of City Hall when they seek funds to help children by strengthening families; reading Rise magazine (www.risemagazine.org) to learn more about the lives of struggling parents; and inviting parents from CWOP or VOW to speak at your church or club to learn more about parents' ideas to help their children.

Without more resources from government, there won't be money to pay for health care, to improve the schools, and to keep children safe and families together. When families fall apart, everyone suffers. Increase the role of government and raise taxes to help children and families? That may sound unimaginable in 2013. But 25 years ago few thought the Soviet system would end. In the 1960s 35% of the elderly in the United States were poor. Improvements to Social Security and the advent of Medicare changed that; in 1995 10% of the elderly were poor, a far greater decline than for any other group.[12] Sweden in the early 1930s had a residual child welfare system and a punitive family policy that, in many ways, was similar to the U.S. social welfare system at the time. A person accepting poor relief in Sweden, for example, lost his right to vote; this rule was not abolished until 1945.[13] Since then the national government created what has become the most preventive, universal social welfare system in the world. Conditions change, governments change, and programs change.

The parent advocate's movement has lifted the pessimism that was pervasive among child welfare-affected parents. The child welfare system has responded to their complaints. They have a voice and are making a difference in their own lives and in the lives of parents throughout the city. It is now the broader population's responsibility to join with them, to increase their strength, and to destroy the pessimism in the rest of the population that thinks things won't improve, that their voices won't make a difference. Parents have overcome enormous difficulties and have helped move an intransigent system. They need the public's support.

Anyone who has experienced his or her own difficulties might think about the times we have been depressed, have not had enough money, have drunk too much, or have broken promises to ourselves. Think about the mistakes each of us has made while parenting. Imagine what our responses might have been without resources to fall back on—skills, money, family, friends, and connections. And think of what would be seen if our lives were constantly scrutinized in public housing, in public hospitals, in public child care, and in our child's public school.

Parenting is challenging under the best circumstances and can be overwhelming for many. It certainly has been for the mothers in this book who have come back "from the other side." They need all the help they can get from us to keep New York's child welfare system on track and to create the satisfying lives we all seek for our children and for ourselves.

Abbreviations

ACS	Administration for Children's Services
AECF	Annie E. Casey Foundation
ASFA	Adoption Assistance and Safe Family Act of 1997
BCW	Bureau of Child Welfare
BMCI	Bushwick Managed Care Initiative
CCC	Citizen's Committee for Children
CCFP	Concerned Citizens for Family Preservation
CDSC	Community Development Support Corporation
CPI	Community Partnership Initiative (later called CPP, Community Partnership Program)
CRI	Children's Rights Inc.
CSC	Child Safety Conferences
CFP	Casey Family Programs
COFCCA	Council of Family and Child Caring Agencies
CRE	Community Resource Exchange
CWA	Child Welfare Administration
CWF	Child Welfare Fund
CWOP	Child Welfare Organizing Project
CYC	California Youth Connection
DHS	Department of Human Services
EMWM	Every Mother is a Working Mother
FTC	Family Team Conference
IOC	Improved Outcomes for Children
MSAR	Maximum State Aid Rate
MSW	Masters of Social Work
NCCPR	National Coalition for Child Protectin Reform
NYCHA	New York City Housing Authority
OCFS	New York State Office of Children and Family Services
OSI	Open Society Institute

PAI	Parent Advocate Initiative
PAN	Parent Advocate Network
PAWG	Parent Advisory Work Group
PIA	Parents In Action
PUC	People United for Children
SSC	Special Services for Children
VOW	Voices of Women Organizing Project

NOTES

INTRODUCTION

1. John Williamson and Aaron Greenberg, *Families Not Orphanages* (New York: Better Care Network, 2010); Wendy Koch, "Troubled Homes Better than Foster Care." *USA Today*, June 2, 2007, http://www.usatoday.com/news/nation/2007-07-02-foster-study_N.htm?csp=34# . Close, citing Joseph Doyle, "Child Protection and Child Outcomes: Measuring the Effects of Foster Care." *American Economic Review* 97(5) (December 2007): 1583–1610, http://www.mit.edu/~jjdoyle/fostercare_aer.pdf.
2. "Somalia to Join Child Rights Pact," November 20, 2009, poundpuplegacy.org/node/41198.
3. Nicholas Pileggi, "Who'll Save the Children?" *New York Magazine* (December 18, 1978): 4.
4. *Wilder v. Bernstein*, in *Federal Supplement*. 1986, U.S. District—S.D.N.Y., p. 1013.
5. Gerald Finch, *Good Money After Bad: An Analysis of Expenditures and Performance in Private-Sector Foster Care* (New York: Office of the New York City Council President Carol Bellamy, May 1979): i.
6. David Tobis, "New York City Foster Care System, 1979–1988: The Rise and Fall of Reform" (PhD dissertation, Yale University, 1989).
7. Celia W. Dugger, "System to Oversee Foster Care Dismantled in Budget Cutbacks." *New York Times*, April 30, 1992.
8. "Keeping Track," *Child Welfare Watch* 1 (Spring 1997): 7.
9. Michael Katz, *In the Shadow of the Poorhouse: A Social History of Welfare in America* (New York: Basic Books, 1986): 26.
10. Duncan Lindsey, "Preserving Families & Protecting Children: Finding the Balance," University of California, Los Angeles, http://www.childwelfare.com/kids/fampres.htm.
10. Duncan Lindsey, "Preserving Families & Protecting Children: Finding the Balance," University of California, Los Angeles, http://www.childwelfare.com/kids/fampres.htm.
11. Nina Bernstein, *The Lost Children of Wilder: The Epic Struggle to Change Foster Care* (New York: Pantheon Books, 2001): xii.
12. New York City Administration for Children's Services, ACS Task Force on Racial Equity and Cultural Competence, Commissioner's Advisory Board. *Race/Ethnicity and the Path through the Child Welfare System CY 2007*, distributed at the task force meeting of June 18, 2008.

13. Alfred Kadushin, *Child Welfare Services* (New York: Macmillan, 1980): viii.
14. David Gil, "The Ideological Context of Child Welfare." In *A Handbook of Child Welfare: Context, Knowledge, Practice*, ed. J. H. Laird and Ann Hartmean (New York: The Free Press, 1985): 31.
15. Charles Loring Brace, "The Children's Aid Society of New York, Its History, Plan and Results," in *History of Child Saving in the United States*, ed. National Conference of Charities and Correction, Report of the Committee on the History of Child-Saving Work, Twentieth Conference, Chicago, June 1983, reprinted (Montclair, NJ: Patterson Smith, 1971): 3.
16. J. Shaw, "Children Ever in Care: An Examination of Cumulative Disproportionality." *Child Welfare* 87(2) (2008): 20.
17. J. Bosman, "As 8-Year-Old Injured in Fall Heals, Her Mother Deals with Investigators." *New York Times*, August 25, 2009.
18. "Advocates React With Concern To Mayor's Executive Budget." *New York Nonprofit Press*, May 1, 2011, http://cscs-ny.org/advocacy/media/2011May09NYNP.php.
19. G. Cameron, *Towards Positive Systems of Child and Family Welfare: International Comparisons of Child Protection, Family Service, and Community Caring Systems* (Toronto: University of Toronto Press, 2006).
20. Martin Guggenheim, "How Children's Lawyers Serve State Interests." *Las Vegas Law Review* 6 (2006): 827.
21. Charles Perrow, "Demystifying Organizations." In *The Management of Human Services*, ed. R.S.Y. Hasenfeld (New York: Columbia University Press, 1978): 110.
22. Fred Wulczyn, "Reunification from Foster Care" (Chicago: Chapin Hall Center for Children, University of Chicago, November 2002): 5; Kendra Hurley, "ASFA Decoded." *Child Welfare Watch* 15 (Winter 2008): 17.
23. C. J. Groak and R. B. McCall, *A Strategic Approach to Characterizing the Status and Progress of Child Welfare Reform in 21 CEE/CIS Countries* (Washington, DC: USAID/University of Pittsburg Office of Child Development, July 2008): 127.
24. David Tobis, *Moving from Residential Institutions to Community-Based Social Services in Central and Eastern Europe and the Former Soviet Union* (Washington, DC: World Bank, 2000): 5.

CHAPTER 1

1. K. O. Murray and S. A. Gesiriech, *A Brief History of the Child Welfare System*. http://pewfostercare.org/research/docs/Legislative.pdf.
2. The history of child welfare legislation is based on the following reports: Child Welfare League of America, Brief History of Federal Child Welfare Financing Legislation, http://www.cwla.org/advocacy/financinghistory.htm; National Coalition for Child Protection Reform: "A Child Welfare Timeline," http://nccpr.info/a-child-welfare-timeline/.
3. U.S. Department of Health and Human Services, Administration for Children and Families, Administration on Children, Youth and Families, Children's Bureau, The AFCARS Report, Preliminary FY 2011 Estimates as of July 2012, No. 19, www.acf.hhs.gov/programs/cb; Thomas C. Attwood, *Foster Care: Safety Net or Trap Door* (Washington, DC: Heritage Society Foundation, March 25, 2011): 2.
4. I. Schwartz and G. Fishman, *Kids Raised by The Government* (Westport: Praeger, 1999), 15.
5. U.S. Department of Health and Human Services, Administration for Children and Families, Administration on Children, Youth and Families, Children's Bureau, The AFCARS Report, Preliminary FY 2011 Estimates as of July 2012, No.

19, http://www.acf.hhs.gov/programs/cb/stats_research/afcars/tar/report19. pdf; Thomas C. Attwood, *Foster Care: Safety Net or Trap Door* (Washington, DC: Heritage Society Foundation, March 25, 2011): 2; "Watching the Numbers." *Child Welfare Watch* 21 (Winter 2011/2012): 35; "Keeping Track." *Child Welfare Watch* 1 (Spring 1997): 7.

6. David Tobis, "New York City Foster Care System, 1979–1988: The Rise and Fall of Reform" (PhD dissertation, Yale University, 1989): 20.

7. New York City Administration for Children's Services, "Executive Plan Fiscal Year 2010." Administration for Children's Services.

8. D. Schneider, *The History of Public Welfare in New York State1609*–1866 (Chicago: University of Chicago Press, 1933).

9. Marilyn Irvin Holt, *Orphan Trains: Placing Out in America* (Lincoln: University of Nebraska Press: 1992): 107.

10. Tobis, "The New York Foster Care System," 50–61.

11. Nina Bernstein, *The Lost Children of Wilder: The Epic Struggle to Change Foster Care* (New York: Pantheon Books, 2001).

12. Jim Purcell (executive director, Council of Family and Child Caring Agencies), email to the author, September 5, 2012.

13. Nat Hentoff, "I'm Finally Going to be a Pastor II." *New Yorker*, March 30, 1987, 44.

14. Ari L. Goldman and Michael Oreskes, "New York Foster Care: A Public-Private Battleground," *New York Times*, April 9, 1987.

15. Tobis, "The New York Foster Care System," Chap. 4, 100–174.

16. Tobis, "The New York Foster Care System," 189–199.

17. C. Nix, "Problems Beset Child-Care Unit Chief." *New York Times*, July 20, 1986.

18. R. Peddicord, *Gay and Lesbian Rights: A Question: Sexual Ethics or Social Justice?* National Catholic Reporter, 1996.

19. *Wilder v. Bernstein*, in *Federal Supplement*. 1986, U.S. District—S.D.N.Y. p. 1013.

20. Celia W. Dugger, "System to Oversee Foster Care Dismantled in Budget Cutbacks." *New York Times*, April 30, 1992; David Tobis, "The Transformation of the Program Assessment System," Chap. 6, 220–244 in Tobis, "The New York City Foster Care System."

21. John Mattingly (commissioner, New York City Administration for Children's Services), interview with the author, November 17, 2008.

22. Children's Rights Inc., *At the Crossroads, Better Infrastructure, Too Few Results* (New York: Children's Rights Inc., July 2007): 31.

23. John Mattingly, interview with the author, November 17, 2008.

24. Children's Rights Inc., *At the Crossroads: Better Infrastructure, Too Few Results* (New York: Children's Rights Inc., July 2007): 56.

25. Leroy H. Pelton, *For Reasons of Poverty: A Critical Analysis of the Public Child Welfare System in the United States* (New York: Praeger, 1989).

26. Kathleen Maher, *How Has Shift Away From Foster Care Affected Funding, Spending, Caseloads?* (New York: New York City Independent Budget Office, October 2011).

27. James Knight, "I could have been Elisa" Foster Care Youth United, January 1, 2001; Angi Batiste, "A Foster Mother from Hell" Foster Care Youth United, March 28, 1004; Marcus Howell, "An Outsider Forever" January 28, 1996, http://www. representmag.org.

28. Tim Ross and Anne Lifflander, *The Experience of New York City Foster Children in HIV/AIDS Clinical Trials* (New York: Vera Institute of Justice, January 2009).

29. "Watching the Numbers." *Child Welfare Watch* 2(Winter 1997): 45; "Watching the Numbers." *Child Welfare Watch* 19/20 (Winter 2010/2011): 35.

30. *The AFCARS Report, Preliminary FY 2005 Estimates as of September 2006.* U.S. Department of Human Services, Administration on Children, Youth and Families: Washington, DC.

31. John Williamson and Aaron Greenberg, *Families Not Orphanages* (New York: Better Care Network, 2010); David Tolfree, *Roofs and Root: The Care of Separated Children in the Developing World* (Aldershot, UK: Save the Children Fund, 1995); David Tobis, *Moving from Residential Institutions to Community-Based Social Services in Central and Eastern Europe and the Former Soviet Union* (Washington, DC: World Bank, 2000).

32. Kathleen Maher, *How Has Shift Away From Foster Care Affected Funding, Spending, Caseloads?*(New York: New York City Independent Budget Office, October 2011): 6.

33. Dennis Culhane and Jung Min Park, *Homelessness and Child Welfare Services in New York City: Exploring Trends and Opportunities for Improving Outcomes for Children and Youth* (Philadelphia: University of Pennsylvania, School of Social Policy and Practice, 2007, http://repository.upenn.edu/spp_papers/118.

34. Mark Courtney, *Midwest Evaluation of the Adult Functioning of Former Foster Youth: Outcomes at age 21, Executive Summary* (Chicago: University of Chicago/Chapin Hall, 2007).

35. National Association of Black Social Workers, "History," http://www.nabsw.org/mserver/Mission.aspx.

36. "Keeping Track." *Child Welfare Watch*, 1 (Spring 1997): 7.

37. New York City Administration for Children's Services, *Progress on ACS Reform Initiatives, Status Report 3. 2001* (New York: Administration for Children's Services, 2001).

38. Victor Groza, "Overview of Adoption." In *Child Welfare for the Twenty-First Century: A Handbook of Practices, Policies and Programs*, ed. G. P. Mallon and P. Hess (New York: Columbia University Press, 2009): 434.

39. Fred Wulczyn, *Reunification from Foster Care* (Chicago: Chapin Hall Center for Children, University of Chicago, November 2002): 5; Kendra Hurley, "ASFA Decoded." *Child Welfare Watch* 15 (Winter 2008): 17.

40. "Watching the Numbers." *Child Welfare Watch* 7 (Winter 2001): 15.

41. "Watching the Number." *Child Welfare Watch*.19/20 (Winter 2010/2011): 35.

42. David Van Biema, Sharon E. Epperson, and Elaine Rivera, "Eliza Izquierdo: Abandoned to Her Fate." *Time*, December 11, 1995.

43. "Watching the Numbers." *Child Welfare Watch*.7 (Winter 2001): 15; "Watching the Numbers." *Child Welfare Watch* 19/20 (Winter 2010): 35.

44. Children's Rights Inc. *At the Crossroads: Better Infrastructure, Too Few Results* (New York: Children's Rights Inc., 2007) 30.

45. "Watching the Numbers." *Child Welfare Watch* 4 (Winter 1999): 15.

46. New York City Administration for Children's Services, *Protecting the Children of New York: A Plan of Action for the Administration for Children's Services* (New York: Administration for Children's Services, December 19, 1996): 8.

47. "Watching the Numbers." *Child Welfare Watch* 4 (Winter 1997): 15.

48. "Watching the Numbers." *Child Welfare Watch* 4 (Winter 1999): 15; "Watching the Numbers." *Child Welfare Watch* 12 (Winter 2006): 23.

49. Children's Rights Inc., *At the Crossroads*, p. 21.

50. Special Child Welfare Advisory Panel, *Special Report on Family Court* (New York: Special Child Welfare Advisory Panel, 2000): 44–48.

51. Children's Rights Inc., *At the Crossroads*, Chap. 4: Family Court, pp. 111–128; "A Matter of Judgment: Deciding the Future of Family Court in New York City." *Child Welfare Watch* 12 (Winter 2005/2006): 1–22.

52. Children's Rights Inc., *At the Crossroads*, p.116.

53. Clark Richardson (former Administrative Judge, Bronx Family Court), interview with the author, February 11, 2009.

CHAPTER 2

1. Isabel Wolock and Berny Horowitz, "Child Maltreatment as a Social Problem: The Neglect of Neglect." *American Journal of Orthopsychiatry* 54(4) (1984): 13.

2. Leroy Pelton, *For Reasons of Poverty: A Critical Analysis of the Public Child Welfare System in the United States* (New York: Praeger, 1989).

3. Child Welfare Information Gateway, *Foster Care Statistics 2010, Adoption and Foster Care Analysis Reporting System (AFCARS)* (Washington, DC: U.S. Department of Health and Human Services, Children's Bureau, 2010). http://www.childwelfare.gov/pubs/factsheets/foster.pdf#Page=9&view=Fit

4. "Race, Bias & Power in Child Welfare." *Child Welfare Watch 3* (Summer 1998): 1.

5. New York City Administration for Children's Services, ACS Task Force on Racial Equity and Cultural Competence, Commissioner's Advisory Board. *Race/Ethnicity and the Path through the Child Welfare System CY 2007*, distributed at the task force meeting of June 18, 2008.

6. *Nicholson v. Scoppetta*. New York City Court of Appeals. 2004 NY Slip Op 07617 [3 NY3d 357] October 26, 2004.

7. Rachel Monahan, "Parents Say Administrators are Siccing ACS on Them to Retaliate for Complaints." *Daily News*, May 30, 2011.

8. Paul Chill, "Burden of Proof Begone: The Pernicious Effect of Emergency Removal in Child Protective Proceedings." *Family Court Review* 41(4) (October 2003). Special Issue: Child Protection in the 21st Century, citing Children's Bureau, U.S. Department of Health and Human Services, Child Maltreatment 2001: Reports from the States to the National Child Abuse and Neglect Data System, Table 6.5, available at http://www.acf.dhhs.gov/programs/cb/publications/cm01/table6_5.htm.

9. NYC Administration for Children's Services, *Flash February 2011* (New York: Administration for Children's Services, March 3, 2011): 19.

10. Administration for Children's Services, *One Year Home Quarterly Data* (New York: Administration for Children's Services, November 2010): 17.

11. Kathleen Maher, *How Has Shift Away from Foster Care Affected Funding, Spending, Caseloads?* (New York: New York City Independent Budget Office, October 2011): 5.

CHAPTER 3

1. Linda Gordon, "The Powers of the Weak: Wife-Beating and Battered Women's Resistance." Chap. 8 in *Heroes of Their Own Lives: The Politics and History of Family Violence* (New York: Penguin Books, 1988).

2. New York City Finance Division, *Hearing on the Mayor's Fiscal Year 2012 Preliminary Budget & Fiscal Year 2011 Preliminary Mayor's Management Report, Administration for Children's Services* (New York: Administration for Children's Services, March 24, 2011): 4. http://council.nyc.gov/html/budget/PDFs/2012/acs_068.pdf.

3. Administration for Children's Services, *Executive Plan Fiscal Year 2010* (New York: Administration for Children's Services, 2010).

4. Martin Guggenheim, "Parental Rights in Child Welfare Cases in New York City Family Courts," 40 *Colum. J.L. & Soc. Probs.* 40 (2007): 508, 520; Beth Rosenthal,

Terry Mizrahi, Diane Williams, and Maggie LaForce, *Consumer Impact and Involvement in the Child Welfare System: A Status Report on Client Organizing* (New York: Education Center for Community Organizing, Hunter School of Social Work, October 1994).

5. Beth Rosenthal, Terry Mizrahi, Diane Williams, and Maggie LaForce, *Consumer Impact and Involvement in the Child Welfare System: A Status Report on Client Organizing* (New York: Education Center for Community Organizing, Hunter School of Social Work, October 1994).

6. Office of the New York State Comptroller, *Children in Foster Care at Voluntary Agencies Not Receiving All Required Services* (New York: Office of the New York State Comptroller, Report No. A-18, May 24, 1994): 12.

7. Martin Guggenheim, *Legal Opinion on New York Law Regarding Employers' Responsibilities When Considering Employing or Retaining an Employee with an Indicated Child Abuse and Maltreatment Report* (New York: New York University School of Law, January 25, 2008).

8. Beth Rosenthal, Terry Mizrahi, Diane Williams, and Maggie LaForce, *Consumer Impact and Involvement in the Child Welfare System: A Status Report on Client Organizing* (New York: Education Center for Community Organizing, Hunter School of Social Work, October 1994).

9. Martin Guggenheim, *Legal Opinion on New York Law Regarding Employers' Responsibilities When Considering Employing or Retaining an Employee with an Indicated Child Abuse and Maltreatment Report* (New York: New York University School of Law, January 25, 2008).

10. Annie E. Casey Foundation, Data Center, Kids Count, http://datacenter.kidscount.org/data/acrossstates/NationalProfile.aspx?cat=35&group=Category&loc=1&dt=1%2c3%2c2%2c4, accessed August 13, 2012.

11. John Mattingly, *Child Welfare Watch Forum* (presentation, New School University, New York City, 2009).

12. Esmeralda Simmons, email message to the author.

13. Chapin Hall Center for Children, *Children First Placed in Care Between 1996–2001* (Chicago: University of Chicago/Chapin Hall Center for Children, 2007).

14. William Bell (presentation, New York, Hunter College, June 10, 2004), cited in *Annual Report* 2004, Child Welfare Fund.

15. *Wilder v. Bernstein*, 1973, S.D.N.Y.

16. John Kelly, "13 Lawsuits that Reformed (or Drained) Child Welfare." *Youth Today*, February 4, 2004.

17. Ibid.; *Child Welfare Watch* staff, "The Marisol Settlement: What It Means Behind the Scenes" (New York: Center for an Urban Future, April 1999), www.nycfuture.org/content/articles/article_view.cfm?article_id=1019.

18. Bernstein, *The Lost Children of Wilder*, 42–43.

19. Martin Guggenheim, *What's Wrong With Children's Rights* (Cambridge: Harvard University Press, 2005); Martin Guggenheim, interview with the author.

20. Marcia Lowry, executive director, Children's Rights Inc., discussion with the author.

21. Children's Rights Inc., *Marisol v. Pataki* Fact Sheet, accessed June 2008, www.childrensrights.org/wp-content/uploads/2008/06/ny_marisol_fact_sheet.pdf Childrensrights.org.

22. *Child Welfare Watch* staff, "The Marisol Settlement: What It Means Behind the Scenes" (New York: Center for an Urban Future, April 1999), www.nycfuture.org/content/articles/article_view.cfm?article_id=1019.

23. *Douglas Nelson to Retire in 2010 as President of the Annie E. Casey Foundation* (Baltimore: Annie E. Casey Foundation, September 16, 2009), http://www.aecf. org/~/media/PDFFiles/Newsroom/Nelson/DWNAnnounceNewsRelease.pdf.

24. Steven Cohen (staff director, Special Child Welfare Advisory Panel), interview with the author, August 13, 2008.

25. Ibid.

26. Child Welfare Organizing Project, *Parents' Observations on the Special Child Welfare Advisory Panel's Report on Placement Issues,* undated but included in a letter, June 30, 1999 to Steven Cohen, staff director of the panel (unpublished).

27. Nina Bernstein, "Old Pattern Cited in Missed Signs of Child Abuse," *New York Times,* July 22, 1999.

28. Mike Arsham (executive director, Child Welfare Organizing Project), interview with the author, August 22, 2008.

29. Nicholas Scoppetta, *Letter to Michael Arsham,* June 5, 2000 (unpublished).

30. Cited in Child Welfare Organizing Project, *Statement to the Special Child Welfare Advisory Panel,* October 17, 2000.

31. Child Welfare Organizing Project, *Statement to the Special Child Welfare Advisory Panel,* October 17, 2000.

32. Special Child Welfare Advisory Panel, *Final Report* (New York: Special Child Welfare Advisory Panel, December 7, 2000): 37.

33. Ibid., 39.

34. Ibid., 41.

35. Ibid.

36. New York City Administration for Children's Services, *Protecting the Children of New York: A Plan of Action for the Administration for Children's Services* (New York: Administration for Children's Services, December 19, 1996): 14.

37. Ibid., 8.

38. "Watching the Numbers," *Child Welfare Watch* 6 (Winter 2000): 15.

39. New York City Administration for Children's Services, *Protecting the Children of New York,* 108–109.

40. Ibid., 10–11.

41. "Watching the Numbers." *Child Welfare Watch* 3 (Spring 1998): 1.

42. New York City Administration for Children's Services, *Protecting the Children of New York.*

43. "Watching the Numbers." *Child Welfare Watch* 9 (Fall 2003): 15.

44. New York City Administration for Children's Services, *A Renewed Plan of Action for the Administration for Children's Services* (New York: Administration for Children's Services, 2001): 19.

45. Jill Chaifetz, *The New York City Foster Care System in Crisis: The Continued Failure to Plan for Children, A Report of the Committee to Involve Clients in the SPR/UCR Process* (New York: The Door, February 1998): 7, 13.

46. New York City Administration for Children's Services, *A Renewed Plan of Action for the Administration for Children's Services* (New York: Administration for Children's Services, 2001): 19.

47. New York City Administration for Children's Services, *Six Years of Reform in Children's Services: 1996–2002 Reform Update* (New York: Administration for Children's Services, 2002): 1.

48. Child Welfare Organizing Project, *Annual Report 2004* (New York: CWOP): 15.

49. New York City Administration for Children's Services, *The First 100 Days* (New York: Administration for Children's Services, 2002): 1.

50. "Watching the Numbers." *Child Welfare Watch* 8 (Fall 2002): 25; "Watching the Numbers." *Child Welfare Watch* 14 (Summer 2007): 31.
51. "Watching the Numbers." *Child Welfare Watch* 8 (Fall 2002): 25; "Watching the Numbers." *Child Welfare Watch* 11 (Summer 2005): 15.
52. New York City Administration for Children's Services, Letter from Viviane DeMilly, director, Office of Advocacy, and Tanya Krupat, consortium Co-Coordinator, Division of Foster Care & Preventive Services, December 2, 2003 (unpublished).
53. New York City Administration for Children's Services, *The First 100 Days* (New York: Administration for Children's Services, 2002): 7.
54. New York City Mayor's Office, *Press Release, Mayor Michael R. Bloomberg Announces the Resignation of Administration for Children's Services Commissioner William C. Bell,* May 11, 2004.
55. New York City Administration for Children's Services, Office of Communications, Administration for Children's Services, February 2006, p. 2.
56. New York City Administration for Children's Services, *Mission Statement.* August 7, 2008, http://nyc.gov/html/acs/html/about/mission/shtml.
57. "Watching the Numbers." *Child Welfare Watch* 18 (Fall 2009): 33; "Watching the Numbers." *Child Welfare Watch* 21 (Winter 2011/2012): 35.
58. *Statistics.* Available from www.nyc.gov/html/acs/html/statistics/statistics_links.shtm.
59. New York City Administration for Children's Services website, http://www.nyc.gov/html/acs/html/statistics/statistics_links.shtml, accessed August 14, 2012; Tobis, "The New York City Foster Care System 1979–1988," 103.
60. Dana Guyet, "At the Table: Policymakers and Parents Come Together for System Change." *Rise* 5 (2006): 7.
61. John Mattingly, interview with the author, November 17, 2008.
62. Bevanjae Kelley, "At The Table." *Rise,* web exclusive (November 2010), http://www.risemagazine.org/featured_stories/At_the_table.html.
63. Christine Gottlieb (professor, New York University School of Law), interview with the author, November 3, 2010.
64. Fred Wulczyn, Sarah Feldman, and N. Qadeer, *Improved Outcomes for Children, Implementation Study, Interim Progress Report* (Chicago: Chapin Hall Center for Children/University of Chicago, July 2008): 15.
65. John Mattingly, interview with the author, November 17, 2008.

CHAPTER 4

1. Beth Rosenthal, Terry Mizrahi, Diane Williams, and Maggie LaForce, *Consumer Impact and Involvement in the Child Welfare System: A Status Report on Client Organizing* (New York: Education Center for Community Organizing, Hunter School of Social Work, October 1994): 2.
2. Terry Mizrahi, *Building a Foundation for an Organized Client Voice in Child Welfare Through Effective Client Involvement: A Strategic Planning and Action Proposal* (New York: Education Center for Community Organizing, 1994).
3. John Courtney (senior advisor, Fund for Social Change) interview with the author, November 9, 2010.
4. http://cwop.org/about/history/
5. Irene Berthel and Bernadette Blount, "Benefits of Being a Parent Leader." *For Parents, By Parents,* Issue 4 (Fall/Winter 2001): 1, http://www.cwop.org/images/issue4.pdf.

6. Nicholas Scoppetta, Letter to Michael Arsham, June 5, 2000 (unpublished).
7. Child Welfare Organizing Project, mission statement, http://cwop.org/about/.
8. Memorandum of Understanding between the Administration for Children's Services and the Child Welfare Organizing Project, April 26, 2007: 4.
9. Ibid., 1.
10. Child Welfare Organizing Project, *A Parent Leadership Curriculum* (New York: Child Welfare Organizing Project, 2006): 3.
11. Child Welfare Organizing Project, *Restoring Partnership* (New York: Child Welfare Organizing Project, 2012): 4.
12. Marina Lalayants, *Child Welfare Organizing Project, Community Connections, Program Evaluation, Final Report, June 2012* (New York: Silberman School of Social Work, National Resource Center for Permanency and Family Connections, Hunter College, City University of New York, June 2012): 7, 31.
13. www.cebc4cw.org/program/child-welfare-organizing-project-parent-leadership-curriculum/.
14. Ronald Richter (remarks, New York, Administration for Children's Services, meeting with ACS senior management and representatives of advocacy organizations, April 30, 2012).
15. Child Welfare Organizing Project, *A Parent Leadership Curriculum* (New York: Child Welfare Organizing Project, 2006): 13.
16. Mike Arsham (executive director, Child Welfare Organizing Project) interview with the author, February 26, 2007.
17. Mike Arsham, presentation to representatives of DHS-Give Us Back Our Children, Philadelphia, PA, May 13, 2011.
18. *For Parents, By Parents* (New York: Child Welfare Organizing Project, 2005): 1.
19. *Nicholson v. Williams*, 203 F.Supp. 2d at 165. United States District Court, Eastern District of New York.
20. Chris Lombardi, "Justice For Battered Women." *The Nation*, July 15, 2002, www.thenation.com/doc/20020715/lombardi.
21. Jill Zuccardy, "An Obligation to Project: An Interview with Jill Zuccardy." *Rise* 6 (Spring 2007): 4.
22. Teresa Bachiller, *Testimony at the Joint Hearing of the General Welfare and Education Committees of the New York City Council*, April 11, 2006.
23. Robert J. Sampson, Stephen W. Raudenbush, and Felton Earls, "Neighborhood and Violent Crime: A Multilevel Study of Collective Efficacy." *Science* 277 (5328) (August 15, 1997): 918–924.

CHAPTER 5

1. *Rise*, masthead, http://www.risemagazine.org/PDF/Rise_issue_15.pdf.
2. Ellen Barry, "Giving Voice to Parents' Side of Child Welfare." *Los Angeles Times*, July 3, 2006.
3. Youshell Williams (writer, *Rise*), interview with the author, June 6, 2009.
4. Bevanjae Kelley, "How to Write for *Rise*," www.risemagazine.org.
5. Erica Harrigan, "Can I Do This? Support Services Helped Me Prepare for Motherhood." *Rise* 11 (Fall 2008): 6–7.
6. Rosita Pagan, "About *Rise*/How to Write for *Rise*," http://www.risemagazine.org/pages/write.html.
7. Latoya Baskerville, "Building a Bridge: A Workbook for Helping Parents and Foster Parents Connect." *Rise* 13 (2009): 3.
8. http://www.uselectionatlas.org/FORUM/index.php?topic=110936.0.

9. Fred Wulczyn, Randi Rosenblum, Matt Rowe, and Ande Nesmith, *The Bridge Builders: To Preserve the Families of Highbridge. Program Year V Interim Progress Report* (Chicago: Chapin Hall Center for Children/University of Chicago, November 2008): 37.

10. Fred Wulczyn et al., *The Bridge Builders: To Preserve the Families of Highbridge. Program Year VI Interim Progress Report* (Chicago: Chapin Hall Center for Children/University of Chicago): draft outcome section, 4.

11. Fred Wulczyn, "Presentation of the Interim Progress Report IV" (Minutes of the meeting of the donors of Bridge Builders; New York: Open Society Institute, January 28, 2008).

12. *New York Nonprofit Press*, January 2005.

13. Letter from Dale Joseph (Assistant Commissioner of the Administration for Children Services) to Richard Altman (CEO, Jewish Child Care Association), November 23, 2010 (unpublished).

14. Susan Lob (former executive director, VOW) interview with the author, September 4, 2008.

15. VOW mission statement, www.vowbwrc.org.

16. Administration for Children's Services, *Special ACS e-Bulletin from Executive Deputy Commissioner Zeinab Chahine*, July 19, 2005.

17. Susan Lob (former executive director, VOW) interview with the author, July 5, 2011.

18. Voices of Women Organizing Project and the Human Rights Project, Urban Justice Center, *Justice Denied: How Family Courts in NYC Endanger Battered Women and Children* (New York: Voices of Women Organizing Project, 2008): 4.

19. Susan Lob interview, September 4, 2008.

20. Voices of Women Organizing Project and the Human Rights Project, Urban Justice Center, *Justice Denied: How Family Courts in NYC Endanger Battered Women and Children* (New York: Voices of Women Organizing Project, 2008): 32.

21. Ibid., 6.

22. A. Ruiz, "Court System Is Another Abuser." *Daily News*, May 15, 2008. www.nydailynews.com/ny_local/2008/05/15/2008-05-15_court_system_is_another_abuser.html.

23. Susan Lob interview, September 4, 2008.

24. Ibid.

25. Raquel Singh (executive director, Voices of Women) interview with the author, December 30, 2010.

26. Raquel Singh interview, July 6, 2011.

27. Raquel Singh interview with the author, August 23, 2012.

28. Voices of Women/Battered Women's Resource Center, *Case Examples: False & Malicious Reports of Child Abuse* (New York: VOW, 2008).

29. Douglas Besharov, "Contending with Overblown Expectations: CPS Cannot Be All Things To All People." *Public Welfare* (Winter 1987): 7.

30. Raquel Singh interview, August 23, 2012.

31. Susan Lob interview, September 4, 2008.

32. Sharonne Salaam profile, Revson Fellow's Program 2001–2002. http://www.revson.columbia.edu/meetthefellows/fellow/sharonne_salaam.

33. Dasun Allah, "Speculation Gone Wilding." *Village Voice*, December 10, 2002, http://www.villagevoice.com/photoGallery/index/172972/0/; Jim Dwyer, "New Slant on Jogger Case Lacks Official Certainty." *New York Times*, January 28, 2003.

34. Sharonne Salaam (former executive director, People United for Children) interview with the author, July 22, 2011.

35. Sharonne Salaam profile, Revson Fellow's Program 2001–2002, http://www.revson.columbia.edu/meetthefellows/fellow/sharonne_salaam; Salaam interview, July 22, 2011.

36. People United for Children, *Proposal to the Child Welfare Fund* (New York: People United for Children, 2005): 1.

37. Sharonne Salaam, *Statement, Listener Candidate for the WBAI Local Station Board*, http://pacificafoundation.org/cand_page.php?id=365.

38. *First Annual Child Welfare Fund Family Unity Awards* (New York: People United for Children, December 15, 2001): 7; *Family Unity Awards* (New York: People United for Children, December 4, 2004).

39. United Stated District Court, Southern District of New York, People United for Children, Inc., against The City of New York, Stipulation of Settlement, 99Civ. 0648 (KTD), 1–2.

40. Ibid., 4–6.

41. Salaam interview, July 22, 2011.

42. United Stated District Court, Southern District of New York, People United for Children, Inc., against The City of New York, Stipulation of Settlement, 99Civ. 0648 (KTD), Declaration of Joan P. Gibbs, Esq., For an Order Approving the Stipulation of Settlement, A-352.

43. Salaam interview, August 26, 2011.

44. United Stated District Court, Southern District of New York, People United for Children, Inc., against The City of New York, Conferences 5C5ODUF1, 99Civ. 0648, A-496-A560.

45. Salaam interview, July 22, 2011.

46. Ibid.

47. New York City Administration for Children's Services, CY 2010 Admissions by Borough/CD of Origin Compare to CY 2009, http://www.nyc.gov/html/acs/downloads/pdf/stats_placement_2010.pdf.

48. http://www.ccfamilypreservation.org/index.php?name=history.

49. Parents In Action, Leaflet for the Stop Family Court Abuse Rally. (New York: Parents In Action, August 25, 2008).

50. Rolando Bini (executive director, Parents In Action), interview with the author, July 6, 2011.

CHAPTER 6

1. Lisa Paine Wells (Consultant, Child Welfare Strategy Group, Annie E. Casey Foundation), interview with the author, February 16, 2011.

2. http://www.childwelfare.gov/pubs/factsheets/foster.pdf

3. "From Rights to Reality: A Plan for Parent Advocacy and Family-Centered Child Welfare Reform." *Rise:* 5, http://www.risemagazine.org/PDF/From_Rights_to_Reality.pdf.

4. James Bell Associates, *Effective Methods for Involving Consumers in Planning and Decision-Making: Lessons Learned from the Family Preservation and Family Support (FP/FS) Services Implementation Study* (Washington, DC: U.S. Department of Health and Human Services, Administration for Children and Families, Office of Planning, Research and Evaluation, January 4, 2002): 3, http://www.acf.hhs.gov/programs/opre/fys/family_pres/reports/effect_meth/effect_meth_b.html, accessed August 30, 2012.

5. "Mama Drama," *Citypaper 1177* (Philadelphia, December 6–13, 2007), www.citypaper.net; Pat Albright and Phoebe Jones (staff, DHS-Give Us Back Our Children), interview with the author, March 17, 2011.

6. Dana DiFilippo, "Is Home Where the Heart Is? Should Poverty and Inability to Find & Keep Appropriate Housing Tear Mother from Child?" *Philadelphia Daily News*, posted February 22, 2010; http://globalwomenstrike.net/content/dcfs-give-us-back-our-children

7. http://everymothernetwork.net/pages/philadelphia.

8. Jones interview, March 17, 2011.

9. Dana DiFilippo, *Philadelphia Daily News*, posted February 22, 2010; http://globalwomenstrike.net/content/dcfs-give-us-back-our-children.

10. Richard Wexler, "Presentation to the Community Dialogue" (Philadelphia, PA, Tabernacle United Church, December 3, 2010).

11. http://www.parentsanonymous.org/pahtml/paMHabout.html.

12. National Council on Crime and Delinquency, "Parents Anonymous Outcome Evaluation: Promising Findings for Child Maltreatment Reduction" (March 2008): 9, http://www.parentsanonymous.org/paTEST/NCCDSpecialReport308.pdf.

13. http://www.parentadvocacy.org/index.html.

14. Vivek Sankaran, "A National Survey on a Parents' Right to Counsel in Termination of Parental Rights and Dependency Cases," http://www.law.umich.edu/centersandprograms/ccl/specialprojects/Documents/National%20Survey%20on%20a%20Parent%27s%20Right%20to%20Counsel.pdf.

15. Ibid.; American Bar Association, Center on Children and the Law, *Legal Representation for Parents in Child Welfare Proceedings: A Performance Based Analysis of Michigan Practice* (2009), http://abanet.org/child/parentrepresentation/michigan_parent_representation_report.pdf.

16. American Bar Association, *Legal Representation* (2009).

17. Letter from Mimi Laver (director, National Project to Improve Representation for Parents Involved in the Child Welfare System, American Bar Association, Center on Children and the Law) to Wanda Mial (Senior Associate of Children Welfare, Annie E. Casey Foundation), undated (unpublished).

18. Mimi Laver (director, National Project to Improve Representation for Parents Involved in the Child Welfare System, American Bar Association, Centre on Children and the Law), interview with the author, April 5, 2011, August 27, 2012.

19. American Bar Association, Center for Children and the Law, *Summary of Parent Representation Models*, undated, http://www.iowacourts.gov/wfdata/files/ChildrensJustice/ParentAttyRepresen/Summary&LinksofParentRepresentationModels.pdf.

20. Nancy Colon, "I Needed My Lawyer to Be My Advocate." *From Rights to Reality* (New York: *Rise)*: 16.

21. E. Cohen and L. Canan, "Closer to Home: Parent Mentors in Child Welfare." *Child Welfare* 85(5) (2006): 867–884; Susan P. Kemp, Maureen Marcenko, Kimberly Hoagwood, and William Vesneski, "Engaging Parents in Child Welfare Services: Bridging Family Needs and Child Welfare Mandates." *Child Welfare* 88(1) (2009): 101–126.

22. Maureen Marcenko, Ross Brown, Peggy R. DeVoy, and Debbie Conway, "Engaging Parents: Innovative Approaches in Child Welfare" (Tampa, FL: Center for Child Welfare): 33, http://centerforchildwelfare.fmhi.usf.edu/kb/bppub/engaging-parents-innovative.pdf.

23. Lynn Usher, Judith Wildfire, and Daniel Webster, *Executive Summary: An Evaluation in Anchor-Site Phase of Family to Family* (Baltimore: Annie E. Casey Foundation, 2009): 2, 22.

24. Elizabeth K. Anthony, Jill Duerr Berrick, Ed Cohen, and Elizabeth Wilder, *Partnering with Parents, Promising Approaches to Improve Reunification Outcomes for Children in Foster Care, Executive Summary* (Berkeley: Center for Social Services Research, School of Social Welfare, University of California at Berkeley, July 2009): 2, 3.

25. *Parent Advocate Program Evaluation, Outcomes for Families Served in Jefferson County [Kentucky], September 2005–April 2008* (August 21, 2008): 1 (no author listed).

26. http://www.dhs.state.ia.us/cppc/.

27. Andrew White, *Scale of Change, Creating and Sustaining Collaborative Child Welfare Reform Across Cities and States* (Washington, DC: Center for the Study of Social Policy, 2008): 35–37.

28. Geri Demer (coordinator, Iowa Parent Partner Program), email March 11, 2011 to Lisa Paine Wells (consultant to the Annie E. Casey Foundation Child Welfare Strategy Group).

29. Sandy Lint (Community Partnership Manager, Iowa Department of Human Services), interview with the author, March 1, 2011.

30. Sandra Jimenez (designer of the training, Building A Better Future, for Annie E. Casey Foundation), interview with the author, September 27, 2007.

31. Lint, interview, March 1, 2011.

32. White, *Scale of Change*, 16.

CHAPTER 7

1. Citizens' Committee for Children of New York, Inc., *The Wisest Investment: New York City's Preventive Service System* (New York: Citizens' Committee for Children of New York, Inc., April 2010): 23.

2. "Keeping Track." *Child Welfare Watch* 1 (Spring 1997): 7.

3. http://www.nyc.gov/html/acs/html/statistics/statistics_links.shtml, accessed August 19, 2012.

4. "Watching the Numbers." *Child Welfare Watch* 7 (Winter 2001): 15; "Watching the Numbers." *Child Welfare Watch* 21 (Winter 2011/2012): 35.

5. New York City Administration for Children's Services, *Protecting the Children of New York: A Plan of Action for the Administration for Children's Services* (New York: Administration for Children's Services, December 19, 1996): 8.

6. http://www.nyc.gov/html/acs/html/about/mission.shtml, accessed August 14, 2011.

7. Citizens' Committee for Children of New York, Inc. *The Wisest Investment* (April 2010): 8.

8. New York City Administration for Children's Services, *Six Years of Reform in Children's Services: 1996–2002 Reform Update* (New York: Administration for Children's Services, 2002): 9.

9. "Watching the Numbers." *Child Welfare Watch* 19/20 (Winter 2011/2012): 35.

10. New York City Administration for Children's Services, *Strategic Management Report* (New York: Administration for Children's Services, September 2009): 3.

11. Citizens' Committee for Children of New York, Inc. (April 2010): 22, 28.

12. Ibid., 39–52; Children's Rights, Inc., *The Long Road Home: A Study of Children Stranded in New York City Foster Care* (New York: Children's Rights, Inc., November 2009): 149–166.

13. http://www.legal-aid.org/media/144423/fact_sheet_2011.pdf, accessed August 15, 2011.
14. Martin Guggenheim, "Parental Rights in Child Welfare Cases in New York City Family Courts." *Columbia Journal of Law and Social Problems* 40 (2007): 508, 520.
15. Editorial, "Giving Overmatched Parents a Chance." *New York Times*, June 17, 1996.
16. Martin Guggenheim, "Parental Rights in Child Welfare Cases in New York City Family Courts." *Columbia Journal of Law and Social Problems* 40 (2007): 508, 520.
17. "Separation Anxiety: Parent Lawyers at a Loss." *Child Welfare Watch* 4 (Winter 1999): 6.
18. Martin Guggenheim (professor of law, New York University School of Law), interview with the author, November 5 and 12, 2010 and May 10, 2011.
19. Martin Guggenheim, remarks (New York, meeting of lawyers, foundation officers, and advocates supporting the Brooklyn Family Defense Project, November 3, 2010).
20. Bryanne Hamill (former New York City Family Court Judge), remarks (New York, meeting of lawyers, foundation officers, and advocates supporting the Brooklyn Family Defense Project, November 3, 2010).
21. http://www.cfrny.org/about-us/our-results/, accessed September 1, 2012.
22. New York City Administration for Children's Services, CY 2010 Admissions by Borough/CD of Origin Compared to CY 2009, http://www.nyc.gov/html/acs/downloads/pdf/stats_placement_2010.pdf.
23. Children's Rights, Inc., *The Long Road Home: A Study of Children Stranded in New York City Foster Care* (New York: Children's Rights, Inc., 2009): 13.
24. T. F. Pettigrew and L. R. Tropp, *When Groups Meet: The Dynamics of Intergroup Contact* (Florence, KY: Psychology Press, 2001).
25. Jane Golden (vice president for child welfare and foster care services, Children's Aid Society), interview with the author, June 17, 2011.
26. Randi Rosenblum, *The Parent Advocate Initiative: Promoting Parent Advocates in Foster Care, Evaluation Report Year II* (Chicago: Chapin Hall Center for Children/ University of Chicago, October 2010): 14.
27. Ibid., 13.
28. Martin Guggenheim, *Legal Opinion on New York Law Regarding Employers' Responsibilities When Considering Employing or Retaining an Employee with an Indicated Child Abuse and Maltreatment Report* (New York: New York University School of Law, January 25, 2008).
29. Rosenblum, *The Parent Advocate Initiative*, 3.
30. Ibid., 16.
31. Golden interview, June 17, 2011.
32. John Mattingly (commissioner of the New York City Administration for Children's Services) interview with the author, November 17, 2008.
33. Ibid.
34. New York Social Services Law (NYSSL) 409-e; 18 New York Code of Rules and Regulations (NYCRR) 430.12(c)(2)(i).
35. New York State Office of Children and Family Services, *Informational letter: 04-OCFS-INF-09, July 12, 2004, Strengthening Service Plan Reviews, A Practice Paper*, http://nysccc.org/wp-content/uploads/Service-Plan-Reviews.pdf.
36. Jill Chaifetz, *The New York City Foster Care System in Crisis: The Continued Failure to Plan for Children* (New York: The Door, February 1998).

37. Mattingly interview, November 17, 2008.
38. Fred Wulczyn, Sarah Feldman, Matt Rowe, and Kerry Monahan-Price, *Improved Outcomes for Children: Implementation Study with Preliminary Outcome Data* (Chicago: Chapin Hall/University of Chicago, July 2008): 6.
39. Fred Wulczyn, Sarah Feldman, and Nadra Qadeer, *Improved Outcomes for Children: Implementation Study, Interim Progress Report, draft* (Chicago: Chapin Hall/University of Chicago, March 2008): 15.
40. Office of the New York State Comptroller, *Children in Foster Care at Voluntary Agencies Not Receiving All Required Services* (New York: Office of the State Comptroller, Report No. A-18–92, May 24, 1994): 12.
41. Christine Gottlieb (professor of law, New York University School of Law), interview with the author, November 2010; Sharonne Salaam (former executive director, People United for Children), interview with the author, July 22, 2011; Kara Fincke (lawyer, Bronx Defenders), (remarks, New York, New School University, meeting of the *Child Welfare Watch* advisory board, February 23, 2010).
42. New York City Administration for Children's Services, *Measures of Success Report, April 2009*, distributed to the IOC subcommittee of the Commissioner's Advisory Board (New York: Administration for Children's Services, May 5, 2009).
43. New York City Administration for Children's Services, Task Force on Racial Equity and Cultural Competence, Commissioner's Advisory Board, *Race/Ethnicity and the Path through the Child Welfare System CY 2007*, distributed at the task force meeting of June 18, 2008.
44. New York State Office of Children and Family Services, 05-OCFS-Adm-04, *Maximum State Aid Rates (MSAR)—Minimum Payment Requirements for Local Social Services Districts Effective July 1, 2005* (New York: Office of Children and Family Services, July 1, 2005).
45. Citizens' Committee for Children of New York, Inc., *The Wisest Investment* (April 2010).
46. Children's Rights, Inc., *The Long Road Home* (November 2009): 7.
47. "Watching the Numbers." *Child Welfare Watch* 10 (Winter 2004–2005): 31; "Watching the Numbers." *Child Welfare Watch* 19/20 (Winter 2010/2011): 35.
48. Children's Rights, Inc., *Recent Data Shows More Work Must be Done to Bring New York City Foster Kids Home Faster,* http://www.childrensrights.org/news-events/press/recent-data-shows-more-work-must-be-done-to-bring-new-york-city-foster-kids-home-faster/, accessed August 20, 2011.
49. Betsy Krebs (executive director, Youth Advocacy Center) interview with the author, February 4, 2008.
50. "Watching the Numbers." *Child Welfare Watch* 2 (Winter 1997): 11; "Watching the Numbers." *Child Welfare Watch* 19/20 (Winter 2010/2011): 35.
51. "Watching the Numbers." *Child Welfare Watch* 8 (Fall 2002): 35; "Watching the Numbers." *Child Welfare Watch* 8 (Fall 2002): 19; "Watching the Numbers." *Child Welfare Watch* 19/20 (Winter 2010/2011): 35.
52. New York City Administration for Children's Services, *A Renewed Plan of Action for the Administration for Children's Services,* (New York: Administration for Children's Services, July 2001): Appendix B.
53. "Watching the Numbers." *Child Welfare Watch* 8 (Fall 2002): 35; "Watching the Numbers." *Child Welfare Watch* 18 (Fall 2009): 23; "Watching the Numbers." *Child Welfare Watch* 19/20 (Winter 2010/2011): 35.
54. New York City Administration for Children's Services, *Strategic Management Report* (September 2009): 4.

55. A. J. Sedlak, J. Mettenburg, M. Basena, I. Petta, K. McPherson, A. Greene, and S. Li, *Fourth National Incidence Study of Child Abuse and Neglect (NIS–4): Report to Congress* (Washington, DC: U.S. Department of Health and Human Services, Administration for Children and Families, 2010): 3–3, http://www.acf.hhs.gov/programs/opre/abuse_neglect/natl_incid/nis4_report_congress_full_pdf_jan2010.pdf.

56. "Watching the Numbers." *Child Welfare Watch* 19/20 (Winter 2010/2011): 35.

57. Children's Rights Inc., *The Long Road Home, A Study of Children Stranded in New York City Foster Care* (New York: Children's Rights, Inc., November 2009): 10, 16.

58. "Keeping Track." *Child Welfare Watch* 1 (Spring 1997): 7; "Watching the Numbers." *Child Welfare Watch* 19/20 (Winter 2010/2011): 35.

59. New York State Office of Children and Family Services, *Differential Response in Child Protective Services in New York State, Implementation, Initial Outcomes and Impacts of Pilot Project, Report to the Governor and Legislature* (Albany: New York State Office of Children and Family Services, January 2011): 1.

60. Ibid., v, vi.

61. "Keeping Track." *Child Welfare Watch* 1 (Spring 1997): 7; "Watching the Numbers." *Child Welfare Watch* 7 (Winter 2001): 15; "Watching the Numbers." *Child Welfare Watch* 12 (Winter 2005–2006): 23; "Watching the Numbers." *Child Welfare Watch* 19/20 (Winter 2010/2011): 35.

62. Children's Rights, Inc., *At the Crossroads* (July 2007): 14.

63. Martin Guggenheim interview with the author, November 2, 2011.

64. Children's Rights, Inc., *At the Crossroads* (July 2007): 21

65. Ibid., 22; "Watching the Numbers." *Child Welfare Watch* 21 (Winter 2011/2012): 35.

66. New York City Administration for Children's Services, *Outcome 5: Low Repeat Maltreatment, Citywide Summary* (New York: Administration for Children's Services, August 14, 2009), http://home2.nyc.gov/html/acs/downloads/pdf/outcomes/out5_citywide.pdf.

67. Children's Rights, Inc., *At the Crossroads* (July 2007): 34; *Citywide Performance Rating, Agency Performance Rating, Administration for Children's Services* (New York: New York City Mayor's Office of Operations, July 2012), http://www.nyc.gov/html/ops/cpr/html/home/home.shtml., accessed August 31, 2011.

68. John Mattingly, "Testimony by John B. Mattingly, New York City Administration for Children's Services" (testimony, New York City, City Council Preliminary Budget Hearing, March 23, 2009).

69. Children's Rights, Inc., *At the Crossroads* (July 2007): 31.

70. New York City Administration for Children's Services, *Child Welfare Indicators Quarterly Report, 2nd Quarter 2011, Indicated SCR Reports by Service Status by Type of Case*, http://www.nyc.gov/html/acs/downloads/pdf/stats_quarter_report2.pdf.

71. Children's Rights, Inc., *At the Crossroads* (July 2007): 31.

72. New York City Administration for Children's Services, *Child Welfare Indicators Annual Report 2011, Indicated SCR Reports by Services Referred by Type of Case* (New York: Administration for Children's Services, 2011): 15, http://www.nyc.gov/html/acs/downloads/pdf/city_council_report_2011_annual.pdf, accessed August 19, 2012.

73. "Watching the Numbers." *Child Welfare Watch* 19/20 (Winter 2010/2011): 35; "Watching the Numbers." *Child Welfare Watch* 21 (Winter 2011/2012): 35.

74. "Watching the Numbers." *Child Welfare Watch* 21 (Winter 2011/2012): 35.

75. New York City Administration for Children's Services, *Flash* (July 2011): 14.

76. "You've Got Mail! ACS RFP Results Shake Up Child Welfare System," *New York Nonprofit Press*, April 22, 2010.

77. John Mattingly, "Testimony by John B. Mattingly, New York City Administration for Children's Services" (testimony, New York: New York City Council Hearing, October 5, 2010): 3.

78. Mike Arsham (executive director, Child Welfare Organizing Project), interview with the author, November 16, 2010.

79. Ibid.

80. New York City Administration for Children's Services, *Renewed Plan of Action* (May 2001), 28.

81. Chapin Hall Center for Children at the University of Chicago, *ACS Community Partnership Initiative: Approach and Preliminary* Findings (Chicago: Chapin Hall Center for Children/University of Chicago, May 2008) http://home2.nyc.gov/html/acs/downloads/pdf/ocp_chapinhall_report.pdf.

82. New York City Administration for Children's Services, *Child Welfare Services with Community Coalition Contractors Services Overview, Section III: Scope of Services* (Administration for Children's Services, Spring 2008): 203.

83. Letter from Patricia Chabla (assistant commissioner, New York City Administration for Children's Services) to Sr. Ellenrita Purcaro (executive director, Highbridge Community Life Center), May 10, 2010 (unpublished).

84. Mosi Secret, "Children's Services Leader Leaving After Seven Years," *New York Times*, April 27, 2011.

85. Richard Wexler, email message to the author, July 24, 2012. See also Richard Wexler, "Foster Care in New York: A Fresh Start for New York City Child Welfare." NCCPR blog, July 26, 2011, http://www.nccprblog.org/2011/07/foster-care-in-new-york-fresh-start-for.html.

86. Tracy Field (director, child welfare strategy group, Annie E. Casey Foundation), interview with the author, October 4, 2011.

87. City of New York, "Mayor's Management Report, Preliminary Fiscal 2012: Administration for Children's Services" (New York: Deputy Mayor for Operations, February 2012): 31.

CHAPTER 8

1. U.S. Department of Health and Human Services, Administration for Children and Families, Administration on Children, Youth and Families, Children's Bureau, The AFCARS Report, Preliminary FY 2011 estimates as of July 2012, No. 19, www.acf.hhs.gov/programs/cb. *Preliminary Estimates for FY 2011 as of July 2012;* Thomas C. Attwood, *Foster Care: Safety Net or Trap Door* (Washington, DC: Heritage Society Foundation, March 25, 2011): 2; David Crary, "Foster Care Population Drops for 6th Straight Year," ABC News.

2. Linda Gordon, *Heroes of Their Own lives: The Politics and History of Family Violence* (New York: Penguin Books, 1988).

3. Commissioner John Mattingly (presentation, New York, New School University, Center for New York City Affairs, Parent Advocate Initiative Forum, March 16, 2011) http://www.youtube.com/watch?v=R_mdtGrpWxY.

4. Commissioner William Bell (presentation, New York, Hunter College, event honoring the Child Welfare Fund June 10, 2004), reported in *Child Welfare Fund Annual Report* (New York: Child Welfare Fund, June 2004).

5. Martin Guggenheim (law professor, New York University School of Law), interview with the author, May 10, 2011.
6. Ibid.
7. "Watching the Numbers." *Child Welfare Watch* 19 and 20 (Winter 2010/2010): 35.
8. Andrew White (editor, *Child Welfare Watch*), interview with the author, April 29, 2011.
9. Mike Arsham (New York, presentation, CWOP Office, meeting with representatives of DHS-Give Us Back Our Children, Philadelphia, PA, May 13, 2011).
10. Kathleen Maher, *How Has Shift Away from Foster Care Affected Funding, Spending, Caseloads?* (New York: New York City Independent Budget Office, October 2011).
11. Robert J. Sampson, Stephen W. Raudenbush, and Felton Earls, "Neighborhood and Violent Crime: A Multilevel Study of Collective Efficacy." *Science* 277 (5328) (August 15, 1997): 918–924.
12. Paul K. Longmore and Lauri Umansky, "Introduction: Disability History: From the Margins to the Mainstream." In *The New Disability History: American Perspectives*, ed. Paul K. Longmore and Lauri Umansky (New York: New York University Press, 2001): 4.
13. Jess McDonald, "Lessons Learned from the Illinois Child Welfare System Turnaround: Comments by Jess McDonald, former director of the Illinois Department of Children and Family Services; 1994–2003," http://www.jessmcdonald.a25hourdaysites.com/f/Lessons_Learned_from_Illinois_-_7-22-05.pdf.
14. State of Illinois, Department of Children and Family Services, "Child and Family Services Review, Statewide Assessment, Final Submission" (Illinois: Department of Children and Family Services, July 15, 2003): 1, http://www.state.il.us/dcfs/docs/swafinal.pdf, accessed August 30, 2012.

EPILOGUE

1. Michael Arsham, "Commissioner Mattingly's Legacy from a Parent's Perspective," NYNP, September 2011, p. 5; Mosi Secret, "Children's Services Leader Leaving After Seven Years." *New York Times*, July 27, 2012.
2. Mosi Secret, "Queens Family Court Judge Is Picked to Lead the City's Child Welfare Agency." New York Times, July 28, 2012.
3. "Richter Succeeds Mattingly," *New York Nonprofit Press*, July 27, 2011, http://nynp.biz/july2711.html.
4. Michael Arsham, "Commissioner Mattingly's Legacy from a Parent's Perspective." *New York Nonprofit Press*, September 2011, p. 5.
5. Letter to Commissioner Ronald Richter, January 31, 2012, from Mike Arsham, Ruben Asturia, et al. (unpublished).
6. Marina Lalayants, "Child Welfare Organizing Project, Community Connections, Program Evaluation, Final Report, June 2012" (New York: Silberman School of Social Work, National Resource Center for Permanency and Family Connections, Hunter College, City University of New York, 2012): 7, 31.
7. Helen Zelon, "Child Welfare Head: Family Court Crunch Escapes Pols' Notice" (New York: City Limits, June 13, 2012): 4; citylimits.org/news/articles/4593/child-welfare-head-family-fourt-crunch-escapes-pol-notice.
8. Ibid., 2.

ANNEX I: THE VISION AND THE STRATEGY

1. Duncan Lindsey, *The Welfare of Children* (New York: Oxford University Press, 2004): 2, 27, 107–110.
2. Ibid., 337.
3. *Rise, From Rights to Reality: A Plan for Parent Advocacy and Family Centered Child Welfare Reform* (New York: Rise, 2010).
4. National Coalition on Child Protection Reform, Foster Care in New York City: Another Retreat from Reform—On Two Fronts at Once, http://www.nccprblog. org/2010/06/new-york-city-retreats-from-reform-on.html, posted June 24, 2010; New York State Office of Children and Family Services, *Differential Response in Child Protective Services in New York State, Implementation, Initial Outcomes and Impacts of Pilot Project, Report to the Governor and Legislature* (Albany: New York State Office of Children and Family Services, January 2011): 1.
5. Mark Courtney, Amy Dworsky, JoAnne, Lee, and Melissa Raap, *Midwest Evaluation of the Adult Functioning of Former Foster Youth: Outcomes at Age 23 and 24* (Chicago: Chapin Hall/University of Chicago, 2010), http://www.chapinhall. org/sites/default/files/Midwest_Study_ES_Age_23_24.pdf.
6. Kathleen Maher, *How Has Shift Away from Foster Care Affected Funding, Spending, Caseloads?* (New York: New York City Independent Budget Office, October 2011): 5, 6.
7. Ibid., 6.
8. New York City Administration for Children's Services, ACS Task Force on Racial Equity and Cultural Competence, Commissioner's Advisory Board. *Race/ Ethnicity and the Path through the Child Welfare System CY 2007,* distributed at the task force meeting of June 18, 2008.
9. "Rally Against Child Care Cuts." *New York Nonprofit Press*, April 7, 20011.
10. "Over 20,000 Turn Out for March on Wall Street." *New York Nonprofit Press*, May 13, 2011.
11. Steven Cohen (staff director, Special Child Welfare Advisory Panel), interview with the author, August 13, 2008.
12. Gary Engelhardt and Jonathan Gruber, "Social Security and the Evolution of Elderly Poverty," March 2004: 2, http://urbanpolicy.berkeley.edu/pdf/ Ch6SocialEG0404.pdf.
13. Mat Forsberg, *The Evolution of Social Welfare Policy in Sweden* (Sweden: Swedish Institute, 1986): 19.

INDEX

Printed in the USA/Agawam, MA
November 11, 2015

626088.013